PYRAMID-LiFE

Cry, Sis

By

ELiSA GRANT

Quiet Money LLC
Copyright © 2025 by Elisa Grant
ISBN: 979-8-218-85477-5

Published by Quiet Money LLC
in the United States of America.

All inquiries and permission requests
should be addressed to the publisher at
quietmoneyconsulting@gmail.com

To R,

My other half, best friend, confidant, biggest supporter, and husband. Thank you for loving me so completely and for being my strength when I'm supposed to be yours. I pray this book does for others what you've done for me - heal. Your love has healed parts of me that you didn't even break. I will gladly face any of life's trials with you by my side.

With love,
Your Lucky Penny

Spotify Playlist: Pyramid-Life Cry, Sis

"Distance and Time" - Alicia Keys

"Slipping Away" - LEISURE

"After Hours" - The Weeknd

"don't be sad" - Tate McRae

"Take Care of You" - Charlotte Day Wilson, Syd

"I Like" - ROE

"Be the One" [Remix] - Sinéad Harnett, Col3trane

"dreamin'" - 53 Thieves

"Sauce" - Ella Mai

"Blue Window" - Duñe, Crayon

"CUFF IT" [Wetter Remix] - Beyoncé

"The Feels" - Labrinth

"feel something" - Bea Miller

"It's You" - Ali Gatie

"Stolen" - Dashboard Confessional

Contents

Preface

My husband was wrongfully convicted and sentenced to life in prison
without parole. He had no record, no history of trouble, no reason
to believe the system could mistake him for anything but human.
Yet, it did.
And in that mistake, it unraveled everything we thought we knew
about justice, safety, and faith.

These pages carry the words that are sometimes too heavy to speak:
the weight of every visitation cut short, every unanswered question,
every quiet night spent holding on to hope. They reveal what it
means to exist in two worlds at once: one bound by love, the other
by a sentence that was never his to serve.

This book is not about proving innocence; it's about surviving
the silence that follows injustice. It's about learning to live
with the echo of someone's absence, and finding beauty
in the spaces grief tries to fill. It's about healing.

If you have ever loved someone through impossible circumstances,
if you have ever screamed into silence or held on to hope
when you couldn't see a light at the end of the tunnel, if you are
working on healing your inner child or your present self—these
words are for you.

— Elisa Grant

start climbing

My Husband Was Sentenced to Die in Prison

The judge's gavel thudded like a closing coffin lid. I had to choke down a sob just typing that—the memory is still too raw, even 3 years later. My husband's sentence: life in prison. A death sentence lived every day. If that's not reason enough to cry, I don't know what is.

We always say, "That could never be me." Or, "I would die. I could never go through that." And then it happens. And somehow you don't die. You survive. You rise. When flight isn't an option, you fight. You show up for your partner, your kids, your pets, your job...or if none of those anchors exist for you, you just show up for yourself. Sure, you can take a break or try to hide from whatever's bothering you, but it never truly goes away. It's always there, lingering. Sitting quietly on the back burner, simmering, waiting for you to face it.

As a child, I idolized powerful adults such as judges, lawyers, law enforcement. Now I see them as just people with too much power. Angry people. Biased, tired, broken people making life-or-death decisions, and such decisions affect real families like mine—my family torn apart by a crime my husband didn't commit. My sweet husband. A man who would never hurt anyone, let alone end someone's life.

We lived in a small southern town. Everyone knew everyone. Our lawyer was pals with the prosecutor. Jurors were neighbors. Conflict of interest? Maybe. But power? Very real. My friend always says, "Look for the silver linings." I prefer gold, but she's right. Life could always be worse. There's always someone wishing for what you have. It's easy to drown in "woe is me." But when life is unfair, as it is, why do we trust that the justice system is fair?

I have a job I love. Yet I yearn for space to feel my sadness, to be invisible on the days when the cross is too heavy to bear. I'm a woman in a man's world, and I can't appear weak, even when I'm crumbling inside. So I email, "I hope this finds you well," and power through. I fight intrusive thoughts with work ethic: sink or swim. I still dream. Lawyer. Rock star. Housewife. Influencer. Best-selling author. Is it ambition? Or dissatisfaction? I'm learning it's okay to chase many versions of me, even in my thirties.

Throughout most of my twenties, I juggled working in an office by day, bartending at night and on weekends, and squeezing in schoolwork whenever I could. I slept 3-4 hours a night and bounced right back the next morning. Now, I need 10 hours of sleep and I still feel spent. When my husband's trial began in September 2022, I was set to graduate in December. I made it…by a thread. But I couldn't feel a thing. I don't remember my final assignments. I numbed myself with booze; I was drowning in pain. I used to chase highs to escape pain. Now I chase joy, contentment, faith. At 27, I quit the habits. The clarity is painful but real. I'm leaning into grief, anxiety, and fighting the urge to numb again. I'm not judging others' coping. I'm just honoring my own.

I used to hate being at home. Now I dread leaving it. I inch outside only when the neighbors aren't watching. I've started and stopped this book so many times. But maybe I'm not writing for an audience. Maybe I'm writing to wake *me* up.

More recently I've learned that it's ok to feel. To mourn. To cry. My husband's love transcends walls. Physically apart, but emotionally inseparable.

We don't get to experience intimacy in the flesh now that he's in prison, yet I feel closer to him now than ever—fulfilled by his hope, words, tenderness, and strength. He's patient. He uplifts me, even from prison, when it should be *me* uplifting *him*. My husband and I say we weren't ready the first time we met. Maybe this nightmare was meant to reset our lives. To focus our priorities. To bring us closer to God and each other.

Some days sparkle. Others are heavy. I fight depression and anxiety—the racing-heart kind. I remind myself, "Everything is predestined." But when it doesn't help, I pray. Then inhale. Exhale. Still feel guilt for not trusting enough. For doubting I'm strong enough. But they say: *God gives his hardest battles to his strongest soldiers.*

So here I stand. Soldiering on. Sink or swim? I swim. Because sinking isn't an option.

Start

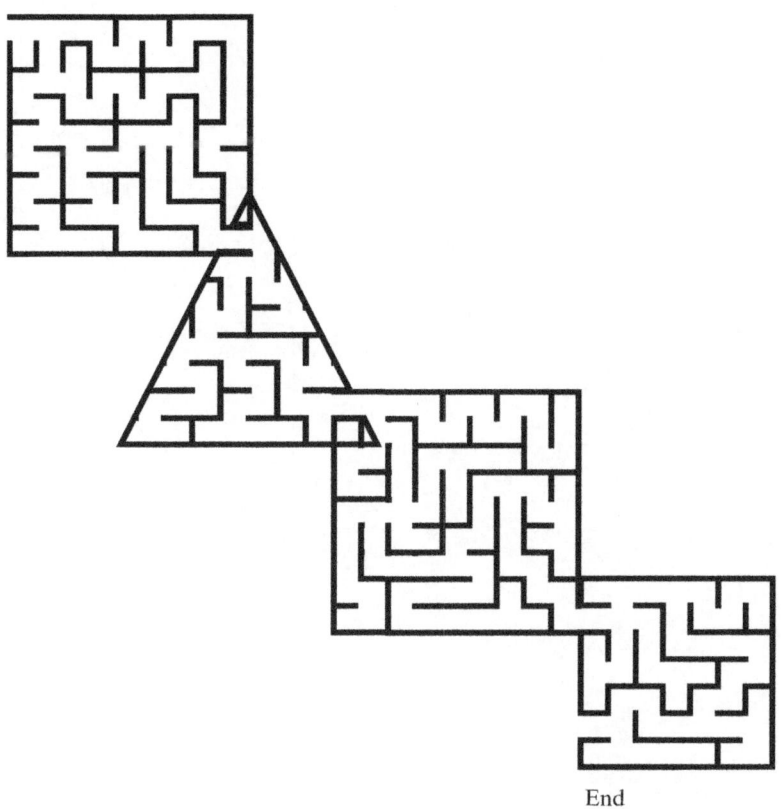

End

There are many twists and turns in life.
Stay focused on what's important and you will find your way.

I Didn't Cry at My Granddad's Funeral

I didn't cry at my granddad's funeral.

That day solidified something I'd known for years: my parents would always expect me to act a certain way, as if the last three decades hadn't proven that I don't fit into their mold. I couldn't live my whole life trying to be someone's perfect daughter when it meant giving up being myself. My mother's sharp glare bore into me, her silent accusation clear: I was embarrassing her by not crying.

But not crying didn't mean I wasn't grieving. Grief is unpredictable for me, shaped by a lifetime of trauma. Sometimes it leaves me numb, unable to cry even when I want to. Other times, it comes in waves - tears and dry heaves that seem never-ending.

Sometimes I can't eat for days, while at other times I overeat as if trying to fill the emptiness inside. One thing remains constant: I grieve best when I'm alone, when I can replay the pain over and over, trapped in a loop of paralyzing anxiety.

Maybe it's a Virgo thing—overanalyzing, overthinking, obsessing over why I can't fix what's broken. I'm a fixer by nature, but I can't fix myself. I envy people who can just let go, who can move on without carrying the weight of loss.

I envy the person I used to be, someone with nothing to lose. Now I have so much to lose. And so much I've already lost.

The sting of losing makes you terrified of loving.

No one asked if I was okay. Because I wasn't crying, they assumed I didn't feel pain. That I could be their strength. Their rock. But how could I be anyone's foundation when I was crumbling inside?

Do they even know what I'm dealing with?

Of course not. I keep it all inside. Maybe they've heard rumors, whispers of my struggles, but no one has dared to ask. No one has said the words: "Are you okay?"

I reached for my phone, texting my husband:
"I need you here with me. I want to run out of here and go home. This is all too much."

He's the only one who can quiet my mind, calm my anxiety, and speak courage into me. His words remind me that I can endure the weight of everyone else's expectations.

I looked up to find my mother's disapproving glance again. She probably thought I was scrolling through social media, completely unaware that I was reaching out to the one person holding me together. That being in her presence had opened the floodgates of past traumas.

Funerals are a harsh reminder of life's fragility—how quickly it comes and goes. My granddad was lucky in some ways. He lived a long life, full of family and memories. Many aren't as fortunate. Some lives are stolen in the blink of an eye, ripped away without fairness or reason.

My husband is living proof of that. His life was stolen, and so was mine, in a single, cruel moment. A three day trial resulting in a life sentence.

I didn't cry at my granddad's funeral. Not because I didn't care, not because I didn't feel the loss, but because I've cried all my tears. I've emptied myself so completely that there's nothing left.

I didn't cry.

Now it's time to write a few affirmations or set meaningful goals for yourself.

At the end of the day, you are the one responsible for your well-being.

Nurture positivity, and let your joy bloom.

And remember, it's ok to cry.

I

T _____

S _____

_____

O _____

K _____

T _____

O _____

C _____

R _____

Y _____

S _____

I _____

S _____

I Got Hitched at a State Prison

A white dress, baggy and oversized. It had to cover everything. God forbid my soon-to-be husband see an inch below my collarbone. Never mind that this man has seen me laid bare in every sense of the word. Modesty was apparently the rule, even on my wedding day.

White, lacy ballet flats pinched my toes, sending me back to high school memories of squeezing into too-small shoes, trying to downplay my awkward frame and big feet. The faint smell of burnt popcorn came with every step, mingling with the butterflies in my stomach. IYKYK.

I sat on the toilet as my sister curled my hair, weaving extensions into the thinning strands that stress had taken from me. She worked with care, ensuring every piece was hidden. Months of anxiety melted away, if only for a moment. Today wasn't a day for stress. Today was a happy day.

The car ride through the countryside stretched long and nerve-racking. Did I remember my ID? What if something went wrong at the courthouse or the prison?

My sisters had traveled so far, and the officiant, who was a rare kind soul willing to marry us in a prison, had come despite a string of rejections from others who "weren't comfortable." Everything had to go right.

The courthouse was rundown, a reflection of the impoverished town around it. A new clerk fumbled with what she needed to do while the main clerk was at lunch. The wait felt endless.

The prison gatehouse loomed. Anxiety clawed at me again. Not him. Please not him. The same officer who'd hit on me twice before greeted me with a smug grin.

"Damn, you look more beautiful every time I see you."

Barf. Clearly I'm in a wedding dress, creep.

I clenched my jaw and went to the bathroom to fix my flower garland. Showtime. Except this wasn't a performance; this was real life. Shoes off. Popcorn. ID. Pat-down.

Garland off. Is my hair a mess now?

No time to check.

I was steps away from my man, but this wasn't just another visit. I was walking in unmarried and walking out as his wife. Plans we made before his trial and dreams of a traditional wedding were distant memories now. But none of that mattered. What mattered was that today, finally, I was marrying the love of my life.

The visitation room felt sterile and impersonal, but when I saw him walk through the door, the rest of the world faded away. My cheeks ached from smiling. My sister and his exchanged knowing looks, probably thinking we were lovesick fools. They weren't wrong.

In that moment, it wouldn't have mattered if we were in an alley wearing potato sacks in the pouring rain. I was becoming his wife.

We'd waited so long for this. We'd known after three months that we wanted to get married, and now it was finally happening.

"No pictures," they said.

I could've cried. How could I not have a keepsake of this moment? But the chaplain, a kind hero, brought a camera anyway. (Getting my hands on those photos would become its own saga, but I did it.)

I went first with my vows, trembling but proud. The words were mine, every syllable coming from the depths of my heart. Then it was his turn.

Four pages of handwritten vows. How could mine compare? His words were eloquent, his love so vivid in every line. All the reassurances he'd given me over the years were now immortalized in those pages. I felt seen, cherished, and so incredibly lucky.

Every year on our anniversary, we reread those vows, reliving the promises we made and the emotions of that day.

"How can a jail relationship last?" they ask. Dedication. Commitment. Love. Honesty. Friendship. Putting the other first. Communication. Perseverance. Strength. Faith.

I got hitched in a state prison.

And

it

was

the

best

day

of

my

life.

Think of a time when you felt undeniable peace and love.
Describe it!

_____

_____

_____

_____

_____

_____

_____

_____

_____

_____

_____

_____

Another Tuesday Morning

The alarm buzzes sharply at 8:00 a.m., jolting me from a restless sleep. I wake with a familiar heaviness pressing against my chest, a weight I've carried every week for months. Tuesday morning. Another Tuesday morning.

I sit on the edge of the bed, staring down at my feet, which feel like they've sunk into the carpet. My phone sits on the nightstand, its glow too bright in the dim light, a silent witness to my bi-weekly ritual of waking up with dread.

The appeals court's decisions are announced every first and third Tuesday and usually arrive by email around 10:30 a.m. Some Tuesdays are just empty, silent markers of more time stolen from us. Other Tuesdays bring news of cases I don't know, names I'll never hear again. But every Tuesday holds the possibility that today might be the day we finally hear something.

I shuffle into the kitchen, my slippers dragging against the floor, and start the coffee maker. The low hum of the machine fills the quiet house as I stare out the window at a world that keeps turning, oblivious to the storm raging inside me.

My heart pounds. I check my email compulsively, though I know it's too early. Refresh. Scroll. Refresh again. The news rarely comes before noon, but still, I check. The inbox is empty, a blank void that matches the knot in my stomach. The headlines blur together, my eyes scanning for the one thing that matters. His name. His case. A word, any word, to tell me if this fight is over.

The day stretches on and I try to distract myself. Work, emails, dishes—mundane tasks to fill the silence. But the doom hangs over me like a storm cloud, dark and looming. Anxiety and panic, causing my heart to race.

At 10:15 a.m., the anxiety sharpens, slicing through the dull ache in my chest. I don't want to keep looking, but I can't stop myself. I sit at the kitchen table, phone clutched tightly in my hand, staring at the screen as if my will alone could summon the email.

And then, at 10:34 a.m., it comes. My breath catches as the email pops up. I don't open it immediately. For a moment, I just stare at it, my mind running through every possible outcome. The seconds stretch into eternity before I finally tap the screen.

Relief, despair, or more waiting. It's always two of the three, yet the anticipation feels new and unbearable every time. The words blur as my eyes skim the names, my heart pounding so loudly I can barely think.

Another Tuesday has come and gone. No news. No answers. The ache in my chest doesn't go away—it just reshapes itself, folding neatly into the quiet corners of my mind, waiting to pounce again in two weeks.

And so the cycle begins again. Another Tuesday morning will come, just like this one, when hope and fear will collide again.

Words are powerful

Think of something you've been struggling with—
whether it's a specific situation or an emotional state.

Start by choosing a negative word that reflects how you
feel about it and write it in the bottom block.

Then, work your way up one block at a time, selecting
words that signify growth and healing.
Finally, in the top block, write a word that represents
your desired state.

The aim is to create a visual journey of transformation, inspiring progress,
strength, and empowerment.

Hey you. It's gonna be ok.

The Childless Mother

Every year, I write my stepson a letter for his birthday.
Letters he never gets. I tuck them away, saving them for
a day when he's old enough to understand. One day,
he'll open them all at once and see the depth of my love
—the things I've done for him and would still do
without hesitation.

He's a piece of my husband—the only piece I may
ever have.

Watching him grow, from a bright-eyed four-year-old
to a nine-year-old wise beyond his years, feels like
watching life pass by on fast-forward. Like catching
glimpses of a favorite show you can never fully follow.
Each milestone, each laugh, each tear—I'm not there for
any of it. He doesn't even know I exist.

How do you love someone so much when they don't
know you? Is this how God feels?

I keep an album of his photos, tracing the changes in
his smile, the way he looks more like his father every
year. I keep a room for him in my home, a place he's
never been but is always ready. Just in case. His father
can't be here, but I can.

He's not abandoned. Not unloved. I'm here— a reflection of his father's love, ready to give him the world.

I'm building something for him. Generational wealth. A future where he'll never worry the way I once did. My parents didn't prepare me for life's chaos. I was born into a plan that wasn't much of a plan at all.
I refuse to pass that on to him.

But how do you fight for someone when you're locked out of their world? How do you make them see the love they're missing when the gatekeepers of their heart refuse to let you in?

It's a dull, aching irony to love so fiercely and be held at arm's length. To want nothing more than to share the truth: his father is not a bad man. His father is an innocent man. Soon he'll understand.

My husband hasn't hugged his son in years, not because he doesn't want to, but because the system stole that from him.

I will never understand the cruelty of keeping love from a child. A parent's love. A bonus parent's love. Love isn't finite—it doesn't run out. Yet some wield it like a weapon, as though more love is a threat.

I could be bitter. I could harden my heart and turn away like so many stepparents do. But that's not who I am. My heart, stubborn as it is, keeps me tethered to this child, loving him with a ferocity he'll never fully understand, at least not yet.

One day, I'll tell him about his father. About the injustice of it all. About the men and women in power who took a good man away for reasons that make no sense to me, let alone to a child. How do you explain to an innocent boy that his hero was betrayed by a system he's taught to respect? How do you make sense of the senseless?

"When is Daddy coming home?"

There's no answer I can give other than "some day." No words that make it okay.

But one day, he'll be old enough to see the truth. And when that day comes, I'll be there. His ally.

His friend. His bonus mom. The one who always believed in him, even when he didn't know I was there.

I pray he'll see how much I love him by the way I love his father. I hope he'll understand that my love for him started the moment I met his dad, and is never-ending.

I love you, L.

—Childless Mother to a Fatherless Child

Write a one-page letter to your younger self.
What would you tell yourself?

_____

_____

_____

_____

_____

_____

_____

_____

_____

_____

_____

Seasons Change

It was a hopeful spring before your trial.
We were ready to grow into our life together,
To claim what we deserved.
Raw, new love blossomed,
Confident, blind to the storm on the horizon.
We didn't know how hard the times would be,
How deep the pain would cut.
Still, we must hold on to hope
That this suffering has an end.

It was a hot summer before your trial.
And the one after was hotter.
Each summer since has burned,
Igniting a fire within me,
A love so fierce, willing to fight for you forever.
This isn't fair.
This shouldn't happen to someone like you.
But here we are, so what do we do?
We keep the fire burning.

It was a stressful fall during your trial.
Like leaves spiraling to the ground,
I prayed to shed this nightmare,
To cast off false accusations.
Out with the old, making space
For something fresh, something healed.
But instead, I've been falling every day since.
Anxiety stealing my breath,
Pinching myself to see if it's real.
We cannot fall apart.
We must stand tall together.

It was a cold winter after your trial.
And the next was colder.
And the third, colder still.
Four winters, five winters.
How many more until you come home?
None, they say.
They've sentenced you to die in prison,
For a crime you didn't commit.
An innocent man, framed,
Stolen from a life we hadn't even begun to live.

But seasons change.
Ours will come.
And when it does,
The world around us will bloom again.

What is your favorite season, and why?
How does it make you feel?
What are some activities you like to do?

_____

_____

_____

_____

_____

_____

_____

_____

Never Satisfied

A subtle win,
A trial or hardship that finally ends.
Feelings of peace begin to sink in—
Never satisfied.

That long-awaited news arrives,
You overcome a fear, survive.
Breaking free, reclaiming your life—
Never satisfied.

"If I just get this, I'll be set,"
Temporary needs, momentarily met.
How sad, how quickly you forget—
Never satisfied.

Comparison steals your fleeting joy,
Envy whispers its next ploy.
The present moment, you can't enjoy—
Never satisfied.

Bigger, better, always wanting more,
Chasing dreams that leave you unsure.
What were we even working toward?
...
Never satisfied.

We all have desires. Take a moment to identify five specific things you want that align with the five categories below.

Wants: Brings:

_____   Income

_____   Peace

_____   Joy

_____   Fun

_____   Fulfillment

Now make sure you are going for these five things first, as they are the most important right now. The core life values above contribute to a balanced and fulfilling life.

It's all about the balance, sis.

EMOtions

Is it better to feel, or to feel nothing at all?
Sometimes the pain cuts so deep you can't even crawl.
Paralyzed by sadness, anxious and confused.
How can this be happening? What did you do?

It strikes like lightning, tight in your chest,
Tears rolling down as you're feeling depressed.
The thoughts replay, the "what ifs" in your head,
What could you have done? What should you have said?

Life has a way of steering its course,
Though detours may feel like an unstoppable force.
You'll stumble, you'll break, but it's all by design,
These trials are yours, a fate intertwined.

The game has no trades; you play the hand dealt.
And when you're wronged, let your strength be felt.
Wipe your tears and dry your eyes,
This isn't the moment to break down and cry.

Emotions fade, situations rearrange,
Now is the time to embrace the change.
With dignity guiding, let yourself rise,
Your power lies in what survives.

Good energy is important and can make the impossible, possible.

Write down 3 limiting beliefs you hold. Then, write the opposite truth as if it's already real. Practice saying the bottom 3 out loud daily.

1. _____

2. _____

3. _____

1. _____

2. _____

3. _____

Apology

There were words I needed but never heard,
soft syllables stitched with regret,
a balm for wounds I didn't know had names.
Wounds that took me years to heal myself.

Instead, silence became your answer,
a weight heavier than any scolding,
pressing down on my shoulders.

You called it strength,
this refusal to look back,
but I call it ignorance,
so I carried the past for both of us.

I waited for you to see me,
to say it wasn't my fault,
to tell me you were sorry
for the storms you unleashed
and the shelter you never gave.
The trauma you inflicted.
The start of me never feeling good enough.

The apology never came,
but I've learned to offer it to myself—
to the child I was,
and to the adult I am.
I am enough.

Is there someone you wish would had apologized to you but never did?
Write down how they hurt you and what an apology would
mean to you as if you were writing to them.

Selfless

How far would you go for the ones you love?
What would you risk, what would you give up?
Life is a series of choices we make.
Would you step aside or put yourself at stake?

No matter how big your dreams, how hard you've worked,
You set them aside, putting others first.
Yet in return comes a feeling undefined,
A warmth that numbs the ache inside.

Why are you so selfless? What are you trying to prove?
Do you give to others because no one gave to you?
You know the sting of abandonment, the ache of being alone,
So you strive to spare others the pain you've known.

After pouring out all of yourself and receiving none in
return,
You ask what went wrong, what lesson you must learn.
But maybe the lesson was never for you.
You've done your part, you've seen it through.

Those you've lifted will carry the weight,
Haunted by your memory, your selfless fate.

UPLIFT CHALLENGE

☐ Compliment a stranger

☐ Donate old clothes to a homeless shelter

☐ Donate to someone's fundraiser

☐ Tell someone they look nice today

☐ Pay for someone's order in line behind you

It feels good to do good.

Free

Freedom is not an open door,
but the choice to walk through it.
It is the quiet defiance of a mind
untangling itself from darkness.

I unlearn the weight of despair,
let it slip from my shoulders
like a coat I no longer care to sport.
Each breath becomes a step forward.

To free myself is to hold space for him,
to believe in a future where
we both walk unbound,
whole and unbroken.

The prison of my mind
has held me long enough.
I step beyond its walls,
into a light I forgot existed.

But freedom is not only mine.
It is a voice echoing from behind walls,
a promise that stone and steel
cannot hold forever.

But his freedom
is not just a metaphor.
It is steel doors swinging open,
the echo of footsteps on concrete,
the taste of the world waiting outside.

A world that refuses to stop,
although his was forced to.
The quiet grief of years stolen pouring out
as he finally breaks free.

I imagine the day his steps
carry him across the threshold,
the sunlight warm on his face,
our world no longer measured in distance and time.

I free myself
as I wait for him to be freed,
both of us unbound,
our lives waiting to begin again.

Freedom is a journey, not just a destination,
for him, for me,

FREEDOM IS COMING.

Postscript

R,

You are everything to me.
Sometimes, I find myself walking back through memories,
to the places I swore I'd left behind.
Childhood traumas, the quiet ache of what I endured
before I ever had the words for it.
Something small will stir it, and suddenly, the ground shifts.
My chest tightens, my heart races, and my thoughts blur
into a language I can't translate.
But you never turn away. You meet me where I am,
in the middle of the storm, with patience instead of pity,
with presence instead of pressure.
You talk me through the noise until it begins to make sense.
You teach me that feelings don't have to be fixed,
they only need to be felt.
They deserve to be felt.
Even while carrying your own pain, you hold space for mine.
You give what you never received, and in doing so,
you show me what healing love looks like:
it's gentle, grounded, unconditional.
Your love is a quiet kind of medicine, a mirror that shows me
how far I've come and how much I still deserve to stay.
You are everything to me, not because you save me,
but because you remind me that I can survive,
and still love,
and still be whole.

Coming Soon

Two worlds. One love.
A thousand unspoken truths.

When her husband is wrongfully convicted
and sent to solitary confinement, their only
connection becomes his letters — pages written
in the silence of a cell.

Through this epistolary erasure piece, **Return to
Sender**, she uses his original letters and turns them
into her responses that unfold across two parallel stories:
The Darkness and *The Light*.

In *The Darkness*, the words reveal the ache of isolation,
injustice, and the slow unraveling of time spent apart and
behind bars.

In *The Light*, those same words become something else —
testaments of love, faith, and resilience that refuse to be
silenced.

Made in the USA
Middletown, DE
23 December 2025

Made in the USA
Monee, IL
08 December 2023

48661774R00100

About the Author

Sharon Wright is a young at heart mother of three: Kathy, Jody and Timothy. Ever since she started reading in grammar school it seems she never stopped. Her love for reading and writing created a long time dream of one day being an author.

Sharon started writing "The Wishing Well" back in 1995. At first it was just a hobby. She never imagined that her hobby would take her so far. To her it was all just a dream.

With the inspiration from her husband, John and long time family friend, LeRoy G. Peterson she got to see her dream become reality. Her family and friends stood by her and encouraged her to keep going and not give up on her "dream."

Today Sharon Wright is sharing her "dream" with you. Enjoy it.

PART ONE

THE WHISHING WELL

Chapter One

Jody had had a long day at the clinic. She got home and kicked off her shoes. She was preparing to take a shower when the phone rang. It was Aunt Debbie.

She said, "Jody, you have to get to the hospital immediately. Your father has had a heart attack. He was driving to the marine base to give a lecture."

Jody said, "Oh! No! Is he alive?"

Aunt Debbie said, "Yes! There was a heart specialist visiting the hospital. He's from New York. They asked him to look at your dad. His name is Doctor Jeff Pierson."

Jody said, "I'm on my way. I love you." She hung up with tears in her eyes. She grabbed her coat and rushed out the door.

When she arrived at the hospital, the desk nurse told her that her father was up on third-floor ICU. She took the elevator up to the third floor ICU. She found the desk nurse and asked her if she could see George Mills.

The nurse asked, "Who are you? Are you family?"

Jody said, "Yes! I'm his daughter."

The nurse had Jody follow her. Then she asked her to wait. She went into the room. Shortly, she came out of the room with Aunt Debbie. They hugged.

Jody asked Aunt Debbie, "How is he?"

Aunt Debbie said, "He's in stable condition. The doctor said you may see him, but only for a short time."

She went into the room. He was all hooked up to many tubes and oxygen. The nurse said, "He's resting comfortably now."

Jody sat by his bed. She held his hand. She said, "I'm here, Dad. It's Jody, who dearly loves you."

There was a knock on the door. In came the intern. He said, "May I speak to you a moment?"

They stepped out into the hall. He said that Doctor Pierson would like to talk to her. He said, "Please come with me to the lounge."

Doctor Pierson set her down on the sofa. He said,

"Your dad has had a mild heart attack. He will be here while we take tests and monitor him." Then he asked her who his regular doctor was.

She said, "It's Doctor Peterson. Has he been called?"

Just then, a nurse came in and said, "Doctor Peterson just arrived."

Doctor Pierson asked Jody to wait while he conferred with Doctor Peterson.

While Jody was waiting for the doctors to return, her aunt came in and sat down beside her. She turned to her and said, "I'm scared. Have you heard anything about Doctor Pierson?"

Her aunt said, "One of the nurses told me he's a heart specialist from New York. He's on vacation. I guess he wanted to see how a small-town hospital works."

The doctors returned. They told her that if it was all right with her, Doctor Peterson would like Doctor Pierson to assist him with the case. She said she would appreciate his help. Then she said, "But what about your practice in New York?"

He said, "Don't worry. I have an able assistant."

While Jody was talking with the doctors, Aunt Debbie went to phone Kathy. She had been on vacation with her family. They were returning that afternoon.

Aunt Debbie phoned Kathy, hoping she was home. The phone rang, and Kathy answered. Aunt Debbie said, "I'm so glad you're home."

Kathy said, "Why? What's wrong?"

Aunt Debbie said, "It's your dad. He's had a heart attack. He's in the hospital in stable condition. Please come ASAP. Jody is here."

When the doctors left, Aunt Debbie told Jody that Kathy was on her way.

Chapter Two

Kathy hung up the phone. She called Mike, "Come quick!"
Mike came in and Kathy rushed into his arms. She was crying, and tears were streaming down her face. He enfolded her in his arms and asked, "What's wrong, sweetheart?"

She choked back a sob and said, "My dad's had a heart attack. I have to go to the hospital."

Mike said, "Get ready. I'll phone for a cab." Then he said, "I'll meet you there as soon as I get a babysitter."

The cab arrived a few minutes later.

Chapter Three

Kathy arrived at the hospital. Aunt Debbie was waiting for her in the lobby. They went up to the ICU. They met Jody outside their dad's room. Jody and Kathy hugged. Jody said, "I'm so glad you're here."

Kathy said, "Can I go in to see Dad?"

Jody said, "Yes!"

They knocked on the door. A nurse answered, and Jody said, "This is my sister, Kathy. Can she see my dad?"

The nurse said, "Yes, for a few minutes."

Jody waited outside for Kathy, hoping her dad was going to be all right. They needed him and loved him very much. Kathy visited a few minutes, and she came out. She wanted to know what was being done for her dad.

Jody said, "Kathy, come into the lounge, and I'll explain everything to you."

Just as Jody and Kathy were going into the lounge, Mike came down the hall. Kathy rushed into his arms. Mike said, "How is he doing?"

Kathy said, "He's stable."

Mike said, "That's a good sign, honey." Then they went into the lounge with Jody. Jody told them all she knew.

Chapter Four

Doctor Peterson went in to see George. He said, "Hi, George. How are you feeling? I want to talk to you about your condition. You've had a mild heart attack. You need to have some tests taken to see what damage has been done. Doctor Pierson was here when you were brought in. He's a cardiologist visiting from New York. Since I'm just a general practitioner, I was happy to hear he was here.

"I have talked with him about assisting me with your case. He has accepted, if it's all right with you. I would like to have him come in and talk to you."

George said, "That's fine with me."

Doctor Peterson told George that he would locate

Doctor Pierson and bring him to meet him.

Later that day, Doctor Peterson phoned Doctor Pierson. They talked about getting all the tests that were needed set up.

Before Doctor Pierson hung up, he said, "Just so you know, I have to leave here to go back to New York in two weeks. I've got a patient that needs open-heart surgery.

I will be here until Mr. Mills is better. If you feel uncomfortable about my leaving, I know a very capable heart specialist who just finished medical school at the top of his class. His name is Doctor Rob Wilson. He's seeking work in a small town. He's available to come at a moment's notice. I will confer with him. I'll also discuss and describe Mr. Mill's condition with him. Is that all right?"

Doctor Peterson said, "That sounds good."

Doctor Pierson said, "Doctor Wilson will do very well with your guidance."

Doctor Peterson said, "I will inform George about what is happening. I'll also tell him of the change of doctors.

I will reassure him that he will be in capable hands."

Doctor Pierson said, "I will see Mr. Mills in the morning." He hung up the phone. Doctor Peterson finished his supper.

The next morning Doctor Peterson went in to see George and said, "Hi, George. How are you feeling?"

George said, "I feel good."

Doctor Peterson said, "I've located Doctor Pierson. He's agreed to see you later this morning. In the meantime, he's going to set up the tests that need to be done.

"I've got some news that I have to tell you. Since

I'm your doctor, I feel it's best that you hear it from me."

George said, "Well, what is it?"

Doctor Peterson said, "Well, if it is all right with you, I'm keeping Doctor Pierson on the case with me. He also knows a young heart specialist who is looking for a place to practice. I'm thinking of having him come here to see if he would work out. What do you think?"

George said, "I think that's a good idea. I'll let him care for me when he comes."

Doctor Peterson said, "Great, George, I was hoping you'd say that."

Chapter Five

Mike called his boss. He told him what had happened to his father-in-law. He said that he needed some time off.

His boss agreed. He said to take as much time as needed.

Jody, Kathy, and Aunt Debbie were at the hospital bright and early. They wanted to find out how George was after his attack. The girls went up to see their dad. Aunt Debbie went up with them. They walked into the room.

He said, "I'm waiting to have the tests done. I'm also waiting to hear from Doctor Peterson."

While they were visiting, Doctor Peterson came in with Doctor Pierson. He said, "Good morning, George. How are you doing?"

He turned to the ladies and said, "I'm glad you're here."

Then he introduced Doctor Pierson to everyone. He told them that he was working with him. He said that Doctor Pierson would be on the case until George went home. He told them that Doctor Pierson knew a young man that had just finished medical school, specializing in cardiology.

He said he would be coming here to practice. "He'll be on my staff as head of cardiology."

Doctor Pierson said, "I will stay and help Doctor Peterson until he arrives."

Everyone thought that was great.

There was a knock on the door, and a nurse came in.

She said, "They are ready to do the tests."

The doctors said, "You ladies may as well go home. We'll let you know the results when they come back."

Jody said, "Fine, I'll see you at the clinic."

They left and went for coffee.

Chapter Six

Jody was at her desk when Doctor Peterson came into the clinic. He said, "Jody, do you have a minute? I'd like to speak to you. Please come into my office."

Jody went into his office. Doctor Peterson said, "Your dad's tests have returned. They look good. Doctor Pierson wants to talk to your dad about the results. He also wants to talk to him about the changes that are required to keep him in good health. He's going to talk to him tomorrow before he leaves.

"I, also, want to tell you about the young man that Doctor Pierson has recommended. I'm hoping he'll stay on at the hospital. I'm hoping he'll head our cardiology department. He will be here in about two weeks. His name is Doctor Rob Wilson.

"When Doctor Pierson leaves, Doctor Wilson will take over your dad's case. I really think he is what I have been looking for to help me. Doctor Pierson said he is looking for a small, friendly town that needs a cardiologist. He wants to start a new life. He wants to feel that he is needed."

Jody went home that night feeling very happy.

A few days later, Jody went to pick up her dad from the hospital and take him home. When they got in, George sat down in his favorite easy chair. He said, "That's better."

Jody said, "I have to phone the clinic to let them know I won't be in." She went to phone the clinic.

When she finished using the phone, she came back into the living room. She said, "Dad, we have to make a list of groceries for you. When do you have to see Doctor Wilson?"

George said, "That's right. Doctor Wilson will have my case. I have to make an appointment in two weeks, but

I have to get my medicine today, but they don't want me to drive for a few days. Could you take me?"

Jody said, "Sure, Dad. Let's go now."

When they got back, Jody asked her dad if there was anything else he needed to have done.

He said, "No, I'm all set."

She said, "All right, I'll call you tomorrow. I love you."

The next two weeks went fast. Jody was getting ready for work. She thought she would call her dad and remind him that Doctor Wilson would be here tomorrow. She called her dad and said, "Dad, you did remember that Doctor Wilson will be here tomorrow, didn't you?"

He said, "Yes, Jody, there's nothing wrong with my memory. How are you doing?"

She said, "I'm doing fine. I just wanted to remind you. I love you. Bye! Bye!"

George said, "Bye! I love you. Have a good day at work."

Jody hung up the phone. She grabbed her coat and headed for work.

Chapter Seven

Doctor Wilson came into the clinic. There was no one at the desk so he looked for Doctor Peterson's office. He found it and knocked on the door. He walked in.

Doctor Peterson looked up from his desk where he was sitting. He said, "Hello, you must be Doctor Wilson. How are you? How was your trip? How did you find the clinic?"

Rob said, "Oh, the cab driver knew where it was. He said he's had a lot of fares that come here."

Jody got back from lunch. She walked into the clinic and said, "I'm back!"

Doctor Peterson called Jody. She went into his office. He smiled and said to Rob, "This is Jody Mills, the best nurse this side of the Mason Dixon Line. She sure keeps me on my toes."

Doctor Wilson took her hand and kissed it. He said, "So nice to meet you."

Doctor Peterson said, "Jody, this is Doctor Rob Wilson. He's going to be going on my staff. I have a feeling he's just what we need."

Then he said to Doctor Wilson, "Would you like a tour of the clinic and hospital?"

Doctor Wilson said, "Yes, I'd like to see where I'll be working."

Doctor Peterson said, "I've got patients to see so

I won't be able to accommodate you, but I'm sure Jody wouldn't mind showing you around."

They walked around the hospital and clinic. She showed him the different departments. As they walked past the chapel, Rob said, "Have you ever been married or ever had a boyfriend or any serious relationship?"

She looked at him. She said, "Right now my work pretty well occupies my time."

He said, "Okay! Miss Mills, point taken, but it would be nice to have you as a friend. We will be working together. By the way, could this friend ask you out for a cup of coffee sometime?"

She said, "Okay, friend."

When Jody got home, she called Kathy.

Kathy answered, "Hello!"

Jody said, "It's me."

Kathy said, "Oh, Jody, is anything wrong?"

Jody said, "Nothing bad, but maybe something good." This had Kathy really puzzled. Then Jody said, "The new doctor from New York is in town. He started at the clinic today. His name is Rob Wilson. He has dark hair and eyes. Not bad to look at either."

Kathy said, "Jody, are you getting feelings for him?"

She said, "No, not right now. I don't even want to think about it. I just thought you'd like to know about him."

Chapter Eight

Jody was just ready to order a pizza when the phone rang. "Hello," said her dad. "How are you?"

Jody said, "Fine, I was just getting ready to order a pizza and a bottle of soda. Is anything wrong? Do you have enough medicine left?"

He said, "Yes, I'm still good on that. Jody, how are you doing? How's work going? How is Doctor Peterson?"

She said, "Doctor Peterson is doing just fine. Now that Doctor Wilson is on the staff, the workload is lighter. I'm doing fine. Work is getting to be more fun with Doctor Wilson around.

"Well, Dad, I'm glad you're doing all right. See you tomorrow. I love you! Bye."

George sat for a while wondering about Jody.

Chapter Nine

Doctor Wilson was fitting in very well. Everyone liked him. Doctor Peterson was very happy with him. He'd taken a big load off Doctor Peterson's hands.

Jody was at her desk when her dad walked in. He said, "I'm here for my checkup with Doctor Wilson."

She said, "Okay, Dad, have a seat. He'll be right with you."

A few minutes later, Doctor Wilson walked out. He introduced himself to George. George said, "Hi! Doc."

Doctor Wilson said, "Will you come with me into my office so we can talk?"

They went into the office, and George sat down. Doctor Wilson said, "How are you feeling?"

George said, "I'm doing fine. I'm getting stronger every day. How did all the tests turn out?"

Doctor Wilson replied, "Everything looks good as long as you stay on your medicine and take it easy. If you don't overdo it, you shouldn't have any problems."

George said, "Okay, Doc."

Doctor Wilson looked at George with a sparkle in his eyes and said, "That's one pretty daughter you have. I'm very attracted to her. I would like to be more than friends. Maybe I could start asking her out on dates.

But, every time I approach the dating subject, she gets defensive and skittish."

George said, "Well, Doc, all you can do is ask her.

You may have to go slow and easy with Jody, but you never know, she may just come around. By the way, now that you want to date my daughter, I guess that gives me the right to call you Rob, ha ha!"

Rob said, "I guess it does. Thanks, George. Call me if you have any questions."

Later that evening Rob phoned Jody. He said, "I'd like to talk to you. Could we meet at Hope Park in front of the wishing well?"

Jody said, "Okay." She hung the phone up. She wondered, "Why in the world does he want to talk to me?

What is he going to say?"

Chapter Ten

When Jody got to the park, she saw Rob tossing a coin into the wishing well. He was deep in thought.

She walked up to him and said, "Hi! A penny for your thoughts."

Rob jumped and looked up and smiled. Jody's face looked puzzled as she sat down. Rob sat down beside her.

He was longing to hold her hand, but knew she wouldn't let him.

They sat just looking at one another. They listened to the birds tweeting and chirping in the background.

After a few minutes Rob said, "I wanted to talk to you. I wanted to tell you that I'm very attracted to you.

I would like to be more than friends. I know we don't know one another or anything about each other yet, but you know there's a way to remedy that. Could we try?"

Jody smiled, with a twinkle in her eyes. She said, "How's that, Doctor?"

He said, "By us going out. How would dinner sound?

We could talk. It would help us to get to know one another."

Jody said, "That sounds good to me. I would like to know more about you. I've seen the TLC you show when you're taking care of patients. It makes me want to know all about you."

Rob said, "Great! I'll call you in a few days because I want to know all about you. Thank you, for the compliment."

They talked a little longer, and then Jody said,

"It's getting late. I'd better go. I need my beauty sleep."

Rob laughed, and they both stood up to leave.

That evening while Jody was getting ready for bed, the phone rang. "Hello, Jody, it's Aunt Debbie. How are you doing? I've been trying to get a hold of you. Where have you been?"

Jody said, "Why what's wrong?"

Aunt Debbie said, "Nothing's wrong, Jody. It's just that I worry when I can't reach you."

Jody said. "I've been busy at work showing Rob, I mean Doctor Wilson, around."

Aunt Debbie said, "Oh! It's Rob now instead of Doctor Wilson? Jody, what's going on? Is there a romance budding between the two of you?"

Jody said, "No, Aunt Debbie, it's too soon. I just met him. We want to get to know each other better. I'm not going to rush into anything until I'm positive it is the right thing for me. He did say he wants to know me better."

Aunt Debbie said, "What did you say?"

Jody said, "I said I'd like to get to know him better too. So he's going to call me. I like him, but I have a lot of feelings to sort out, like what Bill would think or say about my getting involved with another man. I wonder how he would feel about it."

Aunt Debbie said, "Jody, you know yourself that Bill would want you to go on with your life. You know in your heart that Bill would be happy for you. He would tell you to always follow your heart."

Jody said, "Maybe you're right. Thanks, Aunt Debbie. I'll let you know anything else that happens. I love you. Bye!"

Chapter Eleven

J ody woke up Saturday morning from a dream about Rob. She couldn't get it out of her mind. So, to keep busy, she cleaned her apartment and did her laundry.

Later on she got restless. She needed some air so she took a walk. She ended up at the wishing well in the park. She tossed a coin into the wishing well. She made a very special wish.

She started speaking to Bill in her mind. She talked out all her feelings with him, the way she used to do. She finally got the answers she needed to hear. Now she felt better. She walked back home smiling and thinking to herself, *Go for it, girl.*

Then she started thinking about how to tell Rob about Bill.

That evening Rob was restless and decided to take a walk around the town. All of a sudden he realized he was at the park. He went over to the wishing well and sat down. He stayed by the wishing well just thinking about Jody. He was praying that finally he had found someone he could care about -- maybe someone who would care about him. He tossed in another coin. He wished his first wish would come true.

As he walked to his car, he thought, *I'm finally over Tiffany, but before I get too involved with Jody, I want to tell her about Tiffany so I can start over with nothing coming between us.*

When Rob got home, he got all the pictures and things reminding him of Tiffany. He threw them away. He said to himself, *It's over. Now I can start getting to know Jody.*

Chapter Twelve

Rob got up the next morning. As he was getting ready to go to the clinic, he started thinking about Jody. He hoped they could be together soon.

When he walked into the clinic, Jody was already at her desk. She said, "Good morning, Rob, I mean Doctor Wilson. I have some patients that need to see you."

Rob said, "Are there any emergencies? I'd like to talk to you."

She said, "No emergencies."

He said, "Good! Please come into my office."

Jody followed him in and sat down.

Rob sat down and said, "Jody, after the talk in the park yesterday, I've been thinking about us. I would like to take you out for lunch if you don't have anything else to do. How about eleven-thirty? Is that good?"

Jody said, "That would be great." She got up and said, "I had better send in your first patient."

As she left, she had the happiest feeling. She felt her thoughts go to Rob and to lunch. She could hardly wait for the time to pass. She hadn't felt like this since Bill and she had been going together. She got to her desk and sent in Rob's first patient.

Just then Doctor Peterson walked up to her and said, "Good morning! What makes you look so chipper? Did you win the lottery?"

Jody laughed, "No lottery, Doctor, I have a date. I'm going out to lunch."

Doctor Peterson said, "I bet I know who you're going to lunch with. Is it Doctor Wilson?" Jody blushed, and Doctor Peterson said, "That's good. It's about time you started seeing other people. He's a nice boy. You have a good lunch and take all the time you want." He left and went into his office.

A short time later he called Rob. He asked him to step into his office. Rob said, "I'll be right in. I'm between patients." He went into Doctor Peterson's office.

Doctor Peterson said, "Hi, Rob, sit down." Rob sat down, and Doctor Peterson said, "How is everything going so far? Do you mind seeing patients that aren't heart patients?"

Rob said, "No, I like getting to know all the patients. I like getting into all areas of medicine. I also like the small town -- everyone knowing everyone. You asked me once if I thought I could get to like Hope well enough to make my home here. I can honestly say yes. I want to stay here. If you still want a partner, I would love to be your partner in the clinic and head of cardiology."

Doctor Peterson said, "I was wondering about your thoughts on that. I would love to have you stay as my partner and head of cardiology, permanently."

Rob said, "Thanks! I love it here. I didn't tell you, but my aunt and uncle live about fifty miles from here.

They have the Stevens Dairy Farm."

Doctor Peterson said, "I know them. I met them a couple of times when they've come into town for the town picnics. They're a very nice couple.

"By the way, Rob, Jody said you asked her out for lunch. She's a very nice girl. Don't hurt her. She's had a very hard year. Go slow until she feels she can tell you what happened. She is like a daughter to me."

Rob said, "Don't worry; that is the last thing I want to do. Her friendship means too much to me to ever hurt her, but thanks for telling me that. I'll be extra careful with her."

Doctor Peterson said, "Good boy! I won't say anything about our talk to her.

"Now, I would like to announce your being my partner and head of cardiology at the next town meeting. It's next month. I would like you there with me so I can introduce you to everyone."

Rob said, "That's fine with me. Now if you will let me get back to my patients, I only have a half hour until lunch."

Doctor Peterson said, "By all means get back and finish up. Keep up the good work. I'm very happy to have you as my partner."

Rob went back to his office with a happy heart. He had finally found a place where he was happy. He had a job he loved. He was in a town he loved. Then he thought of Jody. Maybe she was the girl who he could love and call his own -- someone to make everything perfect.

Chapter Thirteen

Rob and Jody got to the café and picked a quiet corner booth where they could talk without being disturbed. Rob looked at Jody. He smiled and said, "I'm very glad that we are having lunch together."

Jody said, "I've done some hard thinking and soul searching. I've decided I would like to build on our friendship. Maybe later we could work on a relationship.

I haven't had a man who made me feel like a whole woman since I lost Bill, my past love. I lost him the day before we were to be wed. But I've decided it's time for my heart to go on and forward."

Rob sat there stunned for a few minutes. Then he said, "My gosh! Jody, that must have torn you apart. Now I understand why you have been so skittish. I know it's going to be hard for you to forget about him, but with time maybe I can get into your heart. I promise to give it TLC for as long as you need it."

Then Rob took her hand and said, "Jody, I want to thank you for your honesty. I, too, have something to confess. When I was in New York, before I came to Hope, I was going with a girl named Tiffany. She was good for a while, until she got too possessive. She wanted things her way or no way at all. I had to tell her I run my life. She didn't like that idea, so I finally had to tell her we were over and done with."

Jody said, "I really appreciate you being so honest with me. I think we should both think about our situation; we can talk later. Right now we should be getting back to work before we are fired."

Chapter Fourteen

The next day, Jody phoned Kathy and her dad. They both told her that they were happy that she was part of the living again. She hung the phone up.

She went to the kitchen to start her dinner. The phone rang. It was Aunt Debbie. She said, "Jody, what's going on?"

Jody told her all about Rob and their conversation at lunch yesterday.

Aunt Debbie said, "Are you sure you know what you are doing?"

Jody replied, "I'm not sure, but I want to give it a try. I have to start sometime. Rob seems to be a nice guy.

I told him all about Bill. He was very sympathetic. He also told me about his past girlfriend. He was very honest. I feel we can work through any problems we encounter."

Aunt Debbie said, "Just go slow. Be careful!"

Jody said, "I will, Aunt Debbie. I love you. Bye!"

Rob had just walked in the door of his apartment when the phone rang. It was Aunt Lorraine.

She said, "How are you doing? Are you getting settled in okay?"

Rob said, "I'm doing well. I also have some news for you. I'm settled in. I have decided to stay and make Hope my home. I was offered a partnership and also the head of cardiology. Doctor Peterson is great,

and so is his nurse, Jody. Everyone in the clinic and at the hospital seems very nice and helpful. They made me feel right at home.

I love it."

Aunt Lorraine said, "That's good, Robbie; I'm glad you are staying. What about your girlfriend in New York?

Who is Jody?"

Rob said, "Tiffany is in the past. It is over with us. I want my life here. She didn't want to leave New York. Jody is the nurse at the clinic. I've gotten to know her quite well. She has had a rough time, and I'm trying to get to know her. We went out to lunch and we talked. I told her about Tiffany. I told her that it was over with us. She told me about how hard it has been for her. She lost her fiancé just before their wedding. I told her I'd like to help her get over him. She said that would be nice. She said she'd help me forget Tiffany. I want you to meet her. She's a great girl.

"By the way, Doctor Peterson said he has met you and Uncle Leo at a few of the town picnics. Next week is the town meeting. Are you going? I would like you there because Doctor Peterson is going to introduce me as his partner in the clinic and head of cardiology at the hospital. You could also meet Jody."

Aunt Lorraine said, "Oh! Robbie, I'm so happy about all of it. We'd love to come. I'm glad you are settling down by us. I love you, Robbie. Bye! Bye! We'll talk later. Be good!"

Rob said, "I love you both, too. See you soon."

Chapter Fifteen

The town meeting was coming up in a few days. Rob had been so busy that he hadn't had too much time to talk to Jody. He realized he had missed not talking to her or having lunch with her.

Jody was wondering if he still wanted to be friends or if he was afraid he couldn't be more than just friends. All he had been doing was saying, "Hi!" when he came in.

He was busy going between the clinic and hospital since they had had lunch. That was when they had opened their hearts to one another. She had said hi to Rob this morning. *Maybe I'll see him before we leave,* she thought as she started clearing off her desk.

Rob was finally done with his work for the day. Then he realized that it had been a while since he had been able to take time to see how Jody was doing. He felt bad.

He decided to ask her out to dinner tonight, hoping against hope that she would say yes.

He said to himself, *I have to be a fool to have gotten so busy that I haven't taken time to say more than a passing hi to her for so long. I hope she understands. I really miss talking to her. I'm going to change that right now. Please don't make it too late for me to make it up to her.*

Rob left his office. He headed to the reception desk. He didn't see Jody at the desk. His worst fear came to him. She had left. Just

then, she appeared. She was coming from Doctor Peterson's office. He caught up to her as she reached the door.

He took her coat off the coat rack and said, "May I help you on with your coat?"

As she slipped into her coat, Rob said, "I'm sorry

I've been so busy, but I had to catch up on my work so all is in order for the town meeting next Monday.

"Are you doing anything tonight? Would you like to go out to dinner at the café down the street? We can talk some, if you feel like it, and make up for lost time."

Jody said, "Oh, Rob, I forgot about the town meeting.

I thought you had forgotten about me. Yes, I am doing something tonight. I'm going to have dinner with a very dear friend, and I hope to have a very long talk and maybe a stroll in the park. Thank you for asking me. I've been hoping you'd ask me. I'd love to go to dinner with you.

I'm ready to go now. How about you?"

He gave her a big hug and long kiss. Then he stepped back and apologized for being so forward, but he said, "I missed you very much."

Jody said lovingly, "Don't apologize. I liked it. I hope there will be more. If I'm going too fast, just stop me. I can't help it. I missed you more than I thought I could miss anyone."

Chapter Sixteen

The town meeting was about to start. The parking lot was packed with cars from all over the county. It seemed that a new doctor brought the whole county out. But truth be told, some just wanted to see what he looked like and to see if what they had heard was the truth. And some came just for the dance.

The mayor stood up and called the meeting to order.

He said, "Good evening, ladies and gentlemen. Welcome to the Hope Town Meeting. Now, I will turn this meeting over to Doctor Peterson. He has a few announcements to make."

Doctor Peterson came up. He said, "I have something important to tell everyone." He called Doctor Rob Wilson up to the podium. He said, "I would like everyone to meet the new head cardiologist at Hope Medical Clinic and Hospital and also my new partner."

Everyone clapped.

Rob was stunned; he didn't know what to say. Finally, he said, "Thank you for your welcome. I hope I live up to your expectations."

Doctor Peterson put his hand on Rob's shoulder. He said, "Congratulations! I'm happy to have you here."

Jody rushed up and embraced Rob.

After they finished the other town business, Doctor Peterson announced the dance that was to follow the meeting. Rob whispered in Jody's ear, "You're my dancing partner for the evening. Let's go!"

Just then the mayor caught up with them at the door.

He said, "Congratulations! Welcome to Hope."

After the mayor left, Jody looked at Rob and said,

"All right, hot shot! Were you planning on giving me a chance to say yes or no?"

Rob looked at Jody and said, "Gee, I never thought.

Do you want to be my partner for the evening?"

Jody said, "Don't worry, I'd love to be your partner, whenever and for however long you want me."

Rob looked at Jody lovingly. She looked back at him lovingly, too. Then she said, "Let's go have some fun. It's been a while since I really felt like having any fun."

Chapter Seventeen

When they got to the Hope Community Center, the band was playing a lively polka. Rob held his hand out and said, "Shall we skip the light fantastic, my dear?"

Jody said, "Of course, my love."

Rob smiled. He said, "I like the sound of that."

Rob twirled Jody around the dance floor. Then he started nibbling on her ear. Jody snuggled closer to him. She whispered in his ear, "I'm falling in love with you."

Rob said, "I'm already in love with you." He wrapped her up in his arms. He kissed her long and hard right in the middle of the dance floor.

He said, "Are you sure you are ready for the big step so soon? I don't want to push you too soon."

Jody replied, "I'm definite. You're not pushing me into anything I don't want. I love what I see. I want what

I love. I love you, Rob. You're everything that I will ever need or want."

Rob looked at her lovingly and said, "Okay, all I want is your happiness."

They continued dancing until the music stopped.

After the dance was over, they decided to go out to get some air. On their way out, Rob spotted his aunt and uncle. He said, "Come with me, Jody, I want you to meet my aunt and uncle."

Jody said, "I didn't know you had family here."

He said, "They have a farm near here."

Jody said, "Great! I'd love to meet them."

They walked over to Rob's aunt and uncle, and Rob introduced them to Jody. Jody said, "Very nice to meet you."

Aunt Lorraine said, "It's very nice to meet you, too."

Uncle Leo said, "Boy! You found yourself one fine little lady. You take good care of her and don't let her get away."

Rob said, "I thank God every day for letting me find her."

Then Aunt Lorraine said, "What was happening out there on the dance floor, Rob?"

Rob replied, "I was just dancing with the girl I love. I hope to marry her as soon as she says yes."

Aunt Lorraine said, "I'm so happy for you. You really deserve some happiness."

She gave Jody a big hug and said, "Be kind to him. Rob's a good-hearted man." Rob blushed.

Jody said, "I'll give him TLC for as long as he wants it."

Then Rob said, "Jody, would you like something to drink?"

Jody said, "Yes!"

They headed over to the punch bowl. As they were walking there, Jody saw Aunt Debbie talking to Kathy and Mike. She said, "Well, Rob, are you ready to meet my Aunt Debbie, my sister, Kathy, and her husband, Mike?"

He said, "I remember your aunt and your sister from the hospital."

Jody said, "Aunt Debbie, Kathy, Mike, I want you to meet the man of my dreams, Doctor Rob Wilson."

They all looked at him. Rob was smiling down at her.

They all told her that they were happy that she had finally found someone that would make her happy.

Jody said, "Thanks! I'm so glad you like him. But do me a favor; don't tell Dad. He doesn't know about any of this. I want to tell him myself."

They all said okay, and then they welcomed Rob to the family.

Chapter Eighteen

The next day, Jody was at her desk working when Rob came in. She said, "Good morning!" She gave him a kiss and a big bear hug. Then she said, "Rob, will you be free for lunch?"

He said, "I will make sure that I am."

Jody said, "Great! Dad has an appointment at eleven. That's your last one until two. I want to tell Dad about us and our good news. I've asked him to join us for lunch, but he doesn't know you will be there. So while you see him, hush is the word, okay, honey."

Rob said, "Okay, doll! How about meeting you there at the café?"

Jody said, "Fine, dear. I want to surprise Dad."

Rob said, "Okay, I'll see you there." He gave Jody a loving, lingering kiss and a hug to keep her thinking of him."

She thought, *As if I could forget him, "Not" foreseeable.*

Jody had just sat down at her desk when her dad came in. Jody said, "Hi, Dad! What are you doing for lunch?"

He said, "I have a feeling that I'm going with you."

Jody said, "Yes, Dad! Would you mind if someone meets us there?"

He said, "The more the merrier."

She said, "Great! After you're done with the doctor, we will leave."

Jody and her dad got to the café and walked to the rear booth. They had just sat down when Rob walked in. He came over and sat down next to Jody. He said, "Hi, George!

I hope you don't mind if I join you."

George said, "No, I don't mind a bit."

They ordered their lunch.

Then Jody said, "Dad, Rob and I have something to tell you."

George smiled.

Then she said, "We hope you will like it. I think it will make you very happy.

"I don't know if you know this or not, but we have been seeing each other, I mean dating for a while."

George said, "I figured something was going on."

Then she said, "I know I should have told you before, but I didn't until I knew how it would turn out. But, Dad, we dearly love each other. We hope to be married soon.

I know it may seem quick, but I've made my peace with Bill."

Rob said, "How would you feel about having a new son-in-law?"

George replied, "Nothing would make me happier."

Then Jody leaned over to Rob and whispered, "You don't know how long I've been waiting to hear you say those words. They were the sweetest music to my ears."

George said, "Hot dog! This is just wonderful to hear.

It's about time you start living life again, girl.

"Rob, welcome to our family. I'm so glad it's you making Jody smile again. Now let's eat."

Chapter Nineteen

J ody and Rob had been dating and working together for the last few months. They had become very close. They both felt that the time had come for the big step. Jody had been waiting for Rob to ask that special question. She hoped it would be soon. Waiting was getting very hard.

Rob had decided to ask Jody to marry him at the Christmas Party, but hadn't decided how to do it. The Christmas Party was in a few days.

It was the day of the Christmas Party. Jody was busy putting the final touches on the decorations. She was hanging the banner that said, "Donate from the Heart" and the little "Thank You" hearts on the tree when Rob walked in. He said, "Hi, Angel!" He grabbed her and gave her a kiss and a hug. He said, "I've been waiting to do that all day."

She smiled said, "Me too."

Rob looked around and said, "Is there anything else that needs to be done?"

Jody said, "No, everything is in order except for the catering service, but they don't need anyone to be here."

Rob said, "Good! How about going for a bite to eat?"

Jody said, "Sounds good, Honey Buns. But just a quick one. I've got an appointment with my hairdresser at two. After that I'm going

shopping for a new outfit -- something that will make your eyes pop out when you see me in it."

Rob said, "Oh, baby!"

They went and had lunch. When they finished, he kissed her and said, "Bye, darling. I'll pick you up at four."

When Jody finished getting her hair and nails done, she went to the dress shop. She found the perfect dress.

She went into the dressing room to try it on. She said to herself, *This is the one.* It was a long, red velvet dress with white ruffles around the collar and the sleeves. She also found shoes and a purse to match. Then she headed for home.

It was four. Just knowing that Rob would be at her door any minute sent shivers of excitement through her whole body.

Just then the doorbell rang. Jody took one last look in the mirror and answered the door.

Rob took one look at her and went completely speechless. After a few minutes he said, "Jody, you're a vision of loveliness. My heart is beating like a tom-tom.

I think if we don't leave right now, this minute, we will never get to the party."

Jody blushed and said, "I've been thinking about the same thing. I want to give you the pleasure that I know you will give me."

He said, "Oh! Jody, sweetheart, if I wasn't a gentlemen, with old-fashioned, romantic ideals, I would be taking any and all doubts and fears out of your mind by making love to you right here and now."

She said, "Oh, Rob, you're a real gem."

Rob and Jody got to the hall. Doctor Peterson said, "Hi! Doctor Wilson, hi! Jody. Rob, I would like you to say a few words about our *fundraiser* to get the crowd in the spirit to donate."

Rob and Doctor Peterson went up on stage. Doctor Peterson said, "May I have your attention for a moment, please?"

When the crowd quieted down, Doctor Peterson said, "Thank you. Welcome ladies and gentlemen to Hope's fundraiser and Christmas

party. I hope you have a good time, but remember why you are here. Now a few words from Doctor Wilson."

Rob said, "Thank you very much. The fundraiser is to raise enough funds so we can upgrade our equipment at the clinic and the hospital. We also need a few more doctors and nurses. Our hospital and clinic are growing. Please be generous and have a good time. Enjoy yourselves. Now let's have some fun."

Later Jody was sitting with her dad and their families. She looked around, but she didn't see Rob anywhere. She wondered where he had gone.

All of a sudden the kids were screaming, "Santa! Santa!" as he entered through the door with a big red bag on his back. He sat down in the big red chair beside the Christmas tree. The kids all lined up for a turn on his lap. Santa gave them each a gift -- a small doctor's kit for the boys and a nurse's kit for the girls.

Then Jody's dad and everyone at the table said, "Jody, it's your turn to sit on Santa's lap."

Jody said, "You've got to be kidding."

Everyone said, "Oh, come on, go for it. You may get a big surprise. It may well be worth it."

Rob knew that Jody had no idea that he was Santa.

His surprise would go as planned. Jody walked over to Santa. Santa said, "Well, little darling, come sit on my lap. Tell me your Christmas wish."

She said, "Well, Santa, there's a special someone who I'm dearly in love with. I want him to be my husband."

Rob's heart made a flip. She got up to leave to go back to the table. Santa pulled her back on his lap. He whispered, "I'll see what I can do." Then he let her go to the table, and Santa left.

Rob returned to the table. He said to Jody, "Santa stopped me and said you have a special Christmas wish. I have one, too." He kneeled down on his knee in front of her. He reached into his pocket. He took Jody's hand and said, "This special man would be honored to become your husband, if you will have me. Jody, my love, will you marry me?"

He smiled and he opened the box. It was the biggest diamond Jody had ever seen.

Jody said, teary voiced, "Yes! Oh, yes!"

Rob got up and they embraced. Yips and screams filled the room. Hugs and kisses came from everywhere. Everyone congratulated them and wished them well.

Chapter Twenty

Sunday morning Jody got a call from Kathy; she said, "Hi, Jody. How are you doing this morning?"

Jody said, "I'm doing just fine. How are you? Did you and Mike iron out your problems about the kids?"

Kathy said, "Yes, we did. We sat up half the night until we came up with a solution. Everything is, finally, going well again."

Jody said, "I'm so glad to hear that. Rob and I are doing great. We are planning on announcing the wedding date soon. I've got to go now. Tell everyone I said hi!

See you soon. Love ya! Bye!"

Jody had just sat down to eat her breakfast when the phone rang again. It was Aunt Debbie. She said, "Hi! Jody, how is everything?"

Jody said, "What's wrong?"

Aunt Debbie said, "Nothing is wrong. I have good news to tell you. Do you know Clyde Masters?"

Jody said, "Yes, he owns the computer store. Why, what about him?"

Aunt Debbie said, "Well, we have been dating for a long time now. He's getting pretty serious. I'm hoping to hear him pop the question -- soon."

Jody said, "That's great! I wish you luck and love.

I have to go now. See you soon. Bye, Bye."

That evening Jody and Rob went out for dinner. They started talking about wedding plans. The more they talked, the more they wanted to speed things up. They both decided to have a smaller wedding. Jody asked Rob how he would feel about having a family dinner to discuss wedding plans with both of their families. Rob agreed.

Chapter Twenty-One

The next evening when Jody got home from the clinic, she put her feet up to relax for awhile. Then her phone rang. It was her dad. She said, "Hi, Dad. How are you? Is everything okay?"

Her dad said, "Jody, you worry too much. I'm doing fine. How are you doing?"

She said, "Dad, I'm happier than I've ever been.

I'm truly in love. I'm going to marry the man of my dreams.

"Speaking of that, Dad, what are you doing for dinner next Saturday?"

He said, "I'm free as far as I know."

Jody said, "Good! I'm getting the whole family together for a family dinner so we can all discuss our wedding plans."

He said, "I will be there. Where and what time, Jody?"

She said, "It's the Family Restaurant out on the highway at five. Dad, I don't mean to cut this short, but

I have three more phone calls to make. I love you! Take care, Dad. Bye!"

Then Jody phoned Kathy, Aunt Debbie, and Rob's Aunt Lorraine. She told them about the family dinner next Saturday at the Family Restaurant on the highway at five.

After spending about two hours on the phone, she grabbed a sandwich and a soda for her supper. Then she took a long shower. As

she was lathering up with soap, she started thinking about Rob and how his hands would feel on her. She had to quickly finish her shower before her mind went on other thoughts. She went to bed, but didn't sleep well. She couldn't get thoughts about Rob out of her mind.

Jody was up early the next day. She went to the clinic earlier than usual. She had some paperwork to do on a new patient. It was the first appointment of the day.

She put the chart in on Rob's desk. She returned to her desk and gave herself a couple of minutes for a cup of coffee.

She had just poured a cup of coffee, when Rob walked in. She offered him her coffee. He said, "I'd rather have a kiss from my angel's lips to get my day going."

Jody set the coffee down. She flew into his arms.

Rob said, "What's wrong, sweetheart?"

Jody said, "It's just that I love you so much. I couldn't get you out of my thoughts all night long."

Rob said, "Now I know you love me, especially when you have trouble sleeping. I didn't sleep either." They didn't get to finish their talk because their first appointment was walking in. It was time to start the day. They were busy until five-thirty that day.

The next few days were not much easier. By Friday Rob was overwrought. Jody was tired out as well. They couldn't wait for things to lighten up. Doctor Peterson stopped in to see Rob. He apologized for not being at the clinic more often to help out, but he was overworked also.

Then he said, "By the way, Rob, the new doctor will arrive on Monday. He'll be taking care of the general practice cases. You'll like him. He just finished medical school. He's a lot like you, Rob, young and very caring.

His name is Todd Weston."

Rob let out a sigh. He said, "Thank goodness!"

Doctor Peterson said, "We got enough donations from our fundraiser to hire another doctor and update our equipment and give you and Jody a nice raise. You both are well worth it."

He talked to Jody on his way out. He told Rob and her to get some well-deserved rest over the weekend. He said, "I'll take over tomorrow. The clinic is open only half a day." He thanked them for their excellent work, and he left.

Rob was so tired he slept until ten-thirty on

Saturday morning. He hopped into the shower and got dressed. He reached for the phone and called Jody.

Jody answered on the third ring. Rob said, "Good morning, sweetheart. Were you awake?"

Jody said, "Yes, honey, I just stepped out of the shower."

Rob said, "Did you think of me being in there with you? My hands caressing and roaming over your silky, soft body."

Jody said, "Much more than you can imagine. It's getting harder for me to control my thoughts and feelings about you."

Rob said, "I know and can relate with that because my feelings, for you, are getting really hectic on my manly feelings and functions. I can't wait until we are married. Darling, are you sure you want to wait until everything's planned for our wedding? Wouldn't you rather just elope?"

She said, "Oh, Rob, we can't do that. Our families are expecting the family dinner now, but don't think that your idea doesn't sound sinfully tempting because it sure does."

Rob said, "You can't blame a guy for trying." He gave her a long kiss over the phone.

Then he said, "Honey! Can you be ready by four? I want you all to myself for an hour before our families get here."

She said, "That's an offer I can't refuse."

They arrived at the restaurant at five-fifteen. They walked in and found their families seated and waiting for them.

Jody's dad said something to Mike, and they both looked at them and laughed. The women tried to hush them so Jody and Rob wouldn't be embarrassed. They all thought it was very funny.

After everyone was settled down, they ordered what they wanted. When they finished and were drinking their coffee, their families

started talking. They started discussing and making plans on how and where the wedding should be.

Jody's dad wanted them to have a big wedding. He wanted Jody to wear her mother's wedding dress. Aunt Debbie wanted to hire a wedding coordinator. Aunt Lorraine wanted to know what church and minister they were picking. Jody's dad said, "The church she's always attended."

Kathy was naming bridesmaids. She also said, "How would Rich be for the miniature groom and ring bearer and Robin as the miniature bride?" They all liked that idea.

Both aunts were having a loud discussion over the flower arrangements. What kind of flowers? They agreed on pastel roses.

Uncle Leo suggested red and white tuxedos to fit the

Valentine's day theme. Jody's dad didn't agree. He wanted black tuxedos. They would look better. Mike shouted that he despised wearing a tie.

Kathy wanted red dresses for the bridesmaids. Jody said she'd rather have pink. She liked pastels.

Aunt Debbie said it would be nicer to wait until summer. It would be warm and sunny. Then they could have the wedding in Hope Park. The flowers would be colorful and in full bloom.

Jody's dad wanted to know the wedding date. They both replied, "The most romantic day of the year,

Valentines Day!"

Everyone was talking at the same time. Questions, suggestions, and comments were coming at them faster than a waterfall. By the time everyone left, there still wasn't anything resolved. Rob's head was humming. Jody's nerves were strung tight.

Chapter Twenty-Two

Two weeks later, Rob and Jody were both sitting in the park just thinking, trying to figure out what they should do about both of their families badgering them.

They were trying to take over their wedding.

Jody said, "Rob, this is getting way out of hand. I can't stand our families bickering over our wedding. I know they are only trying to help, and I love them dearly for it. I don't want to upset or hurt them in any way. I know that you wouldn't want to either. But, Rob, it's our wedding. We should have some say in what we want. I just get so fed up with all this mumbo jumbo. I just want to marry you.

"Rob, would you mind if we just call Aunt Debbie and ask her and Clyde to come over? Then we can ask them to stand up for us when we elope and get married."

Rob looked at her and smiled with bursting happiness. Jody said, "That's right, sweetheart, we're eloping."

Rob said, "That sounds great, honey." He gave Jody a hug. Then he said, "But what are our families going to think about this?"

Jody said, "If the family is upset or hurt, we can always renew our vows in June -- if that's okay with you."

Rob said, "Honey, I'd remarry you anytime, anywhere."

When they get to Jody's apartment, she phoned Aunt Debbie. Aunt Debbie answered and said, "Hello!"

Jody said, "Can you get a hold of Clyde?"

She said, "Yes, he's right here with me, Jody. Why?"

Jody said, "We would like to talk to you and Clyde. We have something to ask you."

Ten minutes later Aunt Debbie and Clyde were seated in Jody's living room. Aunt Debbie said, "Okay, you two, what's going on that you need us to hear? What do you have to tell us?"

Jody looked at Aunt Debbie and said, "We have decided to elope to Vegas and get married there. We would like to have you and Clyde stand up for us. But, please, don't tell Dad or Kathy and Mike or Rob's aunt and uncle. We will explain everything to everyone when we get back."

Aunt Debbie said, "You know it's almost the end of January. Are you sure you don't want to wait?"

Both Jody and Rob said, "No! We want to do it now."

Aunt Debbie agreed and said, "Why don't Clyde and I meet you here tomorrow around five in the morning, and then we can leave for Vegas. That will give us plenty of time to find a nice chapel for your wedding. We'll also have time to relax. We can leave for home Sunday afternoon so you don't miss any work."

Chapter Twenty-Three

It was Saturday morning and Aunt Debbie and Clyde got to Jody's apartment. Jody answered the door. They came in and went into the living room.

Aunt Debbie, while holding Clyde's hand said, "I'd like you and Rob to sit down a minute. What I'm about to say may seem like it is awfully quick, but Clyde and I have decided to make it a double wedding if it's all right with you. We have been seeing each other for over a year."

Jody and Rob said, "That's great!"

Then they all got up and left for the car. They were on their way to the airport to catch their plane to Vegas.

They figured that O'Hara, in Chicago, was closest. It was only an hour away. They checked and their plane left at seven in the morning so they would have plenty of time for parking and taking care of checking their bags and getting tickets.

They landed in Vegas. They caught a cab and asked the driver if there were any chapels around with a wishing well. He said, "There is a chapel called 'The Wishing Well Chapel' on the other side of the Strip."

They all said, "Perfect! Take us there."

He smiled and said, "A double wedding, right?"

Jody and Aunt Debbie blushed and said yes.

He took them to the chapel and said, "Good luck!"

They said, "We don't need luck. We have each other."

They got out of the cab and went in. The inside had a platform where there was a park scene with a real wishing well set in the center. The minister came out and said,

"May I help you?"

They told him that they wanted a double wedding. He sat down with them and told them how much it would cost.

He also said that his wife played the organ. If they would like some music, it would be extra. They said they wanted the whole package.

He placed Jody and Aunt Debbie on one side of the wishing well and Rob and Clyde on the other side. He stood between them in front of the wishing well. Before the minister got started, he explained to them all about the ceremony.

Then he asked them if there were any special words they wanted to say to each other. Jody and Rob said, "We do!"

Debbie and Clyde said, "Just the 'I do's.'"

He said, "I'll marry Debbie and Clyde first. Then it is Jody and Rob's turn."

Rob and Jody were ready. The minister performed the ceremony. Then Jody said her heartfelt words to Rob. She said with love in her eyes, "Rob, since you've come into my life, all of my days have been sunny and bright. With you at my side, I know that I'm alive. You've made my heart whole. I haven't made that an easy role. I love you today and for always."

The minister said, "Now it's your turn, Rob."

Rob said, "Jody, with you as my wife, I know I will have a wonderful life. You've given me your heart. I'll be the man of your dreams. You need to wish no more. You've found what you've been wishing for."

The minister said, "Those were the most beautiful words. I don't hear vows such as those very often. Now,

Rob and Jody, I pronounce you man and wife. Rob, you may kiss your bride. Congratulations! Mr. and Mrs. Rob Wilson,

I wish you a long and loving life."

Everyone clapped and wished each other love and a long and happy life.

Then Rob asked the minister if he could call them a cab to go to a hotel-casino. The minister said, "I'd be happy to. Where are you going?"

Rob said, "To the MGM Grand."

Jody was shocked. Rob saw her look. He said, "Don't worry about it. I have been saving for a long time for this day. Just leave everything to me."

Chapter Twenty-Four

The cab came, and they all got in and went to the Palace. The outside was beautiful, but the inside was out of this world. They went to the desk and said they had just been married and needed two honeymoon suites.

The manager had them sign the register. He called a bellboy. He took their bags and showed them to their suites.

Rob said, "Mr. and Mrs. Masters, this is our treat. It's our wedding present to you. After you get settled in, meet us at our room around six. We will all go have dinner.

You guys behave yourselves."

Uncle Clyde and Aunt Debbie said, "We won't do anything that you and Jody won't be doing."

Rob smiled and chuckled.

Rob and Jody went to their room. Rob picked Jody up and carried her over the threshold. Jody said, "Oh, Rob, the room is beautiful."

They took a shower together, both full of the thoughts they had been having for so long. When they were dressed, they relaxed for a short time.

Aunt Debbie and Uncle Clyde met them as they were walking out of their room. They all went to dinner. They had a delicious dinner with lively conversation. When the check came, Rob said, "I'll take care of this."

Uncle Clyde said, "Debbie and I are getting tired, so if you don't mind, we're going to our room. Thanks for dinner. See you in the morning."

Rob and Jody both said, "Sleep well. We love you."

After they left, Rob asked Jody if she would like to see the casino and look around for a while. Jody said,

"That would be fun." They walked around and watched people until around nine. They were getting tired so they went back to their room.

Rob took his shower first and got into bed. Then Jody took hers. She spent time making sure she looked beautiful for her man. She slid into her silky honeymoon nighty. She yelled, "Rob, close your eyes. Don't peek! I'm coming to bed."

The next morning, Aunt Debbie and Uncle Clyde met them for breakfast. They talked about when to leave for home. They all decided they would leave at noon. Then they would have enough time to rest up for work on Monday. They said they'd meet and have lunch. Then they'd leave for the airport and home. They went back to their rooms to pack.

When Rob and Jody got to their room, he said, "Jody, honey, I know that this wasn't much of a honeymoon, but I promise to give you a real romantic honeymoon as soon as I can."

Aunt Debbie and Uncle Clyde were also in their room packing. Clyde came up behind Debbie and said, "Where would you like to honeymoon, my sweet darling?"

Debbie turned around and said, "The rest of my life with you will be honeymoon enough for me."

They all met and went to have some lunch after they packed. Around noon they all stood in the lobby and waited for the cab to go to the airport to catch a plane for Chicago. Then they got their car and headed home.

Chapter Twenty-Five

Rob and Jody were tired when they got home. They sat on the couch cuddling and relaxing. Jody said, "Rob! What are we going to do about our families?"

Rob said, "I don't think they will be too upset, especially when we tell them about having a big wedding in June. They can plan the whole thing any way they wish."

Jody said, "We will call everyone when we go to lunch tomorrow. We'll have them all come over around seven. We can tell them and try to explain so they will understand without being mad or upset."

Before they went to bed, Rob told Jody that he was going to move his stuff in this week and also tell their landlord about their marriage. Rob said, "Now that that's settled, it's time for bed, Mrs. Wilson."

Jody said, "Yes, master."

Rob said, "Hmm, I like that."

The next morning while they had breakfast, Jody said, "Don't forget lunch."

Rob said, "I won't forget. Now let's go to work."

When they got to the clinic, before they went in the door, Rob kissed Jody. He said, "I needed that to get through the day."

Jody said, "I needed that too. I love you."

They walked in and started their day. Jody went to her desk, and Rob went to his office.

Over lunch hour they phoned their families. They told them to be at their apartment at seven that night. They finished lunch. She looked at Rob and said, "I love you, more and more each day."

Rob kissed her and said, "I feel the same way about you, angel."

They walked back to the clinic. Doctor Peterson was waiting for them. He said, "I'm sorry I'm late. I had an emergency at the hospital."

Rob said, "Don't worry about it. I'm getting to know a doctor's life and the emergencies that pop up.

"Doctor Peterson, Jody and I have some wonderful news to tell you."

Jody walked up and showed him her wedding ring. She said, "We eloped to Vegas and got married on Saturday. My Aunt Debbie and Clyde Masters went along with us. They made it a double wedding ceremony."

Doctor Peterson hugged Jody, and he shook Rob's hand. He said, "I'm very happy for you. I knew that girl would get you moving and shaking. Oh! By the way, Rob, what about the families?"

Rob said, "We're telling them tonight."

Doctor Peterson said, "Good luck!"

Rob said, "Thanks, I may need it."

Chapter Twenty-Six

Rob and Jody got home after work. They had a quick supper. They took a shower and freshened up. Jody straightened the apartment up. It was almost seven.

Jody was getting nervous.

Rob said, "Honey, calm down. It's going to be fine, sweetheart."

The doorbell rang. Rob answered the door and greeted everyone. They all sat down. Rob said, "Just a minute, I'll get Jody."

Rob went into the kitchen. He said, "I'll take the tray for you."

They went into the living room, and Rob set the tray of coffee and cookies down on the coffee table. Then they went to sit down. Rob was holding her left hand.

Jody's dad said, "What's up?"

Jody turned to Rob and smiled. Then they both turned to the families. They both said, "We have something to tell you."

Then Rob said, "When you hear what it is, we beg of you, please don't be mad at us or upset with us. Jody and I really love each other. We just couldn't wait any longer to be together. So, Saturday morning, we eloped. We went to Vegas and got married."

Everyone looked stunned for a minute.

Then Jody's dad said, "I'm so happy for you. I'm not mad or upset. I remember being young and in love. I didn't want to wait long to be married either."

Kathy said, "How does it feel to be married, Jody?"

Jody smiled at Rob and said, "It's wonderful, but then you should know, Kathy."

Mike took Kathy's hand and kissed her and said, "She'd better know."

They all got a laugh out of that. It lightened the mood. Then Aunt Lorraine said, "I'm a little disappointed, but I will get over it."

Jody said, "We're so happy you aren't mad that we eloped. We would love it if all of you would get together and plan a wedding so we can renew our ceremony just for you. We will leave you to finish taking care of all the details. If you feel the weather is nice enough, you may go ahead and plan it at Hope Park. I know we have let all of you down, but we want to try to make up for it. We'll leave this one in your hands.

"By the way, Aunt Debbie and Clyde have some news to tell everyone."

Aunt Debbie said, "This may be a shock to everyone, but I've been dating Clyde for over a year now. We were married with them. We stood up for Jody and Rob in Vegas and they, in turn, repaid the favor for us. We're very happy."

George, Aunt Lorraine, and Kathy all said, "This is some night for great news. Congratulations! All of you."

Then they did the hugging, kissing, and the "I love you's."

After they left, Rob said, "Well, honey, do you feel better now? I think it went pretty well. It helped with you telling everyone that they had charge of our big wedding."

Jody said, "I guess it did. I surely hope we are in their good graces."

Rob said, "Oh, honey, they still all love us. You know that. Now come over here and cuddle up beside me, my little love bug." They sat down and watched a romantic movie until Rob started to get romantic. Jody knew it was bedtime.

Rob and Jody walked into the clinic the next day. Doctor Peterson and Doctor Weston said, "Hello, how's the 'Old Married Couple'?"

As soon as they said that, out of the exam room came Aunt Debbie, Aunt Lorraine, Kathy, and George. They said, "Over in the corner is a table full of gifts."

Rob and Jody looked at one another, both thinking,

What gives?

Aunt Lorraine walked over to Jody and gave her a big hug. She said, "Welcome to your wedding shower. It's our way of apologizing for the way we acted at the family dinner and Monday night. We were selfish, only thinking about our pleasures with your wedding. We were plain awful. You and Rob had every right to just run off and get married. We're so sorry. Can you ever forgive us? We're all very happy for you. Jody, you're just what Rob needs. We all love you."

Rob and Jody said, "We love you very much. You're forgiven. After all, you're family."

After the gifts were loaded into Rob's truck, they all left, and Rob and Jody went back to work.

It was a slow day with only a few appointments. Rob went into Doctor Peterson's office. Rob said, "Did you know about this?"

Doctor Peterson said, "Yes, I did, Rob. They wanted to surprise you and Jody. They knew that here would be the best place."

Rob and Jody got home that evening and unloaded the gifts. They fixed dinner together and did dishes. Then they got comfy on the couch and talked about what had happened today. They both went to bed with lighter hearts.

Chapter Twenty-Seven

The next day, after work, Jody helped Rob move his stuff out of his apartment and into theirs. They talked to the landlord about Rob's moving in. They told him that they had just gotten married.

The days passed quickly. February came; it was Valentine's Day. Jody and Rob were having breakfast -- heart-shaped pancakes with strawberries and whipped cream.

Rob said, "Honey, I'm leaving a little earlier this morning. I have something to take care of before going to work."

Jody said, "Okay, honey, so do I." She kissed him.

She said, "Bye, I'll see you at work." He left.

Rob walked into the jewelry store. He looked around, and out of the corner of his eye, he saw the perfect gift for Jody. He bought it, and he went down the street smiling. Then he went to the drugstore and the flower shop. He walked out of the flower shop and headed to work.

Jody walked the aisles of the men's store until she found the right gift for Rob. As she walked to work, she was thinking of tonight and how it would be their first Valentines Day in their own apartment.

It was a slow afternoon at the clinic so Jody went home early. She fixed a special dinner. She lit the red candles. Everything was ready when Rob walked in the door.

Jody grabbed Rob and said, "Happy Valentines Day, sweetheart. Close your eyes and don't peek until I say you can look." She took him into the bathroom so he could shower and freshen up. Then she went

into the dining room. While she was waiting, she put the finishing touches on the table. Then she went into the kitchen. She slipped into the new hot, frilly dressing gown. She heard Rob say, "Can I come out now and open my eyes?"

She said, "Come on out."

As Jody was walking to the dining room, Rob was coming out of the bedroom. Their eyes met. Rob let out a "*Wow*!" He grabbed Jody and said, "Oh, baby!"

They went into the dining room. Rob said, "Oh, how pretty. The dinner looks delicious, but not as tasty as you."

Jody said, "Oh, Rob! Just eat your dinner; dessert is later."

When they finished dinner, Rob said, "Wait here a minute. I'll be right back."

While Rob was gone, Jody went and got his gifts.

She put them by his dinner plate. He came in and sat down beside Jody. He gave her the heart-shaped box of chocolates and red roses. Jody gave Rob his presents. They both opened their gifts.

Rob loved the gifts from Jody which were sexy heart underwear and a shirt that said, "World's Sexiest Man!" on the front and "He's All Mine!" on the back.

Jody opened her heart-shaped box of chocolates. Then she took her red roses into the kitchen. As she was taking them out of the wrapping paper, a small box fell out.

Rob heard a scream. He ran to the kitchen door. As he came through, Jody flew into his arms saying, "Oh, Rob, you shouldn't have. I love it. It's beautiful."

It was a ring, a ruby-red heart with small white diamonds around the heart.

Rob said, "I had to do something special. It's our first Valentines Day together."

Jody said, "Oh, honey! You're too romantic. I love you!" She kissed and hugged him.

They went into the living room, sat, and snuggled on the couch for a while. Then Jody said, "It's dessert time."

Chapter Twenty-Eight

Three months later the family got together for Rob and Jody's "Big Wedding." It was a beautiful, sunny day for a wedding.

Jody was wearing her mother's wedding gown. Rob wore a black silky tuxedo. Aunt Debbie was Jody's matron of honor. She wore a lavender ball gown. Three of Jody's cousins and Kathy were bridesmaids. They all wore pale pink floor- length prom dresses. Four of Rob's cousins were groomsmen. Uncle Clyde was best man. All the men wore black silky tuxedos to match the groom.

Jody had a beautiful bouquet of pale, pink, lavender, and light yellow roses with baby's breath. Her bridesmaids' bouquets were smaller copies of Jody's bouquet. All the men wore multicolored boutonnieres to match the wedding colors.

The ring bearer and miniature groom, Kathy's son, Rich, was dressed just like Rob. He carried a white satin pillow with the double rings lying on it. Kathy's daughter, Robin, was dressed as a miniature bride. She carried a small bouquet that matched Jody's bouquet. The miniature groom escorted the miniature bride down the aisle.

The wedding took place with the wishing well in back of them. A flower arbor had been set up in front of the wishing well. It was made up of multicolored roses. Next to the arbor was a wedding candle on a stand.

The minister of Jody's church stood between the wishing well and arbor. Jody and Rob repeated their vows. Then the minister pronounced

them man and wife. Then they moved over to the wedding candle. Hand in hand they lit it. The minister said, "Let this be a reminder of a long and happy life together. Let the light of love never go out."

The reception was over in the pavilion. It had a dance band with a catered meal served.

After dinner, Jody and Rob opened gifts. Then they danced for a while. Then they went and got the wedding candle so they would be reminded of their undying love daily.

Then they left to go on their honeymoon. No one knew where they went.

Chapter Twenty-Nine

They headed north to a small resort up in Eagle River. They told the manager that they were on their honeymoon. He gave them the best cabin he had.

They enjoyed a week of fun. They swam, hiked, and went horseback riding during the day. In the evenings they had candlelit dinners, went dancing, and took walks in the moonlight. They were sorry to see the week end.

The following Monday, they arrived at work. Everyone was excited and wanted to know all about their honeymoon. They told them about what they had done. They said that the evenings had just been theirs.

Chapter Thirty

The days passed with Rob and Jody becoming more in love each day. They were eager to start a family.

It was just after the Fourth of July when Jody woke up feeling sick. She went to the bathroom. She had been doing this for the past two weeks. Rob got up and asked, "Are you feeling all right?"

Jody said, "I have been feeling ill, but I think it's just a bug. I'll have Doctor Peterson check me out."

Rob said, "You let me know what's going on as soon as you know."

Jody said, "I will. You, my love, worry too much."

That morning when Doctor Peterson came in, Jody told him how she felt and for how long. Doctor Peterson smiled. He said, "I'll take a test, but I can tell you now that it sounds like you are about to become a mother."

Jody said, "I hope so."

Doctor Peterson tested Jody. He was right. He told Jody.

She said, "Don't tell Rob. I want to surprise him." She went to tell Rob she was fine. Then she went back to work. Rob was too busy to talk to her for the rest of the day.

When they got into the car to go home, Rob asked Jody, "What is going on? I know you haven't been yourself."

Jody said, "I have something to tell you, but I want to wait until we get home."

When they got home, Jody had Rob sit down and rest while she fixed dinner. She fixed steak, baked potatoes, and salad. She set the table with crystal goblets, china, and candles. She also chilled a bottle of wine they had saved for a special night. When it was all served, she called Rob into the dining room.

Rob said, "*Wow!* What does this mean?"

Jody said, "It's a very special night for us, honey.

My darling husband, I'm pregnant. You're going to be a daddy. I'm about one month along. I'm due around April twenty-fifth."

Rob jumped up. He hugged and kissed her so long and hard she almost fainted.

They didn't eat much. They were too excited. Before Jody knew it, Rob was on the phone calling everyone, telling them the wonderful news. They were all happy and excited about the coming event.

Through the months, Jody had a wonderful, problem- free pregnancy. In September her Aunt Debbie and Kathy gave a baby shower for her. She got all kinds of goodies for the baby. They had the shower at Rob's Aunt Lorraine's farm.

One winter evening, they were sitting and relaxing, trying to think of names for their baby. They came up with Robert George, if they had a boy and Faith Marie if they had a girl. Just then she felt movement and put Rob's hand on her tummy so he could feel it.

Jody's due date was only two months away. Rob said to Jody, "I want to take you on a getaway trip before our baby arrives. How about the second week in April? Anywhere you want to go."

Jody thought for a minute. Then she said, "I've always wanted to go on a 'Floating Casino' to try my luck playing the slots."

Rob said, "That sounds like a lot of fun and enjoyment."

The next two weeks were busy for them, planning for their trip and packing. Rob was busy making the arrangements and getting the tickets for the riverboat casino. Jody was also busy packing for the unexpected.

They figured on leaving on April 15th and staying until the twentieth to make sure they were back home for the blessed event.

Chapter Thirty-One

They got on the riverboat casino called "Floating Fortune." When Jody saw the inside, her eyes lit up like a Christmas tree. They got settled into their cabin, and they ordered a snack. Then Rob suggested that she take a little nap so she would be refreshed enough to have some fun.

Later that evening, they listened to the riverboat band. They also danced to a few slow numbers. Then they returned to their cabin.

While Jody was getting ready for bed, she started feeling strange. It felt as if something had dropped. She felt really heavy. She had felt back pain, but hadn't had any contractions. She didn't say anything to Rob about it. She went to bed. Rob came out of the bathroom. He saw Jody in bed. He said, "Are you okay, honey?"

She said, "I'm just a little overwhelmed by all of this. I'm also tired."

The next few days they enjoyed themselves looking around the boat, especially at the big paddle wheel. They both gambled most of the time. Jody played the slots while Rob roamed around playing the different games.

It was their last night on the riverboat. They were getting ready for the evening when Jody had a hard pain that took her breath away. She didn't say anything to Rob because she wanted one last chance to play the "Jackpot Slot" before they had to leave.

When they got into the casino, Jody started playing on the Wishing Well slot machine. She asked Rob if he would get her something to drink.

Just after Rob left, she put her coins into the slot.

She pulled the handle, and up came one, two, three wishing wells. She had hit the big one! She got so excited she started getting heavy-duty pain. Everyone came running to see what she had hit. All the lights were flashing, and the bells were ringing.

Just then, Jody had another very hard contraction and screamed. Everyone heard her scream. Floor security came running over. Jody said, "Find my husband, Doctor Rob Wilson; he's at the refreshment bar. Tell him I'm in hard labor."

When Rob got to Jody, he said, "Try to hang on, sweetheart. The doctor's on his way."

While they waited, someone came over and handed Rob a big container of coins. It was the jackpot that Jody had just won -- $1,000,000.

The doctor arrived. It happened to be Doctor Pierson. He went over to see who it was that needed him. He said, "Rob, Jody, it's you!"

Rob turned and said, "Jeff! What are you doing here?"

He looked at Jody. He said, "She's pretty close to giving birth. Her water bag broke while we were waiting for you."

Jeff said, "Then we better hurry and get her into that room right there across the hall."

They had no more than gotten Jody into the room and gotten Rob ready, when Jody delivered.

Jeff said, "It's a girl!

"Rob, you have a daughter."

Rob kissed Jody, and he said, "I love you, honey, and

I thank you for our beautiful daughter."

Doctor Pierson said, "Congratulations! Mr. and Mrs. Wilson."

Rob said, "Thanks! Jeff."

Then he said, "By the way, how long have you been working here? What happened to New York?"

Jeff said, "It's a long story. A woman named Tiffany."

Rob said, "Oh, no! You didn't. I have a feeling I know what happened."

Chapter Thirty-Two

When Rob and Jody and Faith Marie arrived in Hope, they went to her dad's place. Everyone was there to welcome them home. Then Rob looked at Jody and smiled. He said, "I've got a surprise for you."

They went across town to the other side of Hope Park. Rob pulled into a driveway. There was a beautiful log cabin. Rob said, "Welcome home, Mrs. Wilson."

Jody was so surprised, she was speechless. He said,

"I bought it before we left on our trip. Our families moved everything in. They did the nursery, complete with everything a baby needs, while we were gone."

Jody said, "Oh, Rob, you always know what makes me happy."

Later on, Jody was sitting on the porch, swinging with Faith, when Rob came out. He sat beside them. They both looked toward Hope Park and the wishing well.

Rob said, "I don't know about you, honey, but I will always treasure Hope's wishing well. It brought us together in marriage, and it also gave us our Faith Marie, 'Million Dollar Girl.'" Rob gave Jody and Faith a kiss. He said, "I could never wish for more than I have right here."

The Wishing Well Sometimes Does Grant Wishes!

PART TWO

FAITH'S FUTURE

Chapter One

It was eighteen years later; Jody and Rob Wilson were driving their daughter, Faith Marie, to the airport in Chicago. Rob and Jody were both telling her to be very careful on her graduation trip to Africa.

They told her to make sure she called home and they would take care of the expenses, so they wouldn't worry about whether she got there safely. She said she would and not to worry.

They arrived at the airport and walked her to her plane. They made sure she had everything she needed for the flight. The call came for the passengers to board. Rob and Jody tearfully said good-bye and hugged her hard and long. Faith gave them a tearful kiss, returned their hugs and headed for the plane.

It was the weekend after her graduation. Faith was leaving for a safari in Africa where she would learn about the animal kingdom. It would be her life's adventure before she decided on her future.

As she took her seat, she started thinking of all the family and friends she would dearly miss during the upcoming months.

When Faith arrived at the airport in Africa, she retrieved her luggage and got off the plane. She walked to the counter to see if they could locate the person who was to meet her.

The person behind the counter said, "I'll page the person meeting you."

She waited and shortly a young man in safari clothes approached her.

He greeted her, "Hello! Are you, Miss Wilson?"

She replied, "Yes, I am. Are you my guide?"

He said, "Yes, my name is Mitch Walters. Let me take your bags and we'll leave for the compound. I'd also like to welcome you to Africa."

When they reached the compound, he took her to a large house. They went up on a large wrap-around porch. He opened a door and they entered a large living room. A young native boy came in and Mitch told him, "Faith will be staying for awhile. Take her bags to the room she will be staying in."

He took Faith to the kitchen to meet the cook. He asked the cook to put some lunch together for them. He then took Faith to her room to freshen up.

He said, "I'll meet you in the living room."

After she freshened up, she met Mitch in the living room and they went out on the porch for lunch.

After lunch, Mitch said, "I have some things to do."

She said, "I want to get settled in my room."

About three hours later, Faith left her room and went outside to sit on the porch and wait for Mitch. She was astounded at what she saw. There were large fenced areas with different animals romping around. Then she saw a jeep coming. It was her guide, Mitch Walters.

He smiled and said, "It's a little overwhelming, right?

Ha, ha! Well, little miss, I'm at your service and here to show you our beautiful country and all the beautiful creatures of nature."

Chapter Two

The next morning, after waking up to a breakfast gong, Faith quickly dressed and joined Mitch and his workers. Following a big breakfast of ham, eggs and fried potatoes, Mitch asked, "Faith, would you like to join me on a trip to see the zebras, elephants and cheetahs?"

Faith replied, "That's why I'm here. I want to see it all. How are the animals captured?"

Mitch replied, "We chase them until they are roped and then get them in boxed cages without hurting them. Then we study their behavior patterns to make sure all is right with them. If they are injured or sick, we keep them until they are able to go back into the wild. Sometimes they have youngsters that can't be released into the wild. Then we try to find zoos or reserves to take them."

She asked, "What happens if they aren't needed?"

He told her, "We keep them and care for them, and some become pets."

Faith exclaimed, "Wow! This is all very interesting."

He then showed her the rest of the compound.

Over the next three months, Faith asked a lot of questions about the animals she saw. She learned many fascinating facts and information about how to care for the injured and sick animals. She also learned

enough to build on her future of being a veterinarian. Her love of animals also helped.

During their moonlight walks, they started to talk. They talked a lot and were getting to know each other. Mitch asked her about her hometown. Faith told him about Hope and the history of the Wishing Well located in Hope Park.

Mitch said, "It all sounds fascinating. I would like to see all the things you have told me about."

Faith said, "Maybe you will, someday."

Without knowing it, Mitch was growing very fond of Faith. With time, his feelings would get stronger.

Faith was also attracted to Mitch and her feelings were already getting stronger. She thought, *Am I falling in love?*

After Mitch brought Faith back to the house, he went to his room. He started to think about his feelings for her.

He hadn't told her that his Uncle Jim was a veterinarian who had a clinic in Hope. He decided to tell her about him in the morning.

Chapter Three

The next day, Faith realized she was having feelings she didn't understand and she was afraid to venture into them. *If I stay, will Mitch and I start a relationship? I really don't want to think about any of this right now. I know what I have to do. I have to leave; and the sooner, the better for my peace of mind.*

She packed and then found John, one of the other guides. She asked him, "Do you have time to take me to the airport?"

He said, "Yes, Miss Wilson. But give me a few minutes to let Mitch know where I'm going."

Faith said, "No! Please don't tell Mitch until I leave here."

He said, "All right, Miss Wilson."

Faith needed to get home to the safety of Hope and her family. She didn't tell Mitch that she was leaving.

She arrived at the airport just as the plane for the States was about to leave. She got her ticket and boarded the plane.

As the plane taxied down the runway, Faith thought she saw Mitch running toward the plane.

When they landed in Chicago, Faith picked up her luggage and hailed a taxi.

She told the cabby, "Take me to 404 Spring Street in Hope."

She rode down the streets of Hope, smiling and glad to be home again. She thought about what she might have missed out on by leaving

Africa and Mitch. She needed to talk to someone about her feelings and get some advice.

The taxi pulled into her Great-aunt Debbie's driveway.

As Faith got out of the taxi, Debbie stepped out her door.

Faith smiled and said, "Hi!"

Debbie said, "What's wrong? Why are you home early? We weren't expecting you until next month."

Faith replied, "I really need to talk to you."

Debbie put her arm around Faith and said, "Dear girl, let's go into the kitchen. I will put a pot of coffee on and we will sit and talk."

Chapter Four

When Great-aunt Debbie set two cups of coffee and a plate of cookies on the table and sat down, she asked Faith, "What's wrong? Girl, you have the same look on your face that your mother had when there was something wrong or troubling her. From the sound of the letters you wrote, you were doing fine and learning a lot from your guide, Mister Walters."

Faith answered, "I was having a good time. But what I didn't tell anyone is that I got to know Mister Walters, Mitch. We talked and went for moonlight walks, and he kissed me a few times. I started responding. I couldn't help myself. He's so tall and has wavy blond hair and those deep sea blue eyes of his...I started having deeper feelings for him than friendship. It started to scare me and that's why I came home."

Debbie looked at Faith and asked, "What are Mitch's feelings toward you?"

Faith replied, "He's very attracted to me and told me he would have begged me not to leave. But I did leave because I didn't understand my feelings and I still don't."

"Have you talked to your mother about any of this, Faith?" said Debbie.

Faith said, "No, I just got back home and you're the first one that I've talked to and confided in."

Great-aunt Debbie said, "Thanks, Faith, but don't take this the wrong way. I really think you should talk and confer with your mother. I love you and I can give you my advice and wisdom, but my advice to you is to talk to your mother."

Faith gave Debbie a big hug and told her, "Thanks." She then phoned for a taxi.

As Faith was walking out the door, her Great-uncle Clyde pulled into the driveway.

Faith said, "Hi! How are you?"

Her taxi pulled up and she got in and left.

Great-uncle Clyde waved to her. He thought, *I wonder what's wrong? Why didn't Faith give me a hug?*

When he got into the house, he asked Debbie, "What's wrong with Faith?"

Debbie explained everything to him.

He said, "That poor girl."

Chapter Five

Faith knew she needed to see her parents and tell them what had happened and why she came home early. *Tomorrow will be soon enough. Right now, I want to get something to eat and then get a good night's sleep.*

When Faith got out of the taxi at the Family Restaurant, she saw her parent's car. She thought, *Oh!*

Boy!

She walked in and saw her parents with her Aunt Kathy, Uncle Mike, Great-aunt Lorraine and Uncle Leo.

They all said, "Come join us, Faith."

While drinking coffee after dinner, Faith answered many questions about her safari adventure, what she had done, who she had met, and everything else that had happened since she had last written to them.

She thought, *Should I tell them the reason why I'm home a month early before someone asks me? Maybe with other relatives here, my parents won't be as shocked and start freaking out over the reason of my being home a month earlier than planned.*

Faith took a drink of her coffee and then said, "Mom, Dad, I've got something to tell you and I hope you don't get upset."

Rob and Jody looked at one another and then said, "What is it?"

Faith replied, "I met a man I have strong feelings for. His name is Mitch Walters and he was my safari guide. He's twenty-two years old and well educated. Mitch wanted to start a relationship. Between that

and feelings I didn't understand, I got spooked, packed up and came running home."

Both of her parents said, "Oh, Faith! We are so glad you came home. You are too young for a relationship and you have your whole life and future ahead of you. We would like to see you go to vet school and enjoy life before settling down."

Rob said, "Now, if everyone will excuse us, I'm taking my family home."

He took Faith's luggage as they all said good-bye and left.

Chapter Six

The next morning over breakfast, Faith told her parents she was going apartment hunting and also checkout the new veterinarian school.

Rob looked at Jody and said, "I'm going to the clinic early today. I think you and Faith need time alone to have a mother-daughter talk."

Faith said, "No, Dad, don't leave. I really want to talk to both Mom and you."

"Okay!" Rob said and sat down.

Faith thought for a moment, then she said, "Mom...Dad, you didn't say anything about what I told you last night."

Rob and Jody both replied, "We really didn't know what to say. We think you made the right choice by leaving and coming home. We are thankful for that."

Faith said, "Oh, Mom and Dad, I'm so glad that you're not upset."

Rob said, "Your mother and I know it had to have been very hard for you to walk away from what may have developed between you and Mitch."

Faith said, "Yes, in a way it was. We were talking and really getting to know one another and going on long walks in the moonlight. I was to the point where I was responding to his kisses and was returning them. To be honest, in my heart and mind, it felt so right being in Mitch's arms. It's like they say, if Mitch returns to me, then I know we

were meant to be together. But because of the respect and love I have for both of you, I will try to forget Mitch and enroll in vet classes and get my degree and see where life's road takes me. Oh! I'd like to let you know...you're great parents and you're cool!"

Rob looked at the kitchen clock and said, "Mom and I have to leave for work now."

They gave Faith a kiss and hug and said, "See you later. Be good. It's great having you home, Faith."

Chapter Seven

Faith was on her way out the door when the phone rang. It was her Aunt Kathy.

She said, "Faith, I just called to see if you are okay. I didn't know how the talk with your parents would go."

Faith said, "I'm doing fine, Aunt Kathy. Actually, Mom and Dad were pretty cool about it. Thanks for calling, Aunt Kathy. I was just on my way out the door to go enroll in the vet class. Bye, Aunt Kathy. I love you!"

"Bye, Faith. I love you too, and good luck," Kathy said.

Faith had just hung up the phone when it rang again. It was her Great-aunt Lorraine.

She asked Faith, "How are you doing and is everything going okay?"

Faith reassured her, "I and everything else is fine.

I would love to talk longer, but I have to get to the vet school and put my application in for the fall classes."

By the time Faith finished at the veterinarian school, it was lunchtime. She decided to stop at the Hope Clinic to see her godfather, Doctor Peterson, and then ask her mother out for lunch.

When Faith arrived at the clinic, her mother was getting ready to go to lunch.

Doctor Peterson came out of his office and saw Faith. He said, "Well, hi there! How's my goddaughter?" He then gave her a kiss and hug.

Faith replied, "I'm doing fine. I just enrolled in vet school and will start this fall."

Doctor Peterson said, "That's great, Faith!"

Faith said, "I stopped in to ask Mom out for lunch."

Doctor Peterson said, "Have a great lunch. It was good seeing you."

Faith and her mother went to the corner café for lunch. When they were served their burgers, fries and chocolate shakes, Faith said, "Mom, I'm going to check out the dormitory for vet students."

Her mother said, "Honey, are you sure that you want to live there? Dad and I wouldn't mind you living at home one bit."

Faith said, "I know that, Mom, but I'd really like to be on my own for awhile and get to know the world. It will be enough on you and Dad with me being at home all summer."

Her mom said, "I understand, but it's no problem. Your dad and I love having you at home. Faith?"

Faith said, "Yes, Mom?"

Her mother said, "I heard they are looking for an assistant at the vet clinic for the summer. It would be a great experience for you, Faith."

Faith said, "Thanks, Mom. I will call about it when
I get home."

Faith's mother said, "I'd love to stay and talk, but
I better get back to work now." She gave Faith a kiss and said, "See you later."

Chapter Eight

On their way home, Rob and Jody talked about life and what they wanted and hoped for Faith.

Jody told Rob, "I had lunch with Faith. Faith wants to live in the dorm for vet students when she starts fall classes."

Rob looked at Jody and said, "Didn't you tell her that we would like to have her live at home?"

Jody said, "Yes, I did, sweetheart, but she wants to be on her own and get to know the world. No matter how much we want to, we can't coddle her. We have to learn to let her go. Faith's a young woman and has her own mind."

Rob said, "I know, but I don't want her hurt."

Rob and Jody arrived at home and walked into the kitchen to a wonderful aroma.

Faith was putting supper on the dining room table.

Faith said, "Hi, Mom and Dad. Are you hungry? Sit down. It's all ready."

After supper they did the dishes together and talked.

Rob said, "Your mother told me about your wanting to live at the dorm and your reasons why. I understand why, but we would feel better if you stayed at home. Would you reconsider for your mother's piece of mind? That way, it would be easier for you to get yourself established and your feet on firm ground until you graduate."

Faith said, "Oh, Dad!" She hugged him and said, "Okay, just to set your mind at ease, I'll think about it, okay?"

While Faith made a big bowl of popcorn, her parents went into the living room and cuddled up on the couch. When Faith walked into the living room, she set the popcorn and three bowls on the coffee table.

After she filled her bowl, she sat down and told her parents about the job she got for the summer at the veterinarian clinic as an assistant.

Rob smiled at Jody and started laughing.

Faith looked puzzled and said, "What are you laughing about, Dad?"

Rob said, "I was just remembering all the stray cats you always brought home when you were younger. Now, with you working at the vet's, just don't bring home any kittens, Faith."

Faith smiled and said, "Okay, I won't, Dad."

Chapter Nine

It was a warm, breezy, sunny morning when Faith awoke. After breakfast and saying goodbye to her parents, Faith phoned her lifetime friend, Kayla Bradley.

Kayla answered on the fourth ring. She said, "Oh, hi, Faith, I've been waiting to hear from you. We haven't talked or seen each other since your grandfather's funeral."

Faith said, "I've been away, Kayla. I went on a safari in Africa the weekend after graduation."

Kayla said, "Oh, wow! That sounds so *cool*. Tell me about it. What was it like and whom did you meet? Anyone famous?"

Faith replied, "It was fun and interesting and the guide, Mitch Walters, took me on many animal runs. He taught me how to care for them and about their different behaviors. It was going fine until we got to know each other and we talked a lot and we took walks in the moonlight. We both started getting attracted to one another. One night during our walk, Mitch took me into this arms and kissed me."

Kayla exclaimed, "Oh, wow, Faith!"

Faith said, "But it spooked me, Kayla."

Kayla asked her, "Why in the world did it spook you, Faith?"

Faith replied, "Because I started having feelings I liked but I didn't understand."

Kayla said, "Oh, Faith! Was Mitch good looking? How old is he?"

Faith answered, "Yes, Mitch is very good looking. He's tall, has wavy blond hair and deep sea blue eyes that you could get lost in. He's twenty-two years old, well educated and has a great personality. It felt so good being in his arms, like all was well with the world. But I got scared and skittish and packed up and came home."

Kayla said, "Oh, Faith, are you okay?"

Faith said, "I still think about Mitch. Kayla, I'm starting vet school this fall, plus I'm starting a job at the vet's tomorrow. So I'll be busy and won't have much time to think about Mitch and that will help."

Kayla said, "Oh, Faith, that's great! Guess what, Faith, because of my love for animals, I'm also starting classes this fall. I've got an empty bedroom in my apartment. How about being my roomy?"

Faith replied, "That would be great, Kayla. I'll be over later to look at it. Gotta run for now. Bye, Kayla, and thanks!"

Chapter Ten

The next day was busy for Faith. She arrived at the veterinarian clinic at 8:00. She was a little nervous, but after meeting Doctor Walters and his explaining to her what she would be helping him with and do, she felt more at ease.

The day started with Mister Stevens' very lively black lab puppy, Max, who needed a distemper shot.

Faith took Max into the exam room and kept him calm while Doctor Walters got the information he needed from Mister Stevens.

Doctor Walters came into the exam room and told Faith, "Hold Max down tight while I administer the shot."

Faith gave Max a puppy treat and a hug. She then returned Max to Mister Stevens.

After Mister Stevens and Max left, a little girl walked in, hugging her kitty with tears streaming down her face.

Faith went to her, hugged her and asked, "What's wrong, baby?"

The little girl said, "Please help my kitty. She's all swollen up."

Faith looked at the little girl and smiled. She asked her, "What's your name? And what's your kitty's name?"

Tearfully, the little girl said, "My name is Jenny and my kitty is Fluffy."

Faith said, "Jenny, don't worry. We will take extra special care of Fluffy."

Doctor Walters took Fluffy into the exam room. By this time, Fluffy was really meowing.

Faith was petting her and trying to calm her down when she saw a puddle of liquid on the exam table and a little head sticking out.

Faith says, "Oh, my goodness...kittens!"

Doctor Walters said, "Fluffy seems to be doing okay on her own. You're doing fine with keeping her calm. Faith, from what I've seen I have the feeling that you've helped with the birth of kittens before."

Faith replied, "Yes, I have. When I was younger, I was always bringing stray cats home and there were so many kittens. I wanted to keep all of them, but my parents said no. To keep my parents from getting upset, I had to give the kittens away. When my dad heard that I was going to work here, he reminded me not to bring any cats home. I've always loved animals and that's why I want to be a vet."

Doctor Walters smiled and said, "You will be a great vet."

Fluffy gave birth to three new kittens, all very healthy and pretty. Faith found a cat basket and put

Fluffy and the kittens in it.

Doctor Walters told Jenny, "Fluffy is fine and she is a mama of three beautiful kittens." He then phoned Jenny's parents.

Faith placed the basket beside Jenny.

"Thank you," Jenny said and hugged Faith and Doctor Walters.

Jenny sat and played with the kittens while she waited for her parents to take them all home.

Chapter Eleven

Faith and Doctor Walters had a late lunch at the corner café after closing for the day.

Doctor Walters said, "Faith, for your first day of working here, you've done an excellent job. I know that you will pass vet classes with flying colors."

Faith said, "Thank you, Doctor Walters. I enjoy working with you. Bye, Doctor Walters."

Doctor Walters replied, "Bye, Faith, see you tomorrow."

Faith pulled into the driveway and saw her father barbecuing on the patio. The smell of the burgers had her stomach growling with hunger.

She said, "Hi, Dad. Those burgers smell divine."

Faith walked into the kitchen and said, "Hi, Mom. What can I do to help?"

Just then the phone rang. Faith said, "I'll get it, Mom."

Faith answered it. "Hello?"

"Hi, Faith, this is Dennis Mitchell. How are you?"

She said, "I'm fine. How are you, Dennis?"

Dennis responded, "I'm fine. I bet you thought you would never hear from me again, right?"

Faith answered, "Hoped is more like it. What brings you back to Hope?"

Dennis replied, "The job I'm starting on Monday at Hope's Glove Factory."

Faith said, "Wow! I hope they know what they are in for with hiring you!"

Dennis said, "Oh, come on now, Faith. I've changed. I've grown up and matured since getting into trouble with the Fire Department over calling in false alarms, pulling fire alarms, and driving your dad to the edge."

"I hope so," Faith said and laughed.

Dennis said, "I know I have. Would it be okay if I called you again sometime?"

Faith said, "Yes, that would be nice."

Dennis replied, "Then until next time, bye, Faith."

She said, "Bye, Dennis."

Faith hung up the phone and turned to her mom. Faith said, "Guess who's back in Hope."

Her mother answered, "Could it be Dennis Mitchell?"

Faith said, "The one and only."

Just then Faith's dad walked into the kitchen. He said, "The burgers are done."

Faith helped her mother bring the rest of the food to the table on the patio.

Rob asked Jody, "Is there something wrong?"

Jody said, "No, not really."

Faith said, "Mom's a little upset about Dennis Mitchell being back in town and calling me."

Faith's father replied, "I hope you won't be seeing him, he's one bad dude."

Faith said, "Oh, Dad. He said he has grown up and changed."

Rob replied, "Okay, but let your mom and I meet and talk to him before you go anywhere with him, Faith."

Faith answered, "I will do that and if he asks me out, I will tell him to meet me here, okay, Dad? Dennis starts a job at the glove factory Monday."

Rob said, "That's good. I hope he does well. Maybe he's finally settled down."

Faith's mother said, "I'm sure he has grown up and settled down and has turned into a civilized person, Rob."

Faith's parents asked her how her first day at work was.

She told them, "It was interesting." She told them about the little girl's cat and the three kittens. Then she said, "No, Dad, I didn't bring any home!" They all laughed about that.

She told him about Doctor Walters and how nice he was. She said, "He's sixty years old and very patient and understanding for being an elderly man. I enjoy working there."

They said, "That's great!"

Faith said, "I won't be living at the vet dorm."

Faith's mother asked, "Does that mean you will be here at home?"

Faith said, "No, I talked to Kayla Bradley the other day and she has an extra bedroom. She asked me to be her roomy. Would that be okay with you and Dad? You know her parents."

They said, "Yes, Faith, that would be fine with us. We've known her parents for years. We know that Kayla has always been your one true friend."

Faith said, "Yes, she is." With that settled, Faith felt better.

Faith was getting sleepy, so she kissed her parents goodnight and went to bed.

Chapter Twelve

The next morning, Faith was awakened by her mom, who said, "You have a phone call from Doctor Walters. It's an emergency. You're to meet him at your cousin Rich's farm as quickly as possible. One of his cows is having a breech birth."

Faith says, "Oh, tell him I'm on my way."

Faith got dressed and rushed out the door. She put her truck in gear and was on her way.

Ten minutes later she was up to her elbows with helping to pull out a newborn calf butt first.

Rich stood with amazement on his face and said, "You're pretty handy for a girl. When did you start working with Doctor Walters?"

Faith said, "This is my second day. I'm doing this for the summer. This fall I'm starting vet classes. Thanks for your confidence, Rich. It means a lot to me. How is Rita doing?"

Rich replied, "She's up at the house going through another day of morning sickness."

Doctor Walters said, "Faith, you might want to see this."

Faith turned around and saw the calf walking; it was the cutest little thing.

Doctor Walters said, "They are both fine. Thanks for your help, Faith. Good job!"

Rich said, "Thanks, Doctor Walters. Send me the bill."

When Doctor Walters and Faith returned to town, the doctor said, "It's almost lunch time. Howa bout some food? My treat."

Faith said, "Lead the way."

Over lunch, Faith told Doctor Walters her plans and dreams for the future.

Doctor Walters told her, "You will succeed in anything you set out to do. You have great potential and are a fast learner."

They returned to the office. It was slow the rest of the day, just a lot of shots.

Faith was heading out the door when Doctor Walters said, "See you Monday morning, Faith."

Faith said, "Okay, bye, Doctor Walters."

Chapter Thirteen

Faith walked through the kitchen door. She saw her mother sitting at the table drinking a cup of coffee.

She said, "Hi, Faith. You look really tired."

Faith said, "I am, Mom."

Faith's mom said, "Sit down, Faith. I will get you a cup of coffee and we will talk. I want to know how things went today at Rich's farm."

Faith took a sip of her coffee. "Mother, it was touch and go for awhile, but with Doctor Walter's help, I pulled the calf's butt out and the rest followed." Then she said,

"Oh, Mom, it was so thrilling and Mother Nature is so wonderful!"

Faith's mother replied, "It sure is. Faith, how are Rich and Rita doing?"

Faith said, "Rita is having another baby and is fighting morning sickness."

"Oh, my, that poor woman. That's baby number five.

It's a good thing they live on a big farm."

Faith yawned and said, "Rich told me I was handy for a girl."

Faith's mother laughed and said, "That sounds like something he would say!"

While Jody went out to get chicken dinners and soda for dinner, Faith went and filled the tub and added the scented bath beads.

After a long relaxing soak and hair washing, Faith felt much better. Faith was stretched out on the couch when she heard her dad coming through the kitchen door.

He said, "Hi, honey, I'm home!"

Faith looked around the corner and said, "Hi, Dad. Mom isn't home. She went out to get some chicken dinners and soda for our dinner."

Faith's father said, "That sounds good."

Faith asked, "How was your day, Dad?"

Her dad answered, "Busy as usual, but not as eventful as your day was or so I heard."

Faith looked at him and said, "How do you know that?"

Her dad smiled and said, "I saw Doctor Walters at the gas station and he told me what happened. He told me that you were a great asset to him."

Faith replied, "I know, Dad, that's what he keeps telling me." Faith looked out the kitchen window and said, "Mom's home with dinner!"

After dinner, Faith went to see Kayla and look at the apartment. She liked it and told Kayla that she'd be her roommate.

When Faith returned home, she told her parents that she liked the apartment. She then told them goodnight and went to her room.

Chapter Fourteen

Faith awoke to a sunny, warm, breezy August morning. She sat up in her bed, trying to wake up. The smell of blueberry pancakes and hickory smoked bacon made her stomach grumble. By the time she was done showering and dressing, she was ready to eat.

She walked into the kitchen and said, "Good morning, Mom and Dad. Isn't it a beautiful day!"

Her parents said, "Wow! You're really chipper this morning." They smiled at Faith.

Faith replied, "Yeah, guess I am. I start vet school next week and I'm excited." Faith then said, "I'm hungry. Mom, is breakfast ready?"

"As soon as Dad and you sit down, I'll bring it to the table."

After Faith's parents left for work, Faith went to her room to start packing what she needed to take when she moved in with Kayla.

She went to her closet shelves to get her new shoes and something fluffy fell down. It was the little stuffed tiger that Mitch had given her the day before she left.

Faith picked it up and held it to her heart. She put it in her box of memories of things she would never forget and then put the box back on her shelf.

When Faith was all packed, she turned the television on to her favorite show, but she couldn't concentrate on the program. Her mind was on Mitch. She went through the channels, trying to find something to distract her thoughts, but nothing did.

Ten minutes later, Dennis phoned and asked her to have lunch with him. Dennis was the best distraction that Faith could find.

Faith met Dennis at the Lakeside Root Beer Stand. They ordered root beer floats and a burger with the works, just like they had eight years before.

When they were seated on their favorite pier, Faith asked Dennis, "How's your job going?"

He answered, "It's going very well and I'm getting pretty well established here in Hope. I'm looking to put down roots here."

Faith said, "That's great, Dennis. You have really grown up and matured." Faith sipped her float, smiled, and said, "We may have grown up and changed, but this tastes as good as they did eight years ago."

Dennis smiled and said, "Faith, you're still as humorous as you were then. I didn't think you would want to see me again after all the trouble I got you into.

Faith, why did you agree to have lunch with me?"

Faith didn't feel the timing was right to tell Dennis the truth, so she turned to him and said, "Dennis, I wanted to see you because you've always been a friend to me even though you were trouble with a capital 'T.' I was curious to see for myself how you have grown up and looked now that you are older. Beside that, I was hungry!"

Dennis laughed and said, "Okay, Faith. Do I get your approval?"

Faith replied, "I guess you're okay. Thanks for the lunch. See you around."

Dennis said, "Bye, Faith. I enjoyed seeing you again."

Faith was getting into her truck when she heard Dennis call her name and saw him running toward her.

He caught up and said, "Faith, what are you doing next Saturday night? If you're not busy, would you like to go to the annual End of Summer Dance with me?"

Faith replied, "I've got a lot to do. I'm getting ready to move in with Kayla and getting ready to start vet school in a week from now. Let me get settled and going to classes. If I'm organized by then, I'd

be happy to go with you. It might be just what I need. I'll call you, Dennis, okay?"

He said, "Sounds good, Faith. Bye...until I hear from you."

"Take care and be good."

"Say 'hi' to your parents for me."

Chapter Fifteen

Faith was up early Sunday morning. She had her stuff packed and loaded in her truck.

Over breakfast her father asked, "Would you like some help with moving?"

Faith smiled and said, "I think I can manage it on my own. But I know you and Mom are dying to see where I'll be living. How about following me and have a look for yourself and talk to Kayla and her parents."

Faith's mother said, "That sounds like a good idea.

I haven't talked to Donna Bradley for a long time."

Faith's dad said, "My gosh, I haven't seen Paul Bradley in awhile either."

Faith put her breakfast dishes in the sink. She turned to her parents and said, "Are you ready to go? I really need to get this day started."

They all left for Kayla's apartment.

Kayla and her parents greeted them at the door.

They said, "Hi, Jody, Rob. We haven't seen you in awhile. How are you doing?" Donna said.

Jody replied, "We've been busy."

Rob said, "Hi, Paul. How's it going? Has your golf swing improved any?"

Paul laughed and said, "Wouldn't you like to know?"

Rob laughed.

Everyone helped Faith bring her boxes in. Faith and Kayla were soon busy talking and putting things away. By the time everything was settled and all talked out between both girls' parents, it was three o'clock.

Mister Bradley said, "Since it's past lunch time, why don't we all go out for an early dinner? We will go to the new steak house. Rob, before you say anything...it's on me."

Over dinner, Jody, Donna, Rob and Paul all got caught up on the latest news. Faith and Kayla talked about veterinarian school.

Out in the parking lot, Faith's parents told her to be good and that they loved her. Then they hugged and kissed her goodbye.

Faith said, "Bye, Mom and Dad. Enjoy your time alone together. The house is all yours. Have fun!"

Faith smiled and winked.

Her parents said, "Oh, Faith, you have grown up, haven't you!"

Chapter Sixteen

Monday morning Faith was showered and dressed by the time Kayla put the box of doughnuts and bottles of chocolate milk on the table in the breakfast nook. They chatted through breakfast.

Faith arrived at work and said, "Good morning, Doctor_Walters. What's on the agenda for today?"

He said, "We have a few farm calls to go on, starting with the Jackson farm. They have a sick foal."

They arrived at the Jackson farm and were walking toward the house where Mister Jackson met them. As they walked to the stable, he explained the foal's symptoms.

Doctor Walters examined the foal and they found it was a vitamin deficiency. Faith administered two shots and gently rubbed the shot area and said, "You will feel better now, boy."

Mister Jackson said, "Thanks, Doc."

"Good job, Miss Wilson."

Faith said, "Thanks. I'm learning."

They then headed to the McGregor's dairy to check out a cow that wasn't producing the milk amount she should. They arrived and went to the barn.

Faith was learning how to do examinations and it was her turn this time. She determined it was a vitamin deficiency as well and she

recommended a vitamin supplement. She told Mister McGregor its name and where to find it.

He replied, "You have one smart assistant there, Doctor Walters."

Doctor Walters smiled at Faith and said, "Don't I know it!"

They had one more call to make at the Johnson rabbit farm.

Doctor Walters said, "It's getting late and I know you're getting hungry, Faith. Do you want to wait until morning with this call?"

Faith said, "No, it's okay, let's get it done for the day."

Doctor Walters said, "Okay."

They arrived at the Johnson farm. Mister Johnson told them about the sick bunny.

Faith was taking out Thumper when he let one go and Faith jumped back. She saw the dish of pork and beans in the far corner of the cage and said, "Who's been feeding Thumper?"

Mister Johnson started laughing and said, "That's the problem! My two-year-old son Billy has been feeding him."

Faith chuckled and said, "Don't let Billy feed him beans any more! Rabbits like carrots and lettuce."

Faith and Doctor Walters chuckled about it on the way back to the office.

Chapter Seventeen

The rest of the week Faith was busy learning the office routine and it was Saturday before she knew it.

Faith awoke thinking about Dennis and the dance. She jumped in the shower and dressed.

Kayla was in the kitchen making omelets. Faith walked into the kitchen and said, "Those really smell good."

Kayla said, "Thanks, but as the old saying goes, 'the proof is in the taste.' Now sit down and let's eat."

After they ate, Faith helped Kayla with the dishes and clean up the kitchen.

Faith dialed Dennis' number. She told him she would go to the dance with him. Then she told Dennis her address.

Dennis said, "I will pick you up at seven."

Faith then went and looked in her closet to select what she would wear. She decided on her black skirt and ruffled white blouse.

Kayla said, "Faith!"

"Yes, Kayla?"

Kayla asked, "What dress do you like the best? This red one with the little white jacket or the floral pattern?"

Faith told Kayla, "I like the red one."

With what to wear settled, Faith called her mother and told her not to worry. She was doing fine. She told her how work was going and the

funny story about Mister Johnson's bunny. Her mom got a good laugh out of it.

She told her, "Mom, don't tell Dad that I am going to the End of Summer Dance with Dennis Mitchell. But do tell him that I love him. I love you too, Mom." Faith hung up.

Faith and Kayla were ready when their dates arrived.

Dennis pulled up into the driveway in a bright red Corvette. He came up to the door and rang the doorbell.

Faith opened the door. Faith thought to herself, *Wow! He looks good.*

Dennis smiled at Faith and said, as he put out his arm, "Shall we go?"

Faith said, "Let's go."

When they arrived at the community center they could hear the band, The Bugs, warming up.

Faith and Dennis walked through the door. They went over to the food table and each filled a plate. They then sat down where Kayla and her boyfriend Eddie were sitting.

By the time the band started playing, the tables had been put away and the floor was ready for dancing. Faith and Dennis danced until the band took a short break.

Dennis went to the punch table and got two glasses of punch. He then returned to the bench where they were sitting and handed a glass to Faith.

Faith said, "Thanks, Dennis."

Dennis said, "No, I didn't spike it!"

Faith asked, "How did you know that's what I was thinking?" She smiled at Dennis.

Dennis replied, "I know you."

When the band started playing again, Dennis took Faith's hand and walked her to the floor. They danced the last dance.

While walking to the car, Dennis asked Faith, "Did you have a good time?"

Faith replied, "It was just what I needed. Dennis, let me tell you this now. You have grown into a perfect gentleman and I thank you for asking me to the dance."

He said, "Thanks, Faith. I needed to hear that from you. It means a lot to me."

They got to Kayla's driveway and Dennis walked Faith to the door.

Dennis said, "Goodnight!" He then asked, "Can I call you again?"

Faith replied, "Yes." She gave him a kiss and her telephone number.

Chapter Eighteen

It was a chilly morning for September 15th. Faith was getting ready for her first day in veterinarian school. Kayla was also ready for her first day. They were both excited yet nervous. Both ate a light breakfast.

They were walking out the door when Faith asked, "Kayla, are you ready for this?"

Kayla said, "As ready as I'll ever be."

Faith said, "Don't worry. You will do fine. With what I've told you and the books you have read on the subject, you will be okay. If you have trouble, I will help you."

Faith and Kayla arrived at the school and found their classroom. Each took a deep breath and got seated.

The teacher, Mister Douglas, walked in and said, "Good morning, ladies and gentlemen. I know you are all nervous and I will do my best to make these classes easy for you. We will start by you answering these questions on the sheet I'm handing out. That will tell me how much I need to teach you and what you need to work harder on."

Faith's and Kayla's first day went smoothly. Mister Douglas was impressed when he found out Faith was training with Doctor Walters. He told Faith that would be a great help to her with the classes.

For the next month, Faith was very busy between veterinarian classes, working and keeping her family up to date on her progress. Kayla and Faith studied every night.

Chapter Nineteen

Faith awoke to a crisp, snowy Saturday in October. She yawned and was getting out of bed to get in the shower when the phone rang.

She answered, "Hello! Oh, hi, Mom!"

Jody asked, "Faith, how are you?"

Faith said, "I'm doing okay, Mom. I know I haven't talked to you and Dad much lately or even seen you, but

I've been thinking about you. Mom, just bear with me for awhile."

Jody said, "Oh, Faith, your dad and I understand the way it is for you. Let me tell you, we are very proud of you."

Faith replied, "Thanks, Mom."

Jody said, "Faith, if you and Kayla are not busy tomorrow, your dad and I would love to have you girls join us for dinner."

Faith said, "That would be great, Mom. Kayla and I need a break. Besides, I really miss you and Dad."

Jody said, "We miss you, too."

Faith replied, "Okay, Mom. We'll see you tomorrow.

I love you. Bye. Bye."

Just then the doorbell rang. Faith answered the door. It was Dennis.

Dennis said, "Hi, Faith."

Faith said, "Hi, Dennis. This is a surprise visit."

Dennis replied, "I guess it is. I'm here to ask you to the Halloween Ball tonight. I thought, maybe, you would need a break and it's going to be a good time for everyone."

Faith said, "That does sound like fun. I'd love to go."

Dennis smiled and said, "Great! I'll pick you up at six sharp."

Faith answered, "I'll be ready." She shut the door, turned around, and leaned against it.

Kayla came out of the kitchen. She saw Faith standing there and said, "Earth to Faith! What's going on, girl?"

Faith replied, "Just thinking."

Kayla smiled and said, "Okay. Lunch is ready."

They grabbed their plates, turned on the television, and plopped down on the couch to relax and talk about life.

Around four o'clock, they started getting ready and by the time they choose what to wear, the bed was covered by their outfits. They both started laughing. They were finally ready by the time their dates arrived.

They arrived at the mayor's mansion where the buffet and dance was being held. When they walked in, everyone was talking about the fall theme of the dance and about the mayor's wife falling on her tush while doing the Peppermint Twist at last year's dance.

They all greeted the mayor and his wife and thanked them for the lovely ball. They then went to the buffet and got plates of food. After everyone finished eating, they danced.

While walking to the car on sore feet from all the dancing she had done, Faith told Dennis, "I had a very good time." Then she gave Dennis a hug and a kiss on his cheek.

Dennis smiled and said, "That was a perfect ending to a fairy tale evening. Thank you, Faith."

Chapter Twenty

With the holidays over and getting better in veterinarian classes, the year went by quickly and before Faith knew it, it was Valentine's Day.

The doorbell rang and Faith opened the door to find Dennis standing there with a box of chocolates in one hand and a red rose in the other.

He handed her the chocolates, smiled, and said, "Sweets for my sweet and a rose for the one who makes my heart rosy!"

Faith said, "Oh my, Dennis! I think we better have a talk. Come in and sit down."

Dennis sat down and Faith took a deep breath. She said, "I have something to tell you and I hope you will understand. I went on a safari trip a year ago and started having feelings for my guide while I was there. Since then I've been thinking about him a lot more and my feelings have gotten a lot stronger for him."

Dennis asked, "What's his name, Faith?"

Faith said, "His name is Mitch Walters."

Dennis replied, "Well, Mitch is a lucky guy."

Faith said, "I'm so glad you understand, Dennis. Just remember, you will always be my special friend, Dennis."

Dennis hugged her and said, "And you, Faith, will always be my special friend. If you ever need someone to talk to or a shoulder to cry on, I'll be here for you."

When Dennis left, Faith sat down and did some heavy, deep thinking about Mitch. She started to get teary-eyed.

Saturday morning Faith was awakened by Kayla. "You have a phone call from Doctor Walters."

When Faith arrived at the clinic, Doctor Walters said,

"I'm sorry to bother you on a Saturday, Faith. Mister Johnson called me and there's a problem with Thumper again. I've got a feeling that Billy's been feeding him again."

Faith said, "Oh, no!"

On the way back to town, Doctor Walters noticed that Faith seemed quiet and withdrawn and appeared sad. He asked her, "What's troubling you?"

She said, "Oh, I had to break it off with Dennis last night. But after I explained why, he understood and we'll remain friends."

Doctor Walters inquired, "I'm not trying to be nosy, but what happened?"

Faith said, "Well, he was getting way too serious. I don't feel the same as he does."

Doctor Walters replied, "There is someone else? You can tell me about it if it would help."

She said, "About a year ago, I went on a safari. I got involved with the guide. I got scared of my feelings so I came home to forget him. But I can't because my longing for him has grown. Now I wish I knew how he felt. I'm afraid to write to him because he may not feel the same as he did then."

"What is his name?" Doctor Walters asked.

Faith answered, "It's Mitch Walters. He runs a nature reserve."

Doctor Walters exclaimed, "*Wow!*"

Faith asked, "Why 'wow'?"

Doctor Walters replied, "Because my nephew Mitch runs one over there."

Faith said, "No, it couldn't be!" She described Mitch and his reserve.

Doctor Walters responded, "You just described my nephew."

Faith was stunned. She had never put two and two together.

Doctor Walters asked her, "Should I call Mitch so you can talk to him?"

Faith said, "No, I have to think."

Chapter Twenty-One

It was the beginning of March and the small animal hospital and guide services were slow. Mitch had time on his hands, so he decided to write to his Uncle Jim in Hope to let him know that he still thought of him.

He also wanted him to find out if Faith still lived there. It had been July since she was with him. He had tried to forget her, but his feelings for her hadn't faded. He decided to ask his uncle if he could find out if she was still in Hope. He started his letter...

Dear Uncle Jim,
I hope this letter finds you well. I've been
busy. But now it has slowed down. I want to tell you
something. Last summer I took a girl on safari. She
wanted to see the animals and also see how we care
for them and what we do here at the hospital. She
was also interested in what we did with the animals
after we healed them.
We got to be quite close. I thought she was
feeling like we were going for a relationship. Then
before I had a chance to tell her about how I felt
and about you, she slipped away and went back home.
She was from Hope. I want to find her. I can't stop
thinking about her. I hope you can help me find her.

Her name is Faith Wilson and she was going to
go to vet school and work with animals. Do you think
you could help me locate her? If you find her, could
you let me know? Maybe you could let her know I'm
still thinking of her and would she contact me so
I can tell her how I feel.
If she's married let me know.
If you wouldn't mind, I'd like to visit you.
Let me know when. Please write soon and let me
know.
Love, Mitch

Mitch sent his letter out in the next post. He said a small prayer that she wasn't married and would see him. It would be hard if he got there and she was married, but he'd handle it.

It was two weeks later, the middle of March, when a letter from Mitch arrived at Doctor Walters' home. He opened the letter and read it.

He thought, *I better let Faith know about this letter.*

He went to work where Faith was feeding the patients and cleaning cages. He greeted her and asked her to come into his office.

He had her sit down and said, "I heard from my nephew. Have you decided to write to him?"

She said, "I was going to write to him after I told my parents about Mitch asking about me."

He said, "Okay, I won't write him about you."

She said, "Thanks, Doctor Walters. But you can tell him that I'll write to him."

She went home that night and told Kayla about the talk she'd had with Doctor Walters.

Kayla said, "Oh, my gosh, Faith. What are you going to do?"

Faith answered, "I'm going to write to Mitch and find out what his feelings are now."

Before Faith went to bed, she called her mother and told her, "I need to talk to you. I'll see you after work tomorrow."

Chapter Twenty-Two

After work, Faith went to her parent's house. She walked into the kitchen where her mother was fixing dinner.

Faith said, "Hi, Mom. Where's Dad?"

"Your dad had an emergency delivery," Jody replied. Then she said, "You're staying for dinner aren't you, Faith?"

Faith said, "Sure, Mom, but I really have to talk to you...woman to woman."

While Faith helped her mother finish dinner, she told her all about Doctor Walters being Mitch's uncle and the letter he had written to Doctor Walters. She told her, "Mom, I understood your feelings about Mitch. I'd like to hear from him."

Jody said, "Just be careful and make sure he's the one. What about Dennis?"

Faith replied, "He's only a friend. I already told him about Mitch. I'll write to Mitch and go from there. Don't worry, Mom, I'll be careful. I'll tell him I've been thinking of him and would love to see him."

"If he wants to see me when he comes, we can go out for coffee and talk. I can show him around Hope. I won't commit until I'm positive my feelings are real. And, Mom, I will make sure that we both want the same things in life."

Her mother said, "That's my girl."

The phone rang as they were doing dishes.

Jody answered and said, "Hello? Hi, Kathy, how are you?" Jody whispered to Faith, "It's your Aunt Kathy." Jody then said, "We're fine, Kathy. How's everything in Texas? It's good to hear from you, Kathy. It's been way too long!"

"I know, Jody. Mike and I have really been busy running and managing a nightclub."

Jody replied, "Wow, you've really come up in this world."

Kathy said, "Yeah, I guess we did. How's Faith doing?"

"You ask her," Jody answered and handed the phone to Faith.

Faith told Aunt Kathy all the latest news. Kathy said, "I'm glad to hear you're happy." Faith then handed the phone back to her mother.

Jody took the phone and while she was talking to Kathy, Faith said, "Thanks for the talk, Mom, I have to get going."

Faith hugged her mother and said goodbye. "Oh, Mom, tell Dad I said 'hi.'"

It was the end of March. Mitch had been waiting for news from his uncle. He was going through his mail when he spotted two letters from Hope, USA.

He quickly tore one open. It was from his uncle. He read it and put it down.

The other one was from Faith. He began to tear up as he read it. She told him why she left so fast and after she got home, she realized that it was too fast. She said that she tried to forget him with Dennis.

She said she finally told Dennis how she felt about him. She realized her feelings for him, Mitch, were stronger. All she thought about was him. She said she'd love to see him, but she was in veterinarian school and had three more years to go. Maybe after she finished....

Then she said maybe they could write and get caught up and see how things went. She signed it: "Love and miss you, Faith."

She put a P.S. in at the end. It said: "Write soon."

Chapter Twenty-Three

Before going to bed that night, Mitch thought about Faith. He read her letter again, then sat down and answered it.

He congratulated her on starting veterinarian school. He told her that he had heard from his uncle that she had a boyfriend and how he felt about hearing that. But since he read her letter, he would like to correspond with her to see if they could maybe get close again. In other words, start over. Mitch told her he couldn't stop thinking about her.

He signed the letter: "Your Loving Mitch."

It was April when Faith received Mitch's letter.

She read it after her last veterinarian class. By the time she had finished reading it, she was in tears. When she got to the veterinarian clinic she knew what she wanted to say when she answered Mitch's letter.

After she finished at work that evening, she told Doctor Walters about the letter she received from Mitch and what her answer would be.

Doctor Walters smiled and told her, "It sounds like yours and Mitch's feelings are the same."

She said, "I hope so."

Doctor Walters asked her, "Are you sure working so much and school isn't tiring you out?"

She said, "Oh, no, I love working here and it's helping me in school. If I need time off, I'll let you know. I'll see you tomorrow. Bye."

Faith had just walked through the door when Kayla said, "Let's go out to a Friday night fish fry. I'm too tired to cook and you look beat."

Faith said, "That sounds good. I am tired."

On the way to Capt'n Hook's, Faith told Kayla about Mitch's letter. Over dinner they talked about school and their grades.

Faith told Kayla, "I don't know how to tell my dad about Mitch and my stronger feelings for him."

Kayla said, "Just be honest and open with your dad. I'm sure that he will understand."

Faith said, "I hope so."

When they got home, Faith went to bed but she couldn't fall asleep. She kept thinking about Mitch. Finally, she gave up trying to sleep and got out of bed. She turned her desk light on, sat down, and put her thoughts on paper to Mitch.

She told him that Dennis was just a friend and that Dennis knew how she felt. It could go no further than friendship.

She said she had grown since she last saw him, as had her feelings. She said she loved his idea of starting over and going from there. She signed the letter: "Faithfully yours."

Chapter Twenty-Four

Faith arrived at her parent's house just as they were ready to eat dinner. Her mother set another place and then sat down.

When Faith was seated, Rob said, "Now it's more like home."

Jody said, "What's up? Is anything wrong?"

Faith said, "No, but I do have something I need to tell both of you." They both waited to hear what she had to say.

Faith looked at her parents and then she started. She said, "Mom, Dad, I know I haven't mentioned Mitch to you for awhile, but I have received and written two letters to him. I told him my feelings and he has told me his. I also told him about Dennis. I told Dennis we could only be just friends. I told him about Mitch and he understands. He said he'd like to meet Mitch and tell him what a special girl he was getting.

"Mom, Dad, my feelings for Mitch have grown. Oh, Mom, Dad, I love him and I think he loves me. But don't worry,

I will still finish vet school and I will also continue working with Doctor Walters. Mitch understands that and encourages it."

Her parents replied, "We're happy for you, but until you finish school, be careful. It could be awhile until you see each other. Remember, three years is a long time."

Faith said, "I know. I'll be careful and I won't get hurt over not seeing Mitch. I'm determined to finish school. Mitch wants me to

finish school because it will help if and when we end up in Africa on the reserve."

Her parents both let out a sigh.

Faith said, "Don't worry, it won't be for a long while. Besides, you know that sooner or later I'll have to be on my own or going with my husband wherever he went."

Her parents said, "Yeah, we know. But that won't make it any easier when the time does come."

Chapter Twenty-Five

It was April and Faith's birthday was just around the corner on the 19th. In three weeks it would be her "Golden Birthday."

Faith was up and straightening up and fixing a quick breakfast for her and Kayla. She was thinking how much she'd like Mitch to be there for her 19th birthday.

Mitch was feeding the animals when he decided to call his Uncle Jim.

He told him, "I decided to surprise Faith by coming there for her birthday. Do you have a room for me?"

Uncle Jim replied, "I sure do have room. I was hoping you would come over for a visit. You need to see where you stand with Faith."

Mitch said, "I feel the same. Don't say anything to Faith. I want to surprise her. While I'm there, I also want to check out some zoological parks and zoos for my animals. Some of them need a protected area to live in."

His uncle answered, "Yes, that's a very good idea. That means you'll be here awhile. Maybe when you're not running, you could help us out, too."

Mitch said, "Well, if you can put up with me, how about until June. Then if all goes well, I could be there when Faith finishes her first year of vet school. Who knows, maybe the rest of the summer Faith

could spend with me at the reserve, if her parents say it's okay with them. It could help her with her second year of school."

His uncle responded, "That sounds great, Mitch. When can I expect you?"

Mitch replied, "Well, I have to get things settled here. Probably right around the seventeenth or eighteenth of April. I'll call and let you know exactly when."

His uncle said, "Great, Mitch, then I can arrange to meet you in Chicago."

Mitch replied, "That sounds good. But you better let Faith's parents know what's going on."

His uncle said, "Okay, I'll do that right away so they can plan on how to keep Faith busy while I come and get you. It will be good to have you here. I love you, son."

Mitch finished their call, "I love you, too, Uncle Jim; and thanks."

Mitch called in John and Tim. He told them, "I need someone to take care of the reserve because I'm going to be leaving for the States to see my girl and check out some zoos for some of the animals."

Both said, "We can handle it."

Mitch said, "I'll be leaving in about two weeks. Are you sure you can handle it? I'll give you my uncle's number in case of an emergency."

They both replied, "That's a good idea."

Mitch spent the next two weeks getting ready to go. John and Tim drove him to the airport on Friday morning.

Mitch had called his uncle on Thursday night and told him to meet him Monday morning. He said he had the ten o'clock flight.

Doctor Walters called Mister and Mrs. Wilson as soon as he got off the phone with Mitch. He told Rob and Jody,

"I would like to talk to you tomorrow after I finish work."

They said, "Fine, come for dinner."

Doctor Walters arrived at the Wilson's. They all sat down to dinner.

Doctor Walters told them about Mitch coming to Hope on Monday and wanting to be Faith's birthday surprise. He then told them how he was going to keep Faith busy the day he had to pick up Mitch from the airport. Doctor Walters asked, "Is that okay?"

They both said, "Yes. Faith will be so happy."

The next two weeks went quickly.

Faith's mother called her and said, "I'd like you to come over on your birthday around seven."

Mitch called his uncle Friday afternoon just to remind him, "I'll be there April nineteenth at ten."

Doctor Walters said, "Great."

He called Faith's parents, who said, "Great." They had told Faith to come over around seven o'clock. She knew nothing.

Faith got up Monday morning to the phone ringing. It was Doctor Walters.

"Faith, I'm sorry but you will have to hold down the fort because I have to go out of town. I'll be back around one."

Faith answered, "That's fine. I'll be right in. I'll see you later."

Doctor Walters headed out the door for Chicago.

He got to the airport and parked. He went to the terminal. There were still a few minutes before Mitch arrived. When Mitch got off the plane he started looking for his uncle and saw him waiting at the gate. He met him and they embraced.

Mitch said, "Hi, Unc, it's been awhile."

Doctor Walters replied, "Too long. Everything is set. Faith is working today so I could get out of town on business. I told her I'd see her around one. Let's get going. I'll drop you off at home and you can get settled. We're due at her parents at seven."

Mitch exclaimed, "Great! I can't wait until I see her."

They headed for Hope.

Chapter Twenty-Six

Faith left work when Doctor Walters returned. She went home and took a nice long bath and rested until five o'clock. She then got up and dressed. She put on the new dress Kayla had given her for her birthday and finished getting ready to go to her parents for her birthday dinner.

She had no idea what was going on or who was waiting to see her. She thought, *It sure would nice to have Mitch here tonight.*

Faith's parents were getting ready for Faith's surprise party. They had told everyone to be there around 6:30.

It was 6:30. Everyone had arrived...almost.

Mitch and Doctor Walters rang the bell at about 6:45. They were rushed in and Doctor Walters took Mitch into the den. He told Mitch, "Wait here."

Everyone wondered who Mitch was and what was going on. Doctor Walters went and sat down.

Rob saw Faith's truck and he said, "Everyone, hide. When I say 'surprise,' you all come out." He went into the den and told Mitch, "Wait until I come and get you."

Faith got to the door and it was locked. She rang the doorbell and her father let her in. He took her coat and hung it up, then turned to her and said, "Happy Birthday."

Rob and Jody then both yelled, "SURPRISE!"

129

Everyone ran out and wished her a happy birthday.

Rob and Jody went to the den door. They said, "Faith, close your eyes and don't peek."

They motioned for Mitch to come out and had him go to Faith. He gave her a big hug and kiss.

Faith opened her eyes and almost fainted. She asked, "Is it really you?"

Mitch said, "It sure is, sweetheart. I'm really here."

Everyone wanted to know who he was.

Faith said, "This is Mitch Walters. I met him when I went on a safari last summer. He was my guide. He's also the man I love. I also hope to marry him after I finish school."

The dancing started. While everyone was busy dancing, talking and enjoying the party, Faith and Mitch went out on the porch to reminisce. Outside, Mitch took Faith in his arms and he gave her a big hug and a long kiss. They told each other how much they missed each other and talked for about an hour.

When they came back in, Faith went and thanked her parents and Doctor Walters for the best birthday she'd ever had. They said they knew that she'd be very happy and surprised when she saw Mitch.

When the party ended, Mitch said to Faith, "I will see you tomorrow."

Kayla and Faith left for home. Faith was walking on air...all the way home. Kayla couldn't wait until they got home so she could find out how everything went between Faith and Mitch.

When they got home, Kayla said, "What a surprise! Did you have any idea what was going on?"

Faith said, "No, the party and Mitch was a total surprise and a wonderful one!"

Chapter Twenty-Seven

Early Saturday morning Mitch rang Faith's doorbell. Kayla looked out the window and saw who was at the door.

She ran to Faith's room and jumped on her bed.

Faith bolted awake and said, "Kayla, what's wrong?"

Kayla smiled and said, "Your 'lover boy' is at the door."

Faith jumped out of bed and ran to the door. She opened the door for Mitch, who was standing in the early morning sunshine.

Mitch said, "Good morning, sweetheart." He gave her a kiss.

Faith responded, "Hi there, honey. I love your wake-up calls."

Mitch said, "I like hearing that. I know it's early, but I couldn't wait any longer to see you today. So go get dressed so I can take you out for breakfast."

Faith replied, "I'll be ready in the blink of an eye."

Twenty minutes later they were seated at the Doughnut Shop counter. When they finished eating, Mitch turned to Faith and said, "I hope you don't have any plans for today."

Faith smiled and replied, "Yes, as a matter of fact,

I do. I plan on spending the day with the man who I happen to love and plan on spending my every moment with."

Mitch said, "Oh, Faith, I think we better get going."

"I'm all yours. Lead on. Where to?" asked Faith.

Mitch told her, "I would like to see the famous wishing well in Hope Park."

On their way to the park, Mitch asked Faith, "Did you mean what you said?"

Faith answered, "Yes, I did."

They arrived at the park and Mitch helped Faith out of the car. They walked hand in hand along the park path until they reached the bench next to the wishing well. They sat down.

Faith then told Mitch the story of the wishing well and how special her birth was to all of them. She told him how her parents had both made their wish to fall in love and marry someone special. The wishing well made it all come true.

She then told him about her birth and how her mother hit the jackpot on the slot machine named "Wishing Well" and that she was a "million dollar baby."

Mitch smiled and said, "Honey, you sure are."

He stood up, took a coin out of his pocket, walked over to the wishing well, tossed it in, closed his eyes, and made a wish.

Faith walked up behind him and said, "What did you wish for?"

He took a ring out of his shirt pocket and showed it to Faith. He then said, "That you will accept this promise ring until I replace it with an engagement ring."

Faith replied, "Oh, Mitch! Yes!" She then gave him a big hug and kiss.

Mitch exclaimed, "Oh, baby! I like it when you do that. It's gonna be very heard for me to control my feelings for the next three years."

Faith replied, "I will enjoy the feeling of knowing I'm worth waiting for."

Mitch said, "Only for as long as I have to. Now I better get you home."

Mitch walked Faith to her door. He gave her a kiss and said, "I love you. Think of me until we meet again."

Chapter Twenty-Eight

It was a week before the end of her first year of veterinarian school. Faith kept busy between school, working, seeing her parents, and dates with Mitch.

It was June 1st before she knew it -- the last day of school. It was a busy day.

Faith and Kayla got home from school feeling happy and proud. After having a glass of wine, they got ready to go to Faith's parent's house for a get-together celebration.

When Faith and Kayla walked in, the balloons fell down and cheers rang out. Faith and Kayla's parents rushed toward them. Mister Douglas toasted them and wished them luck for the next three years.

Later Mitch sneaked Faith out for a moonlight walk in the park. He kissed her and told her that he was very proud of her.

They sat on the bench to talk. Mitch asked, "Faith, what would you think about taking a trip back to Africa with me until school starts again? If it's okay with your parents."

Faith replied, "Are you kidding? I'd love to!"

Mitch said, "Great, honey! Let's go talk to your parents."

They walked into the house, hand in hand, and sat down in the living room where Faith's parents were.

Faith said, "Mom, Dad, Mitch would like to talk to you and ask you something."

Rob and Jody look at one another. They wondered what Mitch had to say and if they were going to like it.

After an awkward moment of silence, Mitch said, "Mister and Mrs. Wilson, I've talked with Faith about going to Africa for the rest of the summer. I've asked her if she would like to go. She said 'yes.' Now I'm asking for your permission to take her. I hope you know me well enough to trust me. I will protect your daughter with my life. I love Faith and would never hurt her or let her get hurt by anyone or anything."

Rob said, "It's okay with her mother and me. Just take care of her. Above all, you two behave yourselves."

Faith walked with Mitch out to his car. He said, "Do you want a ride home since Kayla already left?"

She said, "No, sweetheart. I want to talk to my parents awhile."

Mitch answered her, "Okay, honey." He embraced and kissed her. "This has to last me until I see you again. Goodbye, my sweet baby. I love you."

Faith replied, "Bye, honey buns, I love you more!"

Chapter Twenty-Nine

It was Saturday morning. Faith awoke to birds chirping. Her first thought was of Mitch and she started to hum. She heard Kayla making breakfast as she jumped into the shower.

When she finished, she joined Kayla at the table.

While they ate, Faith said, "Kayla, I've been wondering, how you would like to work with me and Doctor Walters? I'm sure he wouldn't mind."

Kayla replied, "Well, I think it would be fun."

Faith said, "I'll ask him today."

Faith met Doctor Walters at the door to the clinic. They said "good morning" to each other and then went in.

Faith asked, "Doctor Walters, could I talk to you?"

He replied, "Sure, what is it?"

She said, "Well, I was wondering if we could have Kayla come and help us."

Doctor Walters answered, "I'm sure we can find her some work."

Faith said, "I was hoping she could take over for me once in awhile; maybe two days a week and Saturday's here and there."

He responded, "I know where you're going and I think it can be arranged. Maybe she could start on Monday with us and take over when you and Mitch leave on your vacation in July. See what she says."

Faith replied, "Oh, thank you. You won't be sorry. I'll talk with Kayla tonight and call you with her answer before Monday."

Faith went to work. The day went quickly and it was soon time to close.

She went home where Kayla was waiting for her.

Faith told her, "If you want to start on Monday, we would be happy to have you join us. There is something else I asked Doctor Walters about. I asked him if you could work with him two days a week and a Saturday here and there."

Kayla replied, "That's great! I'd love to work with him."

Faith then said, "I have a favor to ask. You know Mitch wants me to go with him in July to his reserve and help him. How would you feel about working for me until I get back in August for school? After that we can both work with Doctor Walters. What do you say?"

Kayla beamed as she exclaimed, "I can't wait to start!"

Faith called Doctor Walters. She told him, "Kayla will be coming with me on Monday." Then she asked, "Is Mitch there?"

The doctor replied, "Just a minute!"

She said, "Mitch, darling, everything is set with me for the trip. We can leave like we wanted to in July."

Mitch exclaimed, "That's great, honey!"

Chapter Thirty

The next few weeks flew by quickly. Both Faith and Mitch got everything ready to go. Mitch called John and Tim and told them to have the guestroom ready for Faith. They would arrive on the morning of July 7th.

They said, "Great! Everything is going great here."

Kayla was doing great and loving it more every day. She loved the animals and Doctor Walters taught her about their care. She went on farm calls with him and learned just like Faith had.

She told Faith, "I am very thankful for having the opportunity to learn from such great teachers."

Faith and Doctor Walters both laughed and said, "Flattery will get you many things."

It was a normal July Fourth -- picnics, family get-togethers, and fireworks. The next day Mitch and Faith were leaving. Rob and Jody were to drive them to Chicago in the morning.

Faith was up bright and early the next morning, ready to go. They decided to take a flight that had a stopover on the 6th so that they would arrive in Africa the morning of the 7th. Her parents picked up Mitch first and then they picked up Faith.

Faith said, "Goodbye, Kayla." She hugged her. "I'll see you in August."

They arrived at O'Hare with a few minutes to spare. Everyone said their good-byes then Faith and Mitch boarded. They were finally on their way. Faith and Mitch both thought how great it would to be back where they felt they belonged.

Mitch turned to Faith and told her, "I can't wait to see the reserve and to see how everything is going. The first thing I want to do is check the animals out."

He hadn't told Faith yet, but he had a surprise for her. John and Tim had found a female cheetah cub only a few days old. Lions had killed her mother. Luckily for the cub, they found her before the lions did. They had taken her to the reserve and were nursing her by hand.

Mitch had told them to care for her until they got there and he would give her to Faith. She would be about a month old when they arrived.

He was sure that Faith would love her. He would wait until they got to the reserve to show her the cub, then he'd tell her the cub was for her.

Chapter Thirty-One

They arrived at the airport and as they left the plane, Mitch saw John waving at them. He took Faith's hand and they headed for the gate. He got their luggage. He introduced Faith to John. John and Faith each said they remembered the other.

They then headed for the jeep. They arrived at the reserve and took their stuff into the house. Tim met them with a cold drink. They refreshed themselves and had lunch. Afterwards, Mitch showed Faith her room.

While she started to unpack, Mitch went to talk to John and Tim.

They told him that everything was going great. They had animals ready to ship and some to set free in the bush.

He said, "We will go out and see them when Faith is ready."

They were asking him about the cub when Faith came into the room. She asked, "What about the cub? Is it a lion or a cheetah?"

Mitch said, "Just wait and we'll go see her and the rest of the animals. Are you ready to go?"

Faith said, "Yes, I can't wait to see everything. I missed being here more than I thought I did." Quietly she said under her breath, "I don't think I'll want to leave."

Mitch said, "What did you say?"

Faith said, "Oh, nothing. Let's go."

They went out and looked at the animals that were to be shipped. A beautiful female elephant just right for breeding was going to Florida -- Disney's Safari World.

They then went to check out some year-old lions that were going to go to a new zoo in the Midwest. They also had monkeys and some other animals to go out.

Mitch said, ""It looks like everything is ready to go. When do we ship them?"

Tim said, "They are ready to go on Friday."

They went to the area where they kept the orphans. Mitch winked at Tim, who then went into one of the sheds. When he came out, he had a small bundle. He opened the blanket and out popped a little head.

Tim said, "It's a cheetah cub. She's about a month old." He handed her to Faith.

She said, "She's adorable."

Mitch said, "She's yours. Welcome back."

Faith carried her around while they looked at the rest of the animals. When they got back to the house, they fixed up a place for the cub.

She said, "I'll name her 'Bouncer' because when she gets down, she starts bouncing and pouncing on everything she spots."

They all started laughing at her antics. Faith then went to get her a bottle of special formal so she could eat.

They had a busy, hard working week. Bouncer followed Faith around like a little puppy and was underfoot most of the time, but they all loved her.

Friday came and they sent the animals off. They then went out to celebrate.

That evening Mitch and Faith went for a walk to watch the sunset.

Chapter Thirty-Two

The rest of the summer was busy. During the days, they went out in the bush throughout the territory catching animals for the zoos and taking care of the injured animals.

Bouncer needed more attention as she grew. She liked to stalk them. They had to keep track of her or she'd try to pounce on them, usually while they were taking care of an animal. She was becoming a pain too. She caught Tim and gave him some bruises that almost laid him up. They finally had to pen her up while they worked and let her out when they were done.

Mitch and Faith took moonlight walks. They tried to be alone, but Bouncer would follow them. Usually when she met them it would be the end of a romantic walk.

It was almost time for Faith to go back home to Hope. They were finishing up and getting things ready to leave. Faith and Mitch were sitting on the porch watching the sunset. Bouncer was lying down between them taking a catnap.

Faith said, "I'm going to miss all of this, especially not having Bouncer with me. I hope she doesn't forget me."

Mitch replied, "Don't worry, honey, she won't. We can come back on your vacations if all goes right."

"You know, I can see us in the future out here with Bouncer and maybe her mate and our children playing with their cubs."

Faith went to Mitch and sat in his lap. She hugged and kissed him, and said, "I love you more each day."

A few days later all was in order so they could leave. Mitch told the boys, "I'll call you. I will be checking out more places for the animals to go and making trips back to help out when you need it."

Chapter Thirty-Three

Over the next two years, Faith was fully occupied with her classes, studying with Kayla and working with Doctor Walters.

She thought in the back of her mind that she should be spending more time with Mitch, but she knew he understood and was very proud of her. Faith dearly loved him for his understanding ways. Her love for Mitch was growing deeper.

Mitch kept busy with visiting zoos and making sure

John and Tim were taking good care of the reserve and the animals. He went back every time he could.

When Faith had a vacation and during the summer if she was able to, she went with Mitch to be with him for awhile and to make sure that Bouncer was okay. She didn't want Bouncer to forget her. She also wanted to learn as much as possible about the reserve and how it cared for all of the animals. She grew to love Africa more each time they returned.

Faith's fourth and last year was the hardest. She didn't have extra traveling time. She was only free to return with Mitch to the reserve over Christmas vacation and during spring break.

Kayla was enjoying working with Doctor Walters more and more every day and, in turn, Doctor Walters depended more and more on Kayla. Kayla didn't mind. She was doing it for Faith and Mitch so that they could have more time together. Kayla was a dear friend!

Chapter Thirty-Four

It was Thursday, May 31st, the day before graduation and Faith and Kayla were excited and nervous. They were wondering if they passed their final exams.

As they left the school, they discussed what to make for supper. They decided they didn't want to cook and went to Big Burgers. When they had their trays and were seated, Mitch walked in. He came over to their table.

He said, "Hello, ladies. How are you?" He sat down next to Faith and gave her a hug and kiss. He said, "Faith, when you are finished eating, I am taking you on a moonlight boat ride down Hope River."

Faith said, "That sounds romantic." Faith then asked, "Kayla, since Mitch is taking me out, would you mind going home alone?"

Kayla answered, "I don't mind. You two lovebirds have a fun time."

Faith replied, "Thanks, you're great. Bye."

As they left, Mitch smiled, winked, and said, "That's the idea, my love. It will also calm you down for tomorrow night. I have something special planned for after graduation."

Before they went out the door, Mitch turned and said, "By the way, Kayla, thanks for understanding. You're a great friend."

It was Friday night; the Lakeside Veterinary School parking lot was packed when Faith and Kayla arrived.

Before going in, they each took a deep breath and cleared their minds for what was ahead of them. They walked in and got seated with their classmates and smiled at their parents' happy faces.

Mister Douglas took the stage and said, "Good evening, ladies and gentlemen. Welcome to the graduating class of veterinarians."

Everyone clapped as he introduced the class members and handed out their certificates. When he called Faith and Kayla up to receive theirs, he said, "Ladies and gentlemen, I present my two honor roll students."

He gave them each a special veterinarian pin. Everyone was clapping and yelling "*Bravo!* Good going!"

After the crowd calmed down, Mitch found Faith and embraced her tightly. As she walked out the door, Faith saw her parents waiting on the sidewalk.

They each gave Faith a big hug and said, "Congratulations, Faith! We are so proud of you."

Mitch shook Rob's hand. While Faith hugged and talked to Kayla, Mitch asked, "Rob and Jody, why don't you meet us at the Family Restaurant?"

Mitch walked Faith to his car and opened the door for her.

As they drove down the highway, Mitch looked and smiled at Faith. He said, "I've asked your parents to meet us at the Family Restaurant. I've got a big surprise for you."

Faith smiled and asked, "Oh, Mitch, now what are you up to?"

Mitch replied, "Something I know you will love."

Everyone was seated and talked for awhile, then Mitch said, "Mr. and Mrs. Wilson, I'd like to ask for your permission to marry your daughter."

Rob and Jody both smiled and said, "You've got it."

Mitch stood and then knelt down on one knee in front of Faith. He took a gold half heart necklace with diamonds surrounding it out of a box and put it over Faith's head and kissed her.

He put his matching necklace on and said, "They are made to fit together, just like our love will be forever!" He then said, "Faith, this is my way of asking you to become my wife."

Faith said, "I thought you would never ask." She replied, "Yes, oh, yes!"

Jody and Rob asked, "Have you picked out a date?"

They said, "We want to be married on July 15th in Africa on the reserve."

Everyone exclaimed, "What a wonderful place for a wedding!"

Chapter Thirty-Five

It was Saturday morning, a beautiful, breezy, sunshiny day in June. Faith was awake and waiting for Mitch to call when Kayla knocked on her door.

Faith said, "Come in."

Kayla came in and sat on the bed. She was nervous and seemed upset.

Faith asked, "What's troubling you, Kayla?"

She said, "I'm afraid I will not be good enough to be Doctor Walter's partner."

Faith said, "Oh, Kayla, if he feels you are good enough to be his partner, you have nothing to worry about. He wouldn't have asked you if he didn't think you are right for the job. So don't worry."

The phone rang and it was Mitch. Faith said, "Hello, honey buns. Just a minute." She told Kayla, "Get going and I'll see you later."

Kayla left for her first day as Doctor Walter's partner.

Faith went to talk to Mitch. He said, "Are you ready, sweet baby?"

She said, "Yes."

He said, "I'll be over in five minutes."

When he arrived, they went to get tickets and clothes for their trip. Mitch also called John and Tim to have them fix up the guestroom for Faith. He told them they would arrive on the morning of June 15th.

When he hung up, he gave Faith a hug and said, "Well, my little muffin, it's all set...no backing out now."

Faith said, with a loving smile, "There's no way I'll back out. I've waited too long to be with you. I'm yours now and forever."

Mitch said, "Now careful, doll, you know we have waited two years. It will be hard, but we can surely wait another month. We want everything to be perfect."

The next week and a half passed quickly. It was Sunday, the day before Faith and Mitch were scheduled to leave for Africa. They decided to just relax and spend the day with her family. Faith didn't know yet but Mitch had another surprise for her. He had talked to her parents and invited everyone over for a family picnic, so everyone could say their good-byes.

Everyone had a wonderful time at the picnic. They wished them a happy life and a safe trip to their future home.

Chapter Thirty-Six

It was Monday, June 11th -- the big day had arrived. Soon they would be home to see Bouncer and plan their wedding.

They had talked to Rob and Jody about coming over early so they could help with the wedding plans.

Rob told Jody that since he never took her on that special honeymoon after the wedding, they would travel to Europe for a month to see the sights. They were to leave on June 15th for the wedding.

Doctor Walters told Mitch and Faith on the day of the picnic that he decided to close the clinic for July, so he and Kayla and her boyfriend Eddie could fly over for the wedding.

That morning Rob and Jody got up bright and early. They were excited and sad at the same time. They were driving Mitch and Faith to the airport for the last time. They would see them in Africa in two weeks for their wedding.

When they got to the airport, there were a lot of tears, hugs, and kisses. Mitch and Faith boarded the plane. They were on their way home.

When they landed, Faith had a surprise. John and Tim were waiting for them. They had Bouncer on a leash. As they got off the plane, Bouncer spotted Faith and lunged toward the plane. She scared everyone as she ran toward Faith.

Mitch grabbed for her before she could knock Faith down. He tried to quiet her. Faith took her collar and she sat down. Faith hugged her and she settled down. They went to the jeep and left for the reserve.

Everyone started talking at once. John told them about Bouncer's little trips out into the bush.

Mitch asked, "Is everything else going okay? After we rest, we'll take a look around."

Chapter Thirty-Seven

During the next few weeks, they cleaned up the reserve. They also made sure the animals were ready to be shipped out and ready for release into the wild. Faith started getting things set for the wedding.

Bouncer started her nightly trips into the bush again, but she was always back in the morning. She seemed to be getting big in her stomach area.

Mitch told the boys, "I really appreciated your good work on the reserve over the last four years. Faith hopes you will stay on with us after our wedding. We want to make you partners since we all make such a great team." Mitch then asked, "John, will you my best man? And, Tim, will you be an usher?"

They were both very happy to be a part of the wedding. They also both agreed to stay and become partners.

Mitch and Faith asked Pastor Todd of the village church to perform the wedding ceremony. He was delighted to be able to have a wedding in his little church. He told them, "I'll make sure that everything is perfect for your wedding."

They were busy that night checking on the animals when they noticed that Bouncer wasn't gone. She was lying around and sleeping more than usual. They decided to examine her to make sure she was in good health.

They discover that Bouncer was okay; she was just pregnant. They figured she was due -- oh, no! -- right around the time of their wedding.

In the morning, Mitch got a call from his uncle with good news. Mitch told Faith, "After we pick up your parents, we will stay in town and show them around and have lunch because my uncle and Kayla are coming in on the one o'clock flight."

She exclaimed, "That's great! Everyone here at the same time."

Chapter Thirty-Eight

It was July 9th -- only a week until the wedding. They were having a rehearsal at the church and fixing up the church and the house so it would be ready for the wedding.

Bouncer was getting close to her time. Mitch fixed a caged area with a birthing box close to the house so they could keep a close eye on Bouncer. She was doing well. She seemed to know that everyone was there to help her.

Mitch and Faith decided to have vows. They talked to Pastor Todd and he said that would be fine. Mitch and Faith went to the village chief to see if the man who was making their rings had finished them.

The chief took them to see how he was doing. The rings were finished and they were beautiful. Faith's ring was made of ivory. The words were set in gold chips. The outside had "I Love You Forever" and the inside had a small heart on the side, Mitch was on top, then a heart on the other side and Faith below Mitch. It was different and very beautiful.

Mitch's ring was a gold band. Attached to it was a gold nugget shaped like a lion's head. It had two rubies for eyes and a piece of onyx for the nose.

When they saw them, they told him that they were very pleased with the work. When they went to pay, he only took half. He said the rest was a wedding gift to two very special friends of the tribe. Mitch and Faith then invited all of them to the wedding.

The next day, July 15th, was their wedding day. They all got up early and had a quick breakfast. Kayla and Faith's mother came in as Faith was laying out her wedding dress. It had been her grandmother's and her mother's wedding dress.

Mitch and the boys put on their tuxedos. When everyone was ready, they left for the church. They made sure Mitch didn't see Faith until he was supposed to.

Mitch was very excited. He wished time would go faster. He couldn't wait until they said their vows and became one.

Meanwhile the rest of the wedding party got ready to leave for the church.

Faith said, "Wait a minute. I want to check on Bouncer."

She went out to see her. Bouncer seemed very nervous. Faith hoped she wouldn't give birth until after the wedding. She knew it would be today though.

Kayla came out to get her so they could leave together.

She told Faith, "Don't worry; the workers will keep an eye on her. She will be fine."

They left for the church. As Faith got in the car, she said, "In just a short while I will have my heart's desire. I will be Mrs. Mitch Walters."

Chapter Thirty-Nine

Faith, her mother, and Kayla arrived at the church. They entered through the rear door to make certain the men didn't see them.

They were in a frenzy helping Faith get into her wedding dress. Faith's mother was in tears when she said, "Faith, you're a vision of beauty."

Faith heard the start of the wedding march. She became so very excited that she almost tripped walking to her father who was waiting in the foyer.

When he saw her, he looked at her, smiled, and said,

"Faith, my dear daughter, you are absolutely beautiful. Your groom is going to flip his lid when he lays eyes on you."

He kissed Faith and said, "I'm not ready to give you away. But I will walk you to your new life with Mitch."

The church was Old World, built with a wedding arch that was wrapped with roses, the flower of love.

Mitch and Faith stood under the arch during the ceremony. When it was time for vows, Mitch turned to Faith and clearly and loudly said, "Faith, my one and only love, with love as pure as a white dove, I promise my love to you my whole life through. You are my life's partner." The last line was said with deep meaning and teary eyed.

Faith then said her vows, "Mitch, my one true love, my love for you has grown daily. Being your wife will be my pleasure, not only for today, but forever. You are my life's partner."

Pastor Todd then said, "May I present Mr. and Mrs. Mitch Walters."

When Mitch and Faith got to the bottom step of the church, Faith looked up and said, "Oh, my gosh, Aunt Kathy and Uncle Mike!"

They said, "Did you think we would miss our one and only niece's wedding?"

When Mitch and Faith got back home, the first thing Faith did, even before changing out of her wedding gown, was check on Bouncer.

Faith said, "Good girl!"

When Mitch came up behind her and looked, he said, "Good job, Bouncer." Two little cubs were nestled against her, suckling.

Mitch and Faith then walked hand in hand back to the house.

When they got to the house, Mitch asked Faith, "Where would you like to honeymoon? I will go as far as paradise for you."

Faith wraps herself in Mitch's arms and replied, "Well, in that case, I'm already there!"

This book is dedicated to LeRoy G Peterson. The best friend and family member anyone could ask for. Also to my husband John and my kids Kathy, Jody and Tim. Thanks for your encouragement and support

AuthorHouse™
1663 Liberty Drive, Suite 200
Bloomington, IN 47403
www.authorhouse.com
Phone: 1-800-839-8640

First published by AuthorHouse 1/12/2008

ISBN: 978-1-4343-5606-2 (sc)

Printed in the United States of America
Bloomington, Indiana

This book is printed on acid-free paper.

The Wishing Well
and
Faith's Future

Sharon Wright

authorHOUSE®

CONTENTS

BLESSINGS

CHAPTER ONE

Ida Bird stood outside the Fort Defiance Employees' Club at noon, with the July sun just overhead. Nineteen and slender, she wore her shining black hair pulled back tightly by a simple barrette. When Jack Berkowitz walked up to the old wooden building, seeing the girl standing there, he realized this was the young woman Milton Raines had told him about. What struck him was the intensity of her gaze, her serious dark eyes, and her straight shoulders. Her manner and her fair skin, with just a hint of freckles over her high cheekbones, almost led him to think she might not be Navajo. But he had been prepared for this meeting and he knew she was Navajo and a much-celebrated one. The year before at the Navajo Tribal Fair she had been picked as the reigning Queen, Miss Navajo 1953.

"I've been waiting to meet you, Doctor Berkowitz," Ida said. "Mr. Raines told me you could help with my applications to colleges in the East."

"Yes, he told me about you, too. I'm very happy to meet you, Ida. I'll do what I can. But let's go inside where we can talk. The sun is a bit too strong out here."

They mounted the stairs and crossed the broad porch into the lobby. Here the slightly cooler air was stirred by slowly turning ceiling fans. For a few moments they were alone. The regular lunchtime crowd had not yet arrived. They sat on one of the long wooden benches the Club provided for diners to sit on while the meals were made ready. Ida sat stiffly, her hands folded in her lap, waiting for Jack to speak.

"Tell me," Jack began, "what help you've had so far from advisors at your school."

"We don't have any advisors. There's nobody there to help you or encourage you. If you tell them you want to go to college they tell you, 'You're not college material.' They think Indians are too dumb to go to college."

This poor kid, Jack thought. So defeated already. It's hard to believe there isn't *somebody* at that school who can help.

"I'm not sure what I can do," he said. "Maybe I could talk to the principal and get things started in some way."

Ida's head and shoulders drooped forward hearing this.

He sounds like any other white man, Ida thought. Stiff. The same old runaround. 'Principal' this, 'school advisor,' that. They weren't any help before; why would it be any different now?

Jack sensed the coolness of Ida's response. He realized he might be inadequate to the task set before him. He'd depended on his own determination to get through school and college and then on to medical school. He was a doctor now, not an academic advisor. The serious and unhappy girl before him appealed to him. Yet he felt unable to throw himself into the role Milton Raines had cast him.

"Maybe Mr. Raines can help me get started," Jack said, pursuing his own train of thought. "He knows his way around here." With this Ida's face brightened a bit. Milton Raines was a man she trusted.

Raines was one of the people Jack had met shortly after he arrived at Fort Defiance to become the new doctor at the tuberculosis sanatorium. Milton and Jack were regulars at the dining room at the Employees' Club.

"You'll have to meet her," Milt had said of Ida Bird as he showed Jack her photograph in his shop. "She's a honey." Jack remembered his first meeting with Milt and of the visit he made to Milt's tiny, low-ceilinged office and lab at Window Rock some weeks before. He was showing Jack some of the pictures he had taken over his previous twenty-five years on the Navajo Reservation. The pictures always showed the Navajos in their pride and beauty, dressed in their velveteen blouses, wearing their jewelry, seated in front of their looms weaving near their hogans or watering their sheep in shaded streams.

"You see," Milton had said, almost reading Jack's thoughts, "I never take pictures of Navajos drunk in Gallup. I hate those pictures and I hate the photographers who take them."

Jack looked at Ida's photograph again. She'd been working with Milt that summer filing and cataloguing his black-and-white prints and negatives, and beginning to learn printing and enlarging. And there on the wall was Milt's favorite. Jack thought Ida's face a bit too severe, no Honey-like sweetness in it, too much angularity. And her arms in the picture, taken when she was wearing a short-sleeved blouse, had no flesh on them.

"I told Ida about you and that you're from the East. She wants to go on to college there after she finishes high school next year. She has an idea maybe you could help her," Milt said, and so the meeting was arranged.

Rumbling on the wooden stairs outside and on the porch announced the arrival of more guests for lunch. The lobby filled quickly as a group of eight student nurses, recently arrived at the hospital for clinical training, came into the room. They were Indian girls from many tribes, Comanche, Taos, Hopi, but none, Jack observed, as pretty as Ida. They were dressed alike in pink uniforms and white caps, chatting quietly with one another, waiting to be called to the table. The arrival of this large group interrupted the conversation Jack and Ida were having. Soon Mrs. Dunham, an Anglo woman and the chief cook, called out, "Luncheon is being served," and directed everyone to tables set in the dining room.

Ida sat quietly and listened to Jack as he engaged the student nurses in conversation. He was describing his occasional night-call duties in the delivery room at the hospital. She noticed that in contrast to the stiffness and formality of his tone when he'd spoken to her, now he was animated, having fun.

"When you're getting set to deliver a baby, you have to sit on a stool facing the opening where the baby comes out. You've got to have your own legs spread apart so the gown you're wearing is stretched across your thighs like an apron. Because after the head is delivered, the kid squirts out like a greased pig, and you've got to be sure you're there to *catch* it."

Listening to this talk Ida thought, Who is this show-off? Who is he trying to impress? Ida had looked forward so much to this meeting. Columbia University and New York City, where Jack Berkowitz came from, had seemed to Ida like a castle in a land of dreams. Mr. Raines had said the young doctor would know how to help her get there. When she saw Jack walking up to the Employees' Club, Ida liked what she saw. He was reasonably tall, he had curly brown hair, a fresh, friendly smile and he had dimples. She saw that his eyes were blue behind the pink plastic frames of his eyeglasses. But the lunch was turning out to be a waste of time for her. She didn't have a chance to ask any of the questions she had: Where should I write to get an application for admission? How many colleges should I apply to? Where would I have the best chance of getting in? Where can I apply for scholarships? And then all this medical stuff, as if he thought Indians didn't know anything about how a baby is born!

Ida sat silently throughout the luncheon, thinking about what people were saying around Fort Defiance about this young doctor. They said he'd stayed out all night with that homely white girl medical student, the one with the mole on her face, the one who was spending the summer at the hospital at Shiprock, telling people afterward that they had become stuck trying to get over the pass from Mexican Springs. What a story! And then the other story about how he was seen taking out that awful Agnes McKinley, the same Agnes who worked at the Employees' Club as a cook. Ida turned her head to look into the kitchen to see if Agnes was working there that day. Jack, they said, was seen driving Agnes and her two kids around in his new, turquoise blue Chevrolet Bel Air convertible. What was he doing with that old whore anyway? He probably took her to bed. That Agnes would have been easy.

Jack, finishing his story to the nurses, looked in Ida's direction, sensing her disapproval, her disappointment. After lunch he came up to her

"I'm sorry that our conversation got cut off. This is what I'll do. I'll look up the addresses of the registrars at Cornell, Dartmouth, and Radcliff colleges. I'll try to find out about scholarships for Indian applicants. When I have this information I'll get in touch with you. Where will I be able to find you? At Mr. Raines's office? Will I be able to see you again?"

"That will be all right," Ida said in a low voice. She couldn't conceal her disappointment. She wasn't sure she could trust him. At the same time she felt attracted to him. He was "nice" in some ways but, according to the stories, "wild" also. Against her better judgment the "wild" side of him stirred her as she watched his confident stride back to the hospital.

Two days later Jack drove down the tree-shaded main street of Fort Defiance in his convertible with the top down. The leaves of the cottonwood trees rustled above his head as he glided past the hospital and the sanatorium. Up ahead and on his left he saw Ida walking toward the post office with another Navajo girl, plain-faced, wearing glasses.

"Can I give you girls a lift?" Ida tilted her head up, then pointed her lips and chin ahead to the post office and kept on walking.

Jack drove on, sensing the foolishness of his grin as his face fell. Ida's bearing, her stride, moved him. He imagined how he would touch her shoulder when he would put his arm around her for the first time. She would not move away but she would allow his hand to rest there, allow him to feel her smooth skin through her blouse.

Who knows what *that* would lead to, he thought. Why am I, a white man, a Jew from New York, thinking about this Navajo girl, this strange girl from this strange land, sprung like Venus, not from the sea, but from the dry land, this land of mesas and sandstone cliffs?

CHAPTER TWO

Jack Berkowitz had not planned to be a tuberculosis—or "chest"—specialist. He had always sought to avoid clichés. The common saying was, "Tuberculosis is a disease that makes its own specialists." Jack had had tuberculosis himself, and he had been treated with pneumothorax, air injected into the chest cavity to rest the lung, through his years in college. If he sought out special training in tuberculosis after becoming a doctor, and if he went on to declare himself a specialist in the field, he would be doing the obvious. He really didn't want to call attention to his own history. In spite of this, however, in his second year of residency in Boston, he felt a certain sympathy with patients who had any sort of lung or chest disease. He began to attend chest conferences and he gained valuable experience interpreting X-rays of the chest.

On Thursday afternoons at the great Columbia University Medical Center in New York City, the tuberculosis research team would assemble to review the course of all the patients under its care. One day a large package of X-rays was delivered to the conference room. The X-rays were not those of patients hospitalized on the research unit in New York. The films were thrown up on the bank of viewboxes and the names of the patients would appear on the film written in crayon or in ink: *Nellie Yellowhair, Frank Nez, Mary Francisco,* or simply *Chinibah.* The names were exotic. Who were these people? Jack learned that the films were those of Navajo patients at the U.S. Indian Hospital at Fort Defiance, Arizona. Dr. Walsh McDivitt, director of the research team at Columbia, had obtained permission from the Navajo Tribal Council to treat some Navajo patients who had failed to be cured by the standard treatment they'd receive thus far. These patients would be treated by some of the newer drug combinations that were showing promise on the research ward in New York. The Tribal Council agreed to allow such drugs to be used only when they were proven to be safe as well as effective.

Week after week, new sets of X-rays from Fort Defiance were reviewed. New names appeared: *David Tsosie, Jim Blackrock, Esther Manygoats, Ellen Bitsie, Rosita Peaches, Mary Roanhorse, Tony Begay, John Yazzie.* After several months, new films of the first set of Navajo patients appeared. The films often showed gratifying degrees of healing in the lungs and increasing thickness of fat over the ribs. The names and X-rays soon became so familiar that Jack was able to identify the patients by the X-rays of their lungs, and the melody of their names rang in his ears.

Jack accepted the invitation of Dr. McDivitt to continue research in the new drug treatments by taking the job as "Chief of Tuberculosis" at the one hundred-bed sanatorium at the Navajo Medical Center at Fort Defiance. To the exhilaration of the idea of taking on his first job was the added excitement Jack felt making this trip to the West. He wrote the following in a letter to his mother in New York:

"At the state line where the road leaves Texas and enters New Mexico the change is so striking you know you are in the West. It is as if the flat, green, upland plateau of the Texas panhandle had suddenly become gouged out to form wide and open valleys before you. Where ancient streams and rivers had not gouged out the land, the level layers remained as the flat tops of the mesas. I had a curious, sinking sensation as the road dropped down into the brown valleys and the mesas seemed to rise up as if by magic all around me. The Arizona state line and Fort Defiance still lay some four-hundred miles to the west; I knew that I would not get there until some time the next day. So I had the time, driving alone in my convertible with the top down, to take delight in the strange new shapes of the land and in the forms of the thunderheads as they mounted in the sky."

Jack learned soon enough that thunderheads in the West mean the likelihood of rain. First, the chill of cold air ahead of the storm was a welcome change. He'd had enough of the heat in his drive across Texas. When the first cold drops splashed on his head he felt a sudden release, an explosion of joy and he laughed out loud in the wilderness. The West was not, after all, the bone-dry place he'd imagined. He pulled over to the side of the road to put up the top. He was amazed at how quickly puddles appeared all around him, alive with the splashing of raindrops. He drove ahead now with the drumming of the rain on the car's canvas top, headlights on in the swiftly developing darkness, windshield wipers working furiously, wetness shining on the blacktop road ahead. Jack wished the excitement and the drama of the storm to continue. But the fury of the lashing rain ceased, a quieter, softer rain continued for a while, and then he was out in the sun again, this time in a softer light as the day neared its end.

"What's 'chicken-fried steak'?" Jack asked the chef at the motel diner at Moriarty where he stopped for the night. The cook served it up, golden brown and smelling good with a mound of mashed potatoes on the side. It's like my mother's veal cutlet, Jack thought, remembering his mother's cooking, and his mouth began to water. But then the cook smothered the whole plate with white gravy. My God, thought Jack. There must be milk in that gravy! I can't eat meat if it's smothered with milk. But the aroma of crusted batter came through and Jack's appetite returned. He reached for the pepper and the ketchup as antidote for the non-kosher combination and soon he ate his first chicken-fried steak of the West.

In the clear, cool air of the morning, Jack spun down through Tijeras Canyon into the still-sleeping Albuquerque, pink-tinged in the morning sun. He pushed past the empty fairgrounds on

U.S. 66, then past the old brown buildings of downtown Central Avenue, across the Rio Grande, and up again to the open, high desert. The air heated up quickly as the sun climbed overhead, and the glare off the dun-colored sand hurt his eyes. By the time he reached Gallup three hours later clouds began to form giving some relief from the heat. He seemed not as eager now to push on to his destination. He drove very slowly northward from Gallup, taking delight in the coolness and in the sprinkling of rain. He thought it unusual that it would rain in New Mexico and in Arizona in July. He imagined, in a magical way, that it was an omen, that the rain, with its blessing of relief, came just as he was to arrive to take on his new job.

But when Jack drove into Fort Defiance, there were no banners, no fanfares, and no crowds. The main street, only three or four blocks long and lined with fine old cottonwood trees that formed an arched canopy over the thoroughfare, was empty. A red fieldstone, three-story building, the main hospital, rose on the east side of the street. The tuberculosis sanatorium, an older, single-story, white wooden building with its green-shingled, pitched roof and green shutters stretched the length of two blocks on the west side of the street.

Jack now saw that the time had come to take on life in earnest. This was the place where he would spend the next two years of his life. Those two years might be filled with the same loneliness he was feeling just now, seeing the deserted street that lay before him. He was relieved that he had slipped into the little town unnoticed. He wanted not to have to face anybody just yet. He knew that before long he would meet Nellie Yellowhair, Frank Nez, Mary Francisco, Chinibah, David Tsosie, and all the others whose X-rays he knew by heart. He would get to know their faces and they would get to know his. But would he be able to communicate with them, with these people whose names were still so foreign-sounding to him, so exotic? Would he be able to establish that trust that is so important between doctor and patient? He'd been successful so far in establishing that trust, but that was with patients he'd taken care of in Boston and in New

York, people with whom he shared a common language. But would he be able to do that here?

These were his thoughts as he found the apartment that had been assigned to him. It remained cloudy overhead with a sprinkling of rain. He found it dark and cool beneath the vegas of the Southwest-style rooms he entered. He took comfort in this. But as for his magical thinking that the rain was a particular sign of the good news of his coming, he learned soon that rain is common in Arizona, and that in July it often rains every day.

CHAPTER THREE

On Monday morning Jack's new job began. Rounds started with the men's ward on the south side of the building. The high, square room had three rows of white-painted metal beds, one row between the windows on the west wall, one row in the middle, and one row on the east wall. The beds had been made and the patients had been instructed by Miss Moss, the chief nurse, to stand at attention at the foot of their beds, military style. Miss Moss, in a starched white uniform and a stiff-winged nurse's cap stood nearly six feet tall. She was not a Navajo but an Indian from some Oklahoma tribe. She was in her late fifties, stern-faced and all business. She had been in charge of the Fort Defiance sanatorium for more than twenty years. She had seen many doctors come and go. She'd expected that. But she knew that it was *her* dedication, *her* discipline that held the place together. She knew there was advantage to her not being Navajo; the distance allowed her to enforce that discipline. She knew tuberculosis. To survive the disease you had to obey the rules: rest when you were supposed to rest, swallow your pills and take your injections, go to sleep on time, never get drunk or run away. And when the doctor came into the room you were to stand at attention.

Jack looked at the rows of the male patients, mainly young men, a small number of boys, and a few old men. The younger boys and the old men smiled; the young men stood stone-faced. The boys and the young men wore their hair short; some of the older men wore their hair in the traditional Navajo bun or "tsi-yeh." Miss Moss introduced each person by name and Jack responded with one of the first terms he learned: "Yat'eh!" meaning "Hello." Jack was proud that it sounded fairly authentic. The young boys responded with "Hello," and the old men with "Yat'eh-*oh*!," the extra "*oh*!," Jack learned later, was an affirmation, a friendly way to emphasize the pleasure of meeting a person.

The names were all familiar. Those were the names written on the X-rays he had seen in New York. The images of those X-rays flashed through his mind and he found he was busy matching the name, the face, and the lesion in the lung. In the rush of making all those match-ups, Jack had to sort out this difficulty: in New York there were two men named "Leo Nez," and to distinguish between them, the X-rays were labeled "Leo Nez I" and "Leo Nez II." But how could he tell which patient was Leo Nez I and which one was Leo Nez II? After some reflection he figured it out. The X-ray of Leo Nez II showed extensive areas of scarring; this could only mean the man had had his disease a very long time, so Leo Nez II must be the older man. Jack was happy to see that the older Leo Nez looked surprisingly fit, in spite of the extensiveness of the disease on X-ray, and there was a lesson in tuberculosis: a person might tolerate a great deal of injury to the lungs and still look and feel well.

When Jack and Miss Moss turned to leave the room, which had been so quiet during this first formal visit, Jack heard the ward suddenly become alive with murmuring and whispering. He heard or thought he heard a word with a hissing, sibilant quality. He knew they must be talking about him. Later he learned the word was "Ah-zay-ich-*inn*," or "Medicine Maker," the term the Navajos use for "doctor."

So they've looked me over and they're talking about me. What could be more natural?, Jack thought. After all, I've looked *them* over. I've even looked *through* them as well. Maybe they've sensed that. They all know they've been X-rayed. And, indeed, one of next few Navajo words Jack was to learn was the word for X-ray: "Ni-rhad-et-od-*glod*," the light that shines *through.*

A long corridor connected the two wings of the building, the men's ward on the south and the women's ward on the north. The smaller rooms that lay off that corridor housed the older and sicker patients. Here, in contrast to the liveliness of the ward, Jack saw the frightened faces of patients with severe, chronic tuberculosis, patients who in the next few weeks or months would die of their disease.

A second nurse joined Jack and Miss Moss before they entered the women's ward. It was Anna Armijo, the Navajo assistant nursing director. Mrs. Armijo was only five-feet two, and she came along quietly, padding on softer, less perfectly whitened shoes and with a slightly rocking gait.

The women's ward was entirely different. The faces and the eyes of the young women patients, because they were mainly young, were *alive.* In contrast to the stony stares he received on the men's ward, here Jack was greeted with smiles. When he approached each bed and when he was introduced to each girl or woman in turn, he found a radiant grin, a flirtatious smile, or an impertinent, saucy stare. One girl exploded into a giggle and then turned her reddened face away in embarrassment.

"Now girls, behave yourselves!" Miss Moss said sternly in English. Then Mrs. Armijo said something to the girl in Navajo and then to Jack, "Oh, they're just teasing."

Most of the women in the ward appeared quite healthy and, indeed, most were recovering nicely, as Jack knew from his recollection of the X-rays. In the middle of the row by the west wall one girl remained in her bed. She had drawn the blanket up to cover her face, revealing only her eyes, dark and with more than the usual oriental cast. Her forehead was more than usually light-skinned, and very pale. Hers was a direct, placid gaze with a touch of sadness in it.

"This is Ellen Bitsie," Miss Moss said, introducing the girl, and Jack knew she had a large cavity in the right upper lobe of her lung, that her sputum was still positive, and that she was sixteen years old. Ellen said nothing. If she spoke English she was too shy or perhaps she was afraid she would make a mistake.

Over the next several months Jack saw that Ellen was making no progress. Her sputum remained positive in spite of Jack's having added several of the newer, more powerful anti-tuberculosis drugs he had brought from New York. The cavity in the right upper lobe failed to close. On rounds she looked at Jack with that same quiet gaze, never joking, never engaging in playfulness, never flirting. Nor did she ever complain or make any special demands. So it pained Jack that this appealing girl was not getting better.

Jack's office was a large, bright room in the center of the sanatorium building. It contained a large desk, several chairs for visitors, a bank of viewboxes, and a mountainous pile of X-ray films. He took some pride in the plaque, "Chief of Tuberculosis," on his desk though he realized the irony of the of the title. He was "Chief" but also the *only* doctor for the one hundred patients in the sanatorium. One hundred patients! How was he to keep track of all these people? Back in New York he kept a pocket-sized, bound, hard-covered sketchbook in which he recorded the names and a sketch of what patients' chest X-rays looked like. This would be the way he would continue for the two years that lay ahead.

In the afternoons Jack used the office to receive and to speak to relatives of the patients,

"My biggest worry," he explained to Mrs. Bullis, his Navajo secretary, "is that the relatives will take the patients out of the sanatorium before the patients are ready, before they've achieved complete control of their disease. Then all of the time and effort getting them well will have been wasted and the patients will have a greater chance of relapse."

Jack would often watch the horse-drawn wagons come slowly down the tree-lined street of Fort Defiance. A man would drive the team, a woman in traditional Navajo velveteen blouse and ankle-length, billowing cotton skirt, and kerchief over her head would sit beside the man on the seat or on a pile of goods in the bed of the wagon. These would be

Navajos who would have come from great distances, sometimes several days' drive from the interior of the Reservation. Jack would be apprehensive that such Navajos would be less sophisticated, less understanding of the nature of tuberculosis, and that they would be more likely to want to take their relative out of the sanatorium before the patient was cured. Jack's apprehension would increase as these dark, sunburnt Indians climbed down from the wagons and came walking up the front steps of the sanatorium. Then Mrs. Bullis would invite them into the office and they would take their seats quietly.

"These are the abnormal areas of the lung where a cavity exists," Jack often explained showing the patients' X-rays to the relatives. His intention was to impress the relatives with the seriousness of the situation or to explain that, while progress was being made, more time was needed for the patient to become completely well. Mrs. Bullis would interpret into Navajo and when she finished there would often follow a long, carefully delivered oration by the relative, at the end of which Jack would hear a phrase which, in time, became quite familiar to him: "Ah-*shay*-hay, ah-*shay*-hay." Then Mrs. Bullis would report what the relatives had said. They were thankful that the patient was getting better. He or she had been so sick before. They had no intention of taking the patient out before he or she became completely well. "Ah-*shay*-hay," Thank You. Jack soon became less apprehensive when the relatives came. He began to look forward to those long speeches. In time his understanding of Navajo increased to the point where he would be able to answer some of their questions without waiting for Mrs. Bullis' translation. When those long interviews would end there would always be "Ah-*shay*-hay, ah-*shay*-hay!"

So Jack's days piled one upon the other. There were the rounds in the morning with Miss Moss, whom he could respect, and Mrs. Armijo, whose tact and good humor he came to love. He had pleasure seeing most of his patients get well. But he was sad to see that some, like Ellen Bitsie, languished with the disease that, in the past, had borne the name "consumption."

CHAPTER FOUR

Jack knew that the first two months at the sanatorium were the most important for him to do the kind of job he wanted to do.

"Miss Moss, I'm going to need your help," he said at a conference he asked for with his chief nurse. "I want to set aside time in the evenings to examine and to get better acquainted with each patient individually, and I'll need a nurse and interpreter to be with me when I do this."

"Why do you need to do this in the evenings?" asked Miss Moss with a disapproving frown. "Aren't you getting to know your patients on rounds during the day?"

"I am getting to know them," Jack said. "But I feel I'm not really communicating with them. There simply isn't enough time when we see a hundred patients on a morning walk through the sanatorium to know what they're thinking. I know they must have questions to ask, but so many of them are shy, or afraid to ask. And so many of them don't speak English, especially the older ones like Chinibah and Nellie Yellowhair, and the ones like Rosita Peaches who come from remote portions of the Reservation."

"I see your point," said Miss Moss, "but none of the other doctors who've come here asked to do what you propose to do."

"It's the only way," Jack said with enthusiasm, seeing now that he might be recruiting an ally. "There's so much that I need to talk to them about. If their sputum remains positive, they will want to know what the next step will be, what the new drugs might do; if they'll need to have surgery, what the surgery will be like."

"I'm not sure I'll be able to give you the nurses and interpreters at night," said Miss Moss. "The nurses need their time off, and the Navajo interpreters, they deserve to have time with their families. But I'll do what I can."

Stiff as she is, Jack thought, the old girl is fair. Fair to her nurses, and considerate.

Within a few days Miss Moss arranged to provide Jack with the staff he needed for three evenings a week. Jack's first patient was Nellie Yellowhair, a woman of seventy whose long hair was largely grey now though streaked with black. Mrs. Armijo led her slowly into the examining room, chatting with her in Navajo. Jack stood up, extended his hand and motioned for her to sit down and for Mrs. Armijo to sit down as well.

"Yat'eh shi *mah*," (Hello, my mother) Jack said trying the traditional greeting for an older woman. Mrs. Yellowhair smiled and answered, "Yat'eh shi yahzh" (Hello, my son).

"Cha d'eh shahn na a *rhanh*?" (Where is your home?) Jack asked using another new expression he had learned.

"Inh ley Chinle," (Over at Chinle) was the woman's response as she pointed her head to the north and west in the direction of her home. Jack was pleased that Mrs. Yellowhair understood his questions in spite of what he knew was his faulty accent.

"Well, that's about as far as I can go with my Navajo right now," Jack said to Mrs. Armijo with a little smile. "From now on you'll have to help me. Please ask her how she feels since her treatment began here in the sanatorium."

In this way the interviews began. Jack would tell the patient he wanted to listen to the lungs with a stethoscope; then he would put the patient's X-rays on the viewbox and point out where the abnormality showed in the lungs. He showed Ellen Bitsie her X-rays, and the films showed the cavity in the right upper lobe which had failed to close. At sixteen, he did not wish to subject the girl to surgery, the alternative that had to be considered in cases where drug treatment failed.

"Let's give the new drugs a few more months to work," Jack said, trying to reassure himself as well as the girl. Ellen, pale and shy, looked down at the floor and said nothing.

Jack limited these interviews to three or four in an evening, and in six weeks he had given this kind of individual attention to over half of the sanatorium patients. He felt he was getting his work on a solid footing that would last for the coming two years. But he had put off carrying out the promise he'd made to Ida Bird. He did not obtain the addresses of the registrars and information on admission and possible scholarships to colleges in the East. He learned from the conversations he heard at coffee break that the children of some of the interpreters and nurses would be leaving for "off reservation" schools the next day. He realized now that he must try to see Ida before she left for the Fall term.

The growling of diesel engines the following day called Jack's attention to the streams of chartered Greyhound buses driving north up the main street of Fort Defiance toward the boarding school. He was still wearing his white laboratory coat when he rushed out of the sanatorium and followed the buses to where they had parked along the curb, engines running. Parents and teachers were busy herding children and directing them to buses that would take them as far away as Utah, Oklahoma, and California. Jack took some comfort that Ida would only be as far away as the Indian School in Albuquerque, one hundred-forty miles to the east. He searched for her and found her at last, the tallest of the girls, dressed in sweater and skirt, her slim brown legs showing above her Bobby socks. She was a young woman among the crowds of children. Ida saw him, straining to find her face among the others, but she showed him no sign of recognition. Her coldness discouraged him, made him hesitate. He had wanted to speak to her, to tell her he would write to her. But her back was now turned, and in a moment, she climbed aboard with the others and disappeared into the bowels of the bus.

Chapter Five

Aweek later, in the early evening after he finished his work
for the day at the sanatorium, Jack drove up the old
dirt road north from Fort Defiance. He was familiar with the
road and where to find Ida's home because Milton Raines had
brought him up to meet Ida's father, Mr. Joe Bird, the week be-
fore. Milton Raines knew all the Navajos in the Fort Defiance
area and he was an old friend of Mr. Bird. Joe Bird was president
of the Red Lake Chapter, the local self-governing unit, and he
had been instrumental in developing the irrigation project that
brought hundreds of acres of valley land below the Red Lake
dam into production. As part of his official duty to record works
of such importance on the Navajo Reservation, Milton Raines
had often photographed the project and Mr. Bird, its guiding
hand.

Jack found Ida's father, a handsome man in his early sixties,
sitting outside of a rough-hewn cooking shed, enjoying a ciga-
rette. He had regular features, smooth, light skin, heavy eyebrows
and a bit of a mustache. He wore gold-rimmed glasses and a
broad-brimmed felt hat. With his glasses and light skin, Jack
thought he almost looked like a white man. Enjoying his repose,
Mr. Bird sat with his chair tipped backward, taking his pleasure
as the evening sun fell across the valley igniting the pink sand-
stone cliffs with a phosphorescent glow.

Jack was charmed by the old gentleman and by the calm manner in which he seemed to be accepted. At the same time he thought, What am I getting into?

"It's very beautiful up here," Jack began. "It's so quiet. When people rush through this country on Highway 66 or on a train through Gallup they never see anything like this. I feel very lucky to be here."

Mr. Bird nodded quietly in agreement. He held his cigarette between his thumb and forefinger, and though he brought it to his lips from time to time, he didn't seem to inhale. Jack was pleased that he didn't ask any questions, like Where are you from?, or What kind of a name is 'Berkowitz'? Jack would have been willing to answer those questions but he was just as happy enjoying the long silences and the views of the distant cliffs with the light fading upon them.

"I'll be going up to Santa Fe next weekend for the Fiesta," Jack said at last. "I'd like to take Ida with me for the day, but I think the school would want to have a note from you saying that it is all right." Jack had prepared himself this little speech and he congratulated himself that it sounded good. Even though Mr. Bird's expression didn't change much, he was sure now that Mr. Bird would agree.

"I guess that will be all right," was his answer. Jack pulled out a pad and pencil from his shirt pocket and handed it to the older man. Mr. Bird propped the pad on his knee and wrote slowly in large cursive script. They must have emphasized penmanship in the old days at Indian schools, Jack thought.

"Thank you," Jack said when the note was finished. "I think Ida will be happy to get away for the day also." He put the note in his pocket and waited. It would not be polite to just rush off. Just then, down in one of Mr. Bird's fenced fields in the valley below, a mare suddenly broke out into a thundering gallop, her colt gliding swiftly at her side like a shadow.

"Something must have scared her," Mr. Bird explained. " A rattlesnake or a badger." Jack and the older man watched as the horses slowed down to a trot at the far end of the field and began to graze again. The air now still, a mockingbird began its varied song from a juniper tree up on the slope behind them. Jack enjoyed the changing light on the cliffs, the horses' flight, the bird's song, all shared with the fine, placid old man. It was time now for him to leave, and thanking Mr. Bird again, he climbed into his car and headed down to the Fort Defiance road. He had passed this first test of his own will. The white man's enclave, the cluster of houses for the medical staff at Fort Defiance, waited for him.

On the following Sunday, with the note from Ida's father in his pocket, Jack drove back over the road he'd traveled with such apprehension and loneliness six weeks before. The rains of July had stopped and stillness hung over the dry plain on the way back to Albuquerque. He retraced his route, now eastward along U.S. 66, and he dropped off the high ground to cross the Rio Grande, a meandering trickle over a broad swath of sand. The streets of Albuquerque were oppressively quiet, the people having retreated indoors to escape the heat of the August sun. More quiet were the old, 1880s buildings of the Albuquerque Indian School. The two-story, dun-colored stucco buildings with high, pitched roofs and multiple red brick chimneys, showed no signs of life. The baseball fields were deserted, and the lawns beneath the cottonwoods empty.

Jack wondered if anyone would come to the door when he mounted the high front steps of the girls' dormitory and rang the bell. After a wait that seemed longer than the actual five minutes or so, a heavy-set Indian matron came to the door. She kept her graying hair in a tight bun and wore a faded blue dress with an apron, her feet in Keds sneakers. In the dimly-lit lobby behind her Jack could see the shine on the bare wooden floors and on the stairs to the upper story. The odor of furniture polish greeted his nostrils. The girls must be put to work regularly waxing and polishing, he thought.

"Good afternoon," he said as brightly as possible. "I'm Doctor Berkowitz from Fort Defiance. I have a note here from her father that I might take Ida Bird out for the afternoon."

The matron said nothing, but leaned to the side past Jack's shoulder to look at the turquoise blue convertible with the top down parked at the curb at the foot of the stairs.

"No, you may *not* take the young lady out. I don't care *who* you are or *what* note you brought."

"Look, ma'am, we're just going up to Santa Fe for the Fiesta. I'll bring her back before dark."

The matron looked past Jack again at the convertible parked outside.

"I'm in charge here today, young man, and I say 'No!'"

Jack felt the color rise in his neck.

"Isn't Ida here? Won't you please at least call her down so I can say 'Hello' to her?"

"The answer is still 'no' and you'll have to leave now."

Jack turned slowly and walked back down the steps. When he got behind the wheel, he waited a while before turning on the ignition.

Cunt wagon. That's what my brother Howard used to call a convertible, he thought. Let them think what they like. Let them think the worst of me.

His anger subsided as he drove out of the school grounds and south toward Central Avenue. Then he turned west, over the bridge, and back out onto the desert. The wind had picked up and swirling dust-devils marched across the plain. An early afternoon sun bore down on the asphalt of the two-lane highway and produced a shimmering mirage of silvery water ahead. It was the heat and the glare this time that caused him to stop and to put up the top. There was little relief even with this. No cloud or promise of cooling rain greeted him in Gallup or on the road north to Fort Defiance. It would be lonely, hot and quiet there, too.

CHAPTER SIX

When Jack arrived back in Fort Defiance, he saw Ida Bird in his dreams, lying at his side. In his dreams she did not resist when he pulled her toward him and she did not respond when he kissed her mouth. But in her not resisting there was the promise that he could become her lover.

When he awoke he was less able to push her out of his thoughts.

"You're not as peppy today, Doctor," Mrs. Armijo observed at the sanatorium the next morning. And then with a wink, "Has some Navajo witched you?"

With a mock-brooding voice and with a sweep of his outstretched arm Jack intoned, "'La Belle Dame Sans Merci' hath me enthralled."

"What does *that* mean?" Mrs. Armijo asked laughing.

"Like what you said," he answered and said no more.

In his mind Jack was determined to see Ida again.

"I'll be coming to Albuquerque next Sunday," he wrote and mailed the letter the same day. "I hope you'll be free in the afternoon and that I'll be able to take you out for a little while. I don't have any assurance that I'll be any more successful than I was last time, but I'll try. Hope to see you then." He signed it "Sincerely, Jack Berkowitz."

There was a slight murmur, a rustling of the leaves of the cottonwoods that arched over the main street of Fort Defiance. It was a Sunday, the second week of September. Even in Arizona and New Mexico the summer's heat had moderated. Jack drove slowly under that canopy of trees as he drove out of the town on his way to Albuquerque.

At the Girls' Dormitory of the Indian School there was a different matron this time. Yes, the young man *could* take Ida Bird out for the afternoon. She called upstairs and Ida appeared. Ida was scrubbed and clean, her hair shining and smelling faintly of shampoo. She wore a freshly ironed and stiffly starched plaid cotton blouse and a long gray skirt. The penny-loafers on her feet were polished.

He looks different now, she thought. Without his white coat he doesn't look like the show-off he was at the Employees' Club. But he's still trying to impress me with his fancy convertible. There was a hint of a smile on her face as she reached out to touch Jack's hand in greeting.

"It's good to see you again, Doctor. I hope you're not too tired from your trip over here."

"Oh no, I'm not tired," he said smiling, releasing his hand from hers and touching the top of his head. "It's my hair. I drove here with the top down. It's fun that way. C'mon. Get in. I'll show you. He opened the door for her and she slid in onto the blue-and-white vinyl seat.

She saw the spring in his step as he walked around the front of the car to get in on the driver's side. He's showing off now, she thought. Satisfied with himself. I hope he hurries up and gets us out of here. I know those girls upstairs are watching us.

"Where would you like to go? Are you hungry? We can go somewhere to eat."

"Yes, we're always hungry here at the boarding school. I don't know what I would do if my father didn't send a package now and then with little cans of sardines, Vienna sausage, crackers and dried fruit. The other girls come flocking to my room when they find out."

He looked at her intently now, seeing for the first time that the prominence of her cheekbones was more noticeable because of the hollow of her cheeks.

"O.K., let's eat. You suggest a place."

She picked a little café, a dreary, lonely, but clean place on Fourth Street not far from the Indian School. It was almost deserted on a Sunday afternoon.

"What will you have?" he asked as the menus were brought to the table. She looked at the card for a while and then said, "I'll have the rabbit."

Rabbit! Jack thought. That's even worse than ham! A rabbit is a rodent!

Ida saw the confounded and disapproving look on Jack's face but then the look softened. "Sure, that's fine. Rabbit is fine. We'll order that for you. I've never had rabbit, but if you want it that's fine. What's it like?"

What does he have against rabbit? she thought. Well, I'll just explain it to him. "It's very good," she said. "Like chicken. We only eat rabbit in the wintertime. It's easy to catch them then. You follow the rabbit tracks in the snow until you see where he went down into the hole. Then you take a long, pointed stick and push it down until you feel his body. Then you twist the stick until you have the rabbit by his fur. Then you pull him out and kill him. That's how we get them."

Jack was a little shocked at the cruelty of it. Yet he imagined her as a hungry child looking forward to a meal in the cold on a winter's day. Now she was hungry and looking forward to eating rabbit. He looked across the table at her. This was the first time he had a chance to talk to her about her life, and she gave him this gruesome little detail.

"I've been up to your home below Red Lake and it's beautiful," he said. "Milton Raines took me up there one time and I went up again to get the note from your father when I wanted to take you to Santa Fe. Is that where you herded sheep?"

These white people are always asking questions, she thought. What does this doctor want from me? I guess I'll just be polite.

"Yes I've herded sheep up there. I've been herding sheep since I was a little girl. I've herded sheep at the winter sheep camp above Red Lake and at the summer sheep camp up on the mountain. My mother used to pack bedding and supplies on a donkey and my brother Richard and I used to stay up there three weeks at a time. One time I herded three hundred sheep all by myself all the way from Cool Spring back to Red Lake. It was in the winter time and the snow was up to the sheep's bellies. But I never lost a single one."

Looking at the slender, neatly dressed girl with the polished penny-loafers, Jack found it hard to believe that this same girl had pushed her way twelve or more miles over a mountain in the cold, mud and snow.

"And what was your life like back in New York?" she asked. "Did you know anything about Indians when you lived there?"

"Well, I grew up on a street in Brooklyn," Jack began. "There were lots of trees on the street but there wasn't much in the way of land or space around the houses. But I did have a little garden in the back yard about six feet square where I grew radishes one year. Once my parents bought some baby chicks around Easter time that were dyed purple and pink and green. Only one of them grew half way up to be a chicken. Then we had a little puppy, a German shepherd mix who died after he licked rat poison somebody put in the closet where he used to sleep."

That must have been very sad for him, she thought. "It was always sad for us when we lost a pet, too." She remained silent for a while and then she went on, "You know it makes me sad to think that you were so cooped up when you were growing up. We were poor but at least we had the open valleys, the mountain, and the sky, and we always had plenty of animals around." She found it hard to imagine that he did not know her world, her people.

"But what did you know about Indians, or Navajos?"

"Well, I just knew about Indians in the movies, and that wasn't much. And then there was Tonto, the Lone Ranger's friend.

But I didn't learn about Navajos until I began to see their X-rays in the hospital. That's when I heard some real Navajo names. That's when I realized what a terrible time the Navajos were having with tuberculosis. I said to myself, 'This is what I can do. I can get out there, to the Reservation. I'll give it a try for two years. I'll have all the backing of the research team in New York. Maybe I'll be able to help.'"

"You know the Navajos didn't always have tuberculosis. It started when John Collier took away our sheep," Ida said.

"Yes, I read about John Collier's stock-reduction program in the book Dr. McDivitt had me read when I decided to come out to the Reservation. It was Clyde Kluckhohn's book, *The Navajo*. But are you sure it was the sheep-reduction that caused tuberculosis?"

"Of course I'm sure," Ida said, her voice becoming tense and her eyes wider. "John Collier forced the Navajos to set up grazing committees. The committee in our district said my mother's family had too many sheep, so they cut her family down from a thousand to two hundred sheep."

"That still sounds like a lot of sheep for one family."

"Not when you depend on selling lambs and wool for groceries," Ida said. "But we were lucky. We got by because my father went to work on the railroad. We had enough to eat. But those poor families way out on the Reservation began to starve and then they got weak. That's how they got tuberculosis." Ida's face grew sad and she continued, "They took two girls out of our class when they came down with TB. Julie Chee never came back. She died at home last year. Dessie Platero finally came back to school but she was so thin and her chest was all caved in from that operation they did on her ribs."

"I know it's sad." Jack said. "It's always sad when a young person dies. That's why we're using combinations of new drugs so we can cure the disease, so people won't have to have that kind of surgery."

"Then I'm glad you're here," Ida said. "But the Navajos are still angry about John Collier. You know he used to fly around in an airplane himself, to find out where people were hiding their sheep so he could report them."

"It does get you angry, doesn't it?" Jack said, catching her spirit, "to think he was so vindictive."

When Jack took Ida back to the dormitory, they stood on the sidewalk together only a short while, their hands touching in a long, drawn out handshake. He saw that she was looking over her shoulder to the upper story windows where other girls' faces were beginning to appear. Then she drew her hand away quickly and ran up the stairs.

CHAPTER SEVEN

In October, the time of teacher conferences in the schools, Ida came back to the Reservation for half a week with Ginger Jojola, a classmate from the Isleta Pueblo. The weather was still mild and Jack was eager to see more of Ida. Ginger, a girl of eighteen with a ready smile, would be good company, Jack thought. The outing Jack hoped for, to explore the back country around Fort Defiance on horseback, would be just that: an outing, not a date. He didn't want to launch into any serious dating when he and Ida were barely getting to know one another.

"We have some horses," Ida said, "but they're over at Ganado. But we might be able to borrow some from Benjamin Begay, one of my father's friends. He lives right near Fort Defiance."

Benjamin Begay was not at home. His daughter, Lena, a young woman in her late twenties, her face pitted with scars of acne, was busy at home, but she would help.

"Let me finish what I have to do here," she said, a little flushed. She was busy, surrounded by four or five little children, washing diapers in a galvanized iron tub on the kitchen table.

"You'll need three horses, right? Will five dollars for each horse for the day be all right? I'll send my brother, Ben Junior, out to get them." With that, Ben, a muscular young man of seventeen who had been in a back room, got up, lifted a coil of rope from a peg on the wall, and strode off down the hill to a field in the valley.

"I could only catch two of them," he said when he returned. The two rather sad old sorrels he had managed to lasso and lead back were now tied to a rail in the rocky yard, ready to be saddled.

"It's been a long time since I've been on a horse," Jack said. "That was about seven years ago when I was visiting my brother, Elihu. He'd been working in Illinois and he stayed with a family who had a farm and horses. One night they invited me on a ride in the country. We had plenty of moonlight that night. It was a mysterious feeling to be floating along on horseback, in and out of dark shadows beneath the trees. Fortunately the ground was level, the horses went real slow, and they knew the way."

"It sounds like you had a great ride," Ida said, "but this may be very different. These horses don't know us and the ground may be rough in places."

"Could I ride with one of you?" Jack asked, and he stepped sideways and stood closer to Ida. Ginger backed off a step away from the two. There was no further discussion. Without any change of expression, Ida said to Jack, "O.K., you can ride with me."

Ben saddled up the two horses. Jack watched, admiring the way, without any apparent effort, Ida swung herself up into the saddle. "Here, I'll help you," Ben said, offering Jack the help he needed to get up on the horse's back. With a sharp kick in the horse's sides, Ida set the sorrel in motion. Jack grasped the leather saddle thongs to steady himself, and they started off down the hill, Ginger following on the other horse.

The cluster of cabins on a rocky slope at the north end of Fort Defiance gave way, before long, to a valley of fenced fields, some green with oats, some yellow with corn stalks after the harvest. Black Creek ran through the valley, only a narrow stream in a wider, sandy bed whitened with alkali. The ruins of a dam and sluice gate about a mile north of Fort Defiance gave evidence of a Civilian Conservation Corps project of the 1930s. The stones used in the construction of the project were the same red fieldstones as those of the hospital, the boarding school, and the residences of the doctors and nurses. Though the irrigation system was no longer in use, the edges of the wash were still rich with cottonwood and Russian olive. The riders soon entered beneath the canopy of copper of the cottonwood and silver-gray of the olives.

"We'll go north here for a while, on this road that goes to Red Lake," Ida said, "but we won't go all the way. We'll cut over to the east across the valley. There's a place I want you to see."

To their left, a juniper-covered slope rose gradually to the top of the Defiance Plateau, about a thousand feet above the valley. A mid-autumn afternoon sun slanted across the open space to the east and illuminated the pink sandstone cliff that marked the valley's eastern border. Ida turned the horse's head to the right with a gentle tug of the reins. They crossed Black Creek wash and climbed to a level plain of saltbush and sage. Jack was pleased to see how skillfully Ida guided the horse between the tough, waist-high bushes of the plain.

When they had nearly crossed the valley, Ida said, "This is what I wanted to show you." Ida led the horses to the north and east, close to the base of the cliffs. Here they entered a private park whose eastern wall was made of arcades and amphitheaters sculpted into the vertical face of vermillion cliffs, now glowing, phosphorescent in the afternoon sun. The western margin of the park was a shelf of hard, flat, gray sandstone with a line of dwarf piñons running north and south overlooking the valley to the west. In the center of the park and rising straight up from a flat, grassy floor was monolith of sandstone, the same color as the rock of the eastern wall, and three hundred feet tall. Ida led the party around the base of the formation. Jack now saw the form of the rock. It was in the shape of a human figure, a woman! She faced north, wore a full-length, tiered skirt, and carried a burden on her back, a shawl enclosing a baby. A Navajo Madonna! Jack drew in his breath. This new world, this secret place, this sanctuary, Jack thought. She's giving something of herself to me.

Ida's back and shoulders were now a few inches away. In Jack's nostrils was the still fresh smell of Ida's hair mingled with the faintest beginning of perspiration from exertions of the ride. Jack released his grip from the saddle thongs and reached forward slowly, sliding his hands lightly along the sides of the girl's body. Then he clasped his hands in front of her. Jack waited for a response to this move and it wasn't long in coming. Without a word, Ida separated Jack's lightly locked hands and pushed his wrists away, to the side and back. That was that. Jack saw Ginger looking in his direction and she wagged her finger at him. "Naughty!" was the silent word that formed on her lips. Jack shrugged his shoulders, turned his palms up, and tried to put a grin on his face.

The ride ended back on the rocky hills where it started. The light had faded quickly and a wind came up with a chill in it, a hint of the winter that was to come.

In early December Ida returned to the Reservation. The season of the nine-day Yei B'chei healing ceremonies had started after the first snow, and there was word of one such ceremony going on at the summit, in the forest on the divide on top of the Defiance Plateau. Jack remembered the drive on that road through the ponderosa forest during his first trip to the Reservation. It was in March the year before when he'd been driven over the divide on the way to Ganado. It was snowing then as it was now. He'd been amazed to see snow on the branches of the tall pine trees and on the open meadows. Was *this* Arizona? he'd thought. Wasn't Arizona supposed to be a hot, dry desert, an "arid zone?" Now he was driving over that same road with Ida at his side.

"Here's where we turn off," Ida said, pointing to an opening in the fence on the side of the road. An old car tire hung on a fencepost as a marker for where a narrow track ran off to the left. The wheels of Jack's car made a crunching sound as they turned onto the freshly fallen snow. The headlights caught snowflakes flying crazily across Jack's line of sight. The dizzying effect caused him some apprehension. Tracks of whatever car had gone ahead seemed to be disappearing rapidly as the snow fell. Suppose we get stuck or lost in a place like this? In the rearview mirror, however, he caught sight of the headlights of another car.

"There's a car following us. I suppose he's going to the same place we are."

"That's right. Keep going. We're almost there."

Soon they caught up with the taillights of a truck that was making a turn to the right.

"Follow that one."

They made a sharp turn onto a still narrower track that had fresh tire marks. The headlights of Jack's car cut across the cinnamon-colored bark of a great ponderosa pine, then across the dark trunks of younger trees. A few more turns and suddenly they saw the taillights and steaming exhausts of many cars and trucks.

"Pull over there and park next to that pickup that just drove in ahead of us."

All around, dark silhouettes were hitching up their shoulders under jackets and shawls against the cold. Ida and Jack did the same, following the crowd toward the lights. Orange firelight and bright white lights shone from bare electric bulbs that had been strung up between poles and that marked a quadrangle. They stood behind the first row of spectators, families camped around little fires to keep warm, some crouching, some sitting on folding chairs. Singing and prayers came from inside a hogan at the far end of the quadrangle. Jack stood at Ida's side in the semi-darkness, feeling some of the heat of the fires and smelling the perfume of the burning piñon. He gazed at her slender shoulders draped in a scarlet shawl fringed with purple. Her dark hair sparkled with droplets of melted snow and with freshly fallen snowflakes.

"You must have a boyfriend, somewhere, don't you?"

"No, I don't have any boyfriend," she said in a flat tone, looking straight ahead.

To Jack there was something both chilling and, at the same time, encouraging in her reply. He heard her say "boyfriend," singular. That had to mean himself. He wasn't a boyfriend. But there weren't any others either.

From a world away the fragment of a bittersweet, gently ironic lyric of a Jerome Kern, Broadway tune swam into his head, as did the melody of Bing Crosby's crooning, and the melody, for a moment, drowned out the chanting from the hogan:

"A fine romance with no kisses!
A fine romance, my friend, this is!
Why you're as hard to land as the Ile de France:
I haven't got a chance,
This is a fine romance!"

It's O.K., he thought. This romance doesn't have to be. Her life, her people are different from mine. I'm content. I'm content just to stand here tonight next to her.

Shortly before midnight, two lines of eight dancers each entered the quadrangle, and any voices or murmuring from the crowd of spectators hushed. The dancers were hooded with pale blue masks, twin eagle feathers on the backs of their heads, collars of evergreen around their necks and each held a sprig of green in his left hand, and a gourd rattle in his right. They were bare from the waist up and from the knees down, and their skin was painted a ghostly white. They wore short skirts, some with fox tails hanging behind, and they carried silver-studded leather pouches on their left hips. Bells jingled from tassels on their moccasins and the rattles kept a steady beat. Then the dancers raised their eerie, piercing, falsetto chant, "Hoo hoo/hoo *hoo*! Hoo hoo/hoo *hoo*!" as they shuffled toward the hogan and back. Back and forth, back and forth they danced, their voices rising, with the smoke of the fires, into the night sky.

"It's scary, terrifying, beautiful," Jack whispered to Ida, who remained silent at his side.

CHAPTER EIGHT

Ida was home again for the spring break at the end of March.

"Dr. Dawson invited us for a jeep ride in the bottom of the Canyon de Chelly," Jack announced.

"I'd love to go. But who is Dr. Dawson and what's he like?" Ida asked.

"He's the Area Medical Director from Window Rock."

"From his position he sounds like he's a 'high and mighty' type."

"Not at all, Ida. He's really a neat guy. He's got a lot of interests besides medicine. Photography for one. He knows Milton Raines and they like each other."

"If Mr. Raines likes him then I know I'll like him, too."

"And you know he's also a sort of amateur archeologist. He's been in the canyon many times and he wants to show us some things there. There'll be another jeep-load in the party: Dr. Schwartzman and his family. Fred's the pediatrician at Fort Defiance. He's done a lot to stamp out diarrhea that kills a lot of babies on the Reservation."

"Oh, I've heard something about him. He's a kind of loud-mouth who goes around bossing people, telling them what to do and how to live. I know he's trying to do good, but Navajos just don't like the way he does it. I'll just stay with you and Dr. Dawson."

On the morning of the trip, Jim Dawson picked up Jack in Fort Defiance and Ida, who'd caught a ride down from Red Lake.

"I'm glad to meet you, Ida," Dawson said, his merry blue eyes twinkling, as he handed her up into the rear seat of the jeep. Jack climbed in beside her.

"Yes, I think I'll like him," Ida whispered. "He's so short and skinny. And he looks like he's having fun. He's just like a *kid!*"

The road to the Canyon de Chelly from Fort Defiance took the little party past Old Sawmill, through the ponderosa forest at the summit of the Defiance Plateau, then down through sage and scrub to the lower elevation at Chinle. There they entered the mouth of the canyon. At that point the walls of the canyon were low, a dull yellow, and the bottom, a broad expanse of pale sand.

"Let's race them," Dr. Dawson shouted as he waved a challenge to Dr. Schwartzman who was driving in a larger jeep with his family. Jack and Ida held on to the rear-seat rails as they bounced over uneven places in the sandy bottom. They shouted in excitement as they watched the other vehicle carve its tracks and kick up its cloud of dust. Dawson knew how to avoid the soft spots, veered wide to the south, creating a great sweeping curve in the sand. When he gained hard-packed ground, he roared ahead of the other car and he, Jack, and Ida raised their voices in triumph.

When the jeep party entered deeper into the canyon, the rising red rock wall towered over them. The drivers slowed down and the shouting stopped.

"It almost seems as if we're being swallowed up in this place," Jack said.

"It's not that mysterious," Ida said. "My father was raised down here in the canyon, not more than five or six miles from here. I'll take you there one time. But right now it looks like Dr. Dawson is turning up into the Canyon del Muerto."

The Canyon del Muerto entered the Canyon de Chelly as a major branch from the north, its walls, like the main canyon, a thousand feet tall. Dawson turned left and Schwartzman's car followed. Up into that canyon just a few miles, Dawson pointed out a well-preserved Anasazi tower on the left. It was at ground level and it was protected by an overhang of the canyon wall.

"That's Antelope House," he said as he pulled up closer. The party dismounted to take a better look. On the sheer wall above the tower crude stick-figures of rabbits and birds and some circles were painted.

"Those were the original petroglyphs," Dawson explained. "But that beautiful painting of an antelope, the one with the white stripes across its neck, that was done only a hundred years or so ago by some Navajo artist. That's where Antelope House gets its name."

The square stone tower, three stories high, dominated the ruin. Jack got up close, peered into a ground-floor opening and looked up at the inside of the tower which had no roof.

"Look at the plaster on the inside walls!" he exclaimed. "The plaster is still intact! And the wooden lintel of the windows are still firm and they hold up the weight of the stones above them." Ida held back a little.

"Navajos aren't supposed to get too close to what was left by 'The Old People.'"

"But don't some Navajos work alongside the archeologists excavating these ruins?"

"Some of them do but they do it at their own risk."

"Do you really think anything will happen to them if they do dig here?"

"Most Navajos don't take any unnecessary chances," Ida said. "The dead are 'ch'indi,' forbidden to us," she explained. "That's our belief. We just keep away."

"Look over here!" cried Dr. Schwartzman's nine year old son who was doing some exploring on his own. He was standing on the rim of an open, circular, stone-lined pit about fifteen feet in diameter and pointing at a stone bench inside."

"That's a *kiva*," explained Dawson. "That's where the Anasazis held their religious ceremonies, just the way the Hopis and the Pueblo Indians do today. There used to be a roof over this kiva and people used to go down into it by a ladder through a square opening in the roof."

"But what's this over here?" shouted the boy. He was pointing at a dried wooden board resting on the opposite edge of the kiva. It was about a foot long and partly covered by some very brittle brown cloth.

Everyone rushed over to take a closer look. The object, it seemed, had been dug up by the excavation crew and just left there on the rim of the kiva. The covering cloth had been partly pulled aside.

"It's a baby!" Jack cried. The skull, the lower jaw and some of the limb bones, delicate, dry, perfectly formed, lay on the burial board. Ida tugged at Jack's sleeve and pulled him away.

"Let's get out of here," she whispered through her teeth, her jaw tight. "I'm sorry I saw that baby. It's real 'ch'indi.' I shouldn't have been here at all."

The two then walked away from the ruin and the rest of the party out into the middle of the canyon. There the two figures appeared to shrink, walking out toward the junction with the Canyon de Chelly, enveloped by the vast space between towering walls.

"They can pick us up later," Jack said.

Chapter Nine

O n a Saturday evening in the spring, on the grounds of the Fort Defiance Boarding School, there was a breath of cool moisture in the air. The cottonwoods that grew thickly on the campus had just put out their new leaves and they had shaded the grass of the lawn during the day. Most of the children had gone home for the weekend; the campus was largely deserted. But up the flight of stairs to the gymnasium building, bright lights poured out of the open, double doors.

"I hope you'll have a good time," Jack said as he led Ida up the steps. "Have you done any square dancing?"

"Oh yes. We're taught all sorts of dances at school, including square dancing."

When Jack led the girl into the long, high-ceilinged gymnasium, he felt all eyes turning in his direction. They were the youngest couple, and Ida, in her fresh white blouse and billowing, ankle-length skirt, the prettiest woman by far.

Mark Torkelson, the Navajo Area Assistant Director, was dressed as Jack had never seen him. Torkelson, originally from Minnesota, on this night wore a Western shirt, Western trousers of tan gabardine with slant side pockets, cowboy boots, a broad-brimmed cowboy hat, and a red bandana. He placed a scratchy record on the phonograph turntable and turned up the volume.

The gymnasium's hardwood floor helped to amplify the compelling beat and the merry sound of fiddle-playing. Mark lifted the microphone to his lips and in a mock-Western accent began his call:

"Now choose yer pretty lady,
Bow to her an' smile,
Hold her little hand,
We're gonna dance a little while."

The lilt, the merriment, the fun of the old country dance music filled Jack's chest with joy. He'd been totally unprepared for his friend Mark's new talent. He took Ida's hand as they and three other couples squared the set. He felt Ida bounce on her toes to the beat of the music waiting for the caller's next command.

"Now bow to yer partner,
And wave one and all,
To that purty gal yonder,
Way acrosst the hall."

With the first set Jack felt how perfectly light Ida was on her feet. He watched her face with its serious, attentive look as she listened to the caller's commands. She was perfect in executing the "dos-y-dos" and the "a-la-main-lefts."

"That's wonderful," he shouted, his right arm around her waist, his left arm raised holding her hand in the "swing-yer-partners" and in the "promenades." Ida said nothing, concentrating on the caller's next command.

Jack and Ida became aware of some jostling on the part of the other couples to join them in the next square set. They were the center of attention.

Between dances, when steaming hot cider and pumpkin pies were brought out on long tables at the side of the hall, the white ladies and the bolder of the men came up to Ida to engage her in conversation.

"Oh, I know your father."

"How is your family?"

"When will you graduate from school?"

When the dancing resumed, Jack delighted again in circling Ida's waist in the swinging and in the promenades, but especially between the square sets when the couple dances were held. The two of them moved as one to the waltzes and to the courtly Varsouvienne and all eyes were upon them.

"What are you doing with that teenager?" Anna Armijo asked Jack at coffee after morning rounds a few days later. She did her best to keep a straight face as she teased, but soon her broad, bronzed face broke out into a grin.

"Please pass the jam," Jack said after he'd buttered the fresh fried bread that had been set before him. "You know she's just a beautiful girl,"was his response. Though he tried to keep a straight face when he said this, a bit of a grin betrayed him.

"You'd better behave yourself, though. You know she's a T'senjikinnie. That's my husband's clan. And I'm related to her through her father."

Jack got up to answer a knock on the door of his Fort Defiance apartment.

"Is my sister here?" asked a tall young man. He wore the starched, short-sleeved, light khaki summer uniform of a Marine private first class. He had high Indian cheekbones but light skin and light hazel, almost yellow eyes. Judging by his muscular shoulders and by what Jack guessed to be a height of six foot-three, Jack figured the man must weigh two hundred twenty pounds.

"No, she's not." Then, after a pause, "You must be Richard. Ida said you'd be here on furlough soon." Jack began to talk a little faster. "Can I get you something to drink, some soda or water? Come in and sit down for a while. It must be getting hot outside."

Jack's thoughts raced through his head. Why does he think Ida is here? Word's gotten around that I've been seen with her. Does he think I've been sleeping with her? What would happen if he started getting ugly, started to push me around, started running through the house looking for her. What a scene that would be! A brute like that could crush me in a minute.

"No, that's all right," Richard said. "I'll just go on up to Red Lake. She's probably up there."

Jack paced about in the living room after the door had closed. He tried to pick up a book he'd been reading or to listen to his classical music records. He realized why he'd not insisted on Richard's coming inside. He was afraid of the man. But he and Ida had *not* been sleeping together. Guilt, guilt, guilt! Even the thought of sleeping with her, the dreams he'd had of her, made him feel guilty. And that led him to fear he'd be punished for it. What an encounter! Then he went into the kitchen to make himself a glass of iced tea.

"Now it's time for me to take *you* to a dance," Ida said to Jack when she was home on another weekend from school.

"I'm willing. Where at?"

"At the Catholic Indian Center in Gallup. And I hope you'll like it."

"I like any kind of dancing. My father is a great dancer. He taught me that if you can do the two-step, you can dance to any music."

"This will be a Western Dance. Have you ever done Western dancing?"

"I'm not sure, but if I haven't, I know I'll be able to fake it."

"O.K., let's see if you can."

The dance was held in the recreation room of the Center. The young faces in the crowd were all Indian except for Jack and a group of Anglo ranch kids who stood quietly in the corner while everyone else danced.

"You're doing all right with your two-step," Ida said.

When, in circling around the dance floor, Jack heard, above the loud beat of the music, a curious, angry hiss, he didn't realize it was directed at himself. At the next turn around the floor he heard it more distinctly: "*Squaw*-man!" He was singled out again: not "*Jew*-boy" or "*Mockie*" or "*Kike*" as in his childhood and youth in New York, but "*Squaw*-man." Until this time Jack had felt entirely welcome in the West. He was a doctor. He was needed. He was doing a good job. Now it was "*Squaw*-man!"

"Just keep on dancing," Ida commanded, having heard the epithet herself. Her face changed. When they circled past the group of jeering kids again, she looked at them straight in the face with a look of fierce defiance. Jack was proud of her toughness. She has more guts than I have, he thought. She challenged those little rednecks and she stared them down.

CHAPTER TEN

❧

With school out in May, Ida was home from Albuquerque for good. Jack made the now-familiar trip up to Ida's home on the slope above the Red Lake valley.

"I want you to meet my mother," Ida said, leading him to a round-faced woman in her sixties dressed in the traditional three-tiered, ankle-length skirt and velveteen blouse. Her mother spoke no English but must have understood some. She smiled when Jack said, "Yat'eh, I'm pleased to meet you."

"Yat'eh, shi yahzh," she replied.

"That means 'my son,' doesn't it? I've heard older women say that to me at the sanatorium," Jack said, turning to Ida.

"That's right. You don't have to worry, though. She's not thinking of you as a son-in-law," and Ida laughed.

Mrs. Bird walked back to the cooking shack and smoke soon rose from the stovepipe as she fired up the large, cast iron Army woodstove. Soon the aroma of sizzling chicken, onions, and potatoes drifted through the open door. Jack heard a regular slapping sound from within the kitchen.

"What's that sound?"

"My mother has started to shape the dough for tortillas. I'd better get in there and help her," and with that Ida disappeared into the cooking shed.

"'Na'acho'chai,' 'neh'massi,' 'na n'es'kah'dah.' Chicken, po-
tatoes, tortillas. Say that, Jack," Ida said when she came out. "My
mother wants you to come in for lunch." The table was set with
a bowl of pieces of fried chicken, another bowl of fried potatoes,
a platter stacked high with chewy, flat tortillas and a jar of straw-
berry jam.

"We'll wash this down with tea. Navajo tea," Ida said.

"What's Navajo tea like?"

"It's something like regular tea, except it's boiled instead of
brewed. We pick the plant that grows in some places around
here at this time of year. The plant has little yellow flowers but
you have to be able to tell the tea plant from many others that
also have yellow flowers. We never pull the plant out by the roots.
We cut the stem above the ground. That way the plant will grow
and we'll have more tea the next year. We fold the whole plant,
flowers, stem, and leaves into a little bundle and dry it. Then we
boil it."

The clear, orange tea had a distinctive, slightly grassy aroma
to Jack, but a clean, refreshing taste. Washed down after a help-
ing of strawberry jam on a tortilla, it was the perfect ending to a
meal.

"I want to thank your mother," Jack said. "How do you say
'It was delicious'?"

"D'li kahn lah," Ida said and Jack repeated this to Ida's
mother, "D'li kahn lah. Ah-*shay-* hay!"

"Oh, shi yahzh," was Mrs. Bird's response with a smile.

Jack stepped out of the kitchen and looked down at the
fenced fields in the valley. Ida's father and brother, Thomas, were
plowing with a team of horses. Even at the distance of half a
mile the freshly-turned earth gave out its warm, spring smell.
The cottonwoods in Black Creek wash had just put out their
delicate, yellow-green crowns. A line of Russian olives, which
Ida's father had planted for flood-control in the valley years
before, added silver to the scene. Now they pumped their heavy
spring perfume into the air.

This is Ida's home, Jack thought. This is what she'd been taken away from when she was sent to boarding schools. No wonder she'd been so lonesome in those places when she was growing up. Now she's likely to have to leave again, to get a job, to go to school or college, or to marry. She might marry someone out of her own tribe or even a non-Indian.

Ida found him in this pensive mood when she came out of the kitchen where she'd been helping her mother wash the dishes.

"I've never seen you looking so sad. Cheer up. It's nearly summer time. There are so many Indian 'doings' going on. The rodeos are great fun. I could take you to the ones at Steamboat and at Lukachukai. They're not far away."

"I'm sure you're right, Ida," he said, coming out of his reveries. What about the Flagstaff Rodeo and Pow-Wow that's coming up the Fourth of July weekend? Jim Dawson said the rodeo was a national event. I've never been to Flag. I hear it's beautiful there, too. Do you think we could ask your parents to let you come with me?"

"I'd love to go. I've never been there either. But I've invited my friend, Bernice Litsui, from Ramah, to spend that weekend with me here at Red Lake. I bet she'd want to come with us. I'll ask my parents. I'm sure with her along my parents will say it's all right."

Jack liked the idea. He was, in fact, a little relieved. Another person, a chaperone. That would be the right way to do it.

When the weekend approached, Mrs. Bird packed the girls' bedding, a food package of tortillas and sheep ribs and plenty of water. Jack was not free to leave until he was finished at the sanatorium after five the next day, on Friday.

"We're off!" he said at last, and the mood was gay with two girls in the convertible driving out of Fort Defiance. There was still plenty of daylight left but they would be driving into the night to get to Flagstaff. "Let me know when you girls get tired. We can pull off to the side of the road anywhere and camp." They took the paved road to Window Rock, over the divide to Ganado when, in the gathering darkness, Ida directed Jack to turn south on the unpaved road to Klagetoh. There were no road signs.

"I hope we're not going to get lost down this way," Jack said.

"No we won't," Ida said reassuringly. "Just keep going straight and don't turn off on any side road."

They drove nearly two hours without seeing another car or house or hogan. The girls were tired but they didn't want to stop in what seemed such a strange and lonely place. At last they saw lights up ahead. It was Holbrook and Route 66. With spirits lightened, they turned west on the highway and drove another two hours. Finally, exhausted, they pulled off the highway and drove what seemed a safe distance from the road. They rolled out their bedding and sleeping bags and were happy to sleep on the hard and open ground.

"Look over there," Bernice whispered to Ida in the morning. The two girls had laid out their blankets close to one another and about twenty feet away from Jack. "Look," she said. "His eyes are so *blue!*" Jack had just opened up his eyes. He'd not had a chance to put on his glasses and he was looking straight ahead at where the girls were. Ida laughed.

"Do you see now what I have to put up with?"

The spot they'd picked to camp was only about twenty miles from Flagstaff. The morning was bright and cheerful and from the open car Jack and the girls could smell the faint odor of pine as they drove into town. The main street was thronged with gay crowds and colorful banners were hung everywhere. The rodeo grounds were cool, shaded with tall ponderosas. The parking areas were filling up rapidly. Navajos and Indians from other tribes piled out of their cars and trucks, heading for the concession stands. It was not easy to resist the aroma of hot coffee and fresh fried bread.

A slender, dark woman in her late twenties caught up with Jack. Ida and Bernice were a pace or two ahead.

"Long time no see!" said the woman. It was Agnes McKinley and she reached out to touch Jack's sleeve. Ida spun around in time to see who it was.

"Yeah, 'Lone time no see!'" Ida mimicked. She directed a steady glare at Agnes and Agnes disappeared into the crowd.

Jack found it hard to suppress a grin.

The morning events, the calf-roping, bull-riding, and bronco-riding hadn't begun but the loudspeaker boomed the announcer's call to the competitors, the Navajo, Hopi, Apache and Paiute cowboys, to get ready.

After a pause, the announcer's tone changed to a lower pitch.

"Is there a Doctor Barkwit, or Dr. Bennet from Fort Defiance here? Please come to the announcer's booth. Dr. Bennet, please."

Ida, Jack, and Bernice were just making their way to the stands when they heard the request. Jack could hardly make out the words over the general noise of the crowd. Surely the rodeo announcer couldn't be calling him. Why would they want a doctor from Fort Defiance? But Ida had sharper ears, sharper instincts. She'd heard "Fort Defiance" and she knew there must be some connection with themselves. She knew that Navajos would have some difficulty pronouncing "Berkowitz." She'd had enough trouble learning and practicing the name herself when she was preparing to meet Jack the year before. A cloud of fear passed over her face. She rushed to the announcer's booth. She nearly staggered on her way back, her face dead white, her eyes streaming.

"Richard! It was about Richard!"

"What about Richard? What's happened?"

"Richard! He died!"

"How? How did it happen? When did it happen?"

"Yesterday. Yesterday." That was all she could say, choked and sobbing.

Jack and Ida learned the details later. Richard and two other Navajos at Camp Pendleton, on a weekend pass, thought to come out to the Pow-Wow, since Flagstaff, in western Arizona, was not far from California. The three were killed instantly in a head-on collision near Barstow. The California Highway Patrol notified the Navajo Tribal Police in Window Rock, and word was brought up to Mr. and Mrs. Bird at Red Lake. Knowing where Ida was, with Dr. Berkowitz at the Flagstaff Pow-Wow, Mr. Bird made the request for Jack to be paged there.

Stunned and silent, with eyes nearly swollen shut, Ida faced the journey home. They took the fastest way back, on the paved highway, U.S. 66, through Holbrook to Gallup.

"Richard, Richard," she sobbed over and over. "We used to herd sheep together, ride donkeys together." After a long silence she laughed, a curious, painful laugh. Jack feared that Ida was losing her mind.

"We used to play tricks on each other, roll down the hill together inside of truck tires!" The laugh changed instantly to sobbing and more sobbing.

At a stop for gas that evening they entered a nearby café.

"You've got to take something to eat, some coffee," Jack said. She said nothing, ate nothing, drank nothing. Under the fluorescent lights of the café Jack saw that her eyes had swollen completely shut. He had to lead her back to the car.

Richard's image came to Jack, too.

Wiped out! Just like that, Jack thought. That handsome giant of a young man. The man I'd been afraid of. The one that Ida loved, the one whose death was killing her. Jack's throat tightened up and he, too, mourned for Richard, and for Ida. Gone! Just like that! he repeated to himself. From Gallup they drove on up to Red Lake where Ida flew into her father's arms.

CHAPTER ELEVEN

⬥

In the days following Richard's death and his burial in the veterans' cemetery, Jack saw nothing of Ida. He thought of her when he passed the burial ground on the hill south and east of Fort Defiance on the road to Window Rock. Little plastic flowers had been placed over the grassless, rocky mounds, and little American flags fluttered in the wind. He had failed once before to face a grieving family.

He seemed not to have learned his lesson. Mordecai Israelson, his friend in the choir at the Hillel Foundation at City College had fallen out of a rowboat and drowned at the age of nineteen. Jack had lacked the courage to face death, to go to Mordecai's funeral, to comfort his family by being there. This time he gave himself excuses: I don't feel comfortable attending Mass at a Catholic church; I don't know the family well enough.

Know the family well enough indeed, a voice told him. Know the family well enough to ask their permission when it came to taking their daughter out for fun; well enough to dream about taking her to bed, the voice went on. But he stayed away.

Ida appeared at the apartment in Fort Defiance two weeks after the funeral. She was dressed as usual in a fresh white cotton blouse, ankle-length denim skirt, and clean penny-loafers. She stood next to him as he folded his arms around her. She

63

rested her head on his shoulder. He smelled the fresh odor of her hair as he kissed her head. She did not resist, just like in his dream. When he touched her shoulder he felt the skin of her arm through her blouse.

Jack led her inside and closed the door behind him. They sat together on the living room couch.

"I've missed you. Why didn't you come?"

"I'm a coward. I just couldn't face the grief."

"You should have come. I needed you. They had to pull me away from the coffin. Richard's face was so perfect. I couldn't believe he was dead. I couldn't understand how he could have been killed and yet not have a scratch on his face or on his skin. When I reached out to touch him they pulled me away. All I could do was touch the sleeve of his uniform. It wasn't enough. It wasn't enough!" and the tears fell hot and wet upon her face and on her blouse.

Jack held himself stiffly as he sat next to her. He wanted to hold her, to comfort her, but he felt unworthy. He had stayed away. He wasn't there when she needed him. But as he stared straight ahead she reached up and kissed him, her tears against his face. He wept now for her, for Richard whom he hardly knew, for himself that he'd been so weak.

"I was a coward," he repeated.

"It's all right. I just need you to be with me now," she said. He folded his arms around her shoulders, gently because he wasn't worthy of her. But she pulled herself against him and pressed her face against his. He slid his arms now to her waist and held her more tightly, his chest against hers, his thighs against hers. He felt her response with every increase in the tightening of his arms. He couldn't believe that she showed no anger, no resentment. His vision blurred. He felt himself being swept into a whirlpool. She wanted him. She accepted him. Neither feared the future.

Later that day they drove to the high pass on the way to rodeo at Lukachukai. Jack pulled the car over, took Ida's hand and they climbed the hill. They threaded their way between the

Gambel oak and found a place where they could not be seen from the road below. Here they lay down and together watched the sway of the upper branches of the ponderosas as a rising wind made a steady whoosh through the trees. The rodeo beneath the red cliffs at Lukachukai could wait. Here, their shoulders touched, and their hands. They would kiss once in a while. They had made their world.

Chapter Twelve

❧

"We heard about that Marine who died, Joe Bird's son," Anna Armijo said to Jack before rounds at the sanatorium the next morning. "He was Ida's brother, wasn't he? Have you seen her? How is she doing?"

Ida's image swept before his face. How her eyes were swollen shut on the drive back from Flagstaff; how, two weeks later, looking up at the swaying of the ponderosa boughs, she wore that sad, calm, but distant look. Her life had changed and so had his.

"Well, you know, she's not very well. She's not that teenager you once said she was. She's a different person now. She seems calm enough on the outside but she's been injured in spirit." He touched Mrs. Armijo's hand. "Thanks for asking." Fine woman, he thought. She has all the right instincts. Knows when to be funny, when to be understanding. At the right moment she always knows the right thing to say.

Jack and Ida were together now every weekend. He watched her closely, hoping he would see signs of healing. And there were signs. She was busy reaching outward from herself, busy arranging for ways for Jack to see more of Navajo life.

On a bright summer Sunday morning Ida found a squaw dance that was being held in the foothills east of Fort Defiance. They arrived at the site of the ceremony at a quiet time. Families were camped about small fires around a large, open area where the larger bonfires, the outdoor singing, and the dancing had taken place the night before. Ida set out a blanket on the ground some distance from where the Navajo families were settled. "Wait here," she said, and she walked to the far end of the field where smoke from cooking fires curled up from a long, low brush structure. Jack admired the confidence with which she walked. Some of the Navajos in the nearby family groups had turned and were looking in Jack's direction. Though they didn't stare, they knew that Ida had brought a white man to their gathering. How strong she is, Jack thought. She is not in the least uncomfortable to be seen with me. Ida returned from the outdoor kitchen a few minutes later with steaming bowls of thin mutton stew and fresh-smelling, newly-made fried bread. Chunks of mutton and diced potato swam in a clear broth that had little or no visible fat, and the flavor and aroma were delicate. The round, golden, deep-fried bread was the perfect companion for the stew.

"Do you know the people back there in the kitchen?" Jack asked. He was grateful for the meal. He was hungry in the brisk early morning mountain air. "I recognized some of the ladies in the kitchen, but I don't know them very well," she replied. "But they are busy cooking and serving all the time, and anybody who comes is fed. If you are a family member, though, you are expected to help cook or bring food with you. I'll take you to a squaw dance where my clan, the T'senjikinnies, are sponsors and you'll see."

The squaw dance the T'senjikinnies sponsored was held a few weeks later in open, sagebrush country between Cross Canyon, west of the forest-covered Defiance Plateau, and Ganado. Ida had been in the cooking shed since early morning joining the women in the continuous bustle in the kitchen. Some women kneeled or sat on the ground in front of open fires making fried bread. First they mixed white flour, baking powder, salt and water, kneaded them into dough in large wooden bowls, and then pulled off pieces of dough and rolled them into balls. These were patted and stretched into discs and laid carefully into hot lard in cast-iron skillets. The women watched the dough rise, savored the fresh odor as the bread smoked and turned brown, and then, with long-handled forks, turned the bread over to brown on the other side. When they were done, the discs of fried bread were stacked onto piles, ready to be served. Other women worked chopping mutton for the stew, stirring the great stew pots over wood-fired stoves, boiling water for coffee, clearing the tables where everyone was invited to sit down and eat and serving the guests. When one round of guests were finished, the tables were cleared, dishes were washed and new arrivals seated and fed. Jack now received the call from Ida.

"Come on in. It's time for you to eat."

"When you're through," Ida said, "I want you to see something that will be going on pretty soon. It always thrilled me as a little girl. I want you to see the riders and the horses." She led Jack to where a crowd was gathering near the prayer hogan where singing had been going on most of the morning. The eager crowd was soon rewarded by the approach of the riders, seventeen in all, thundering over the hill from the east, raising clouds of dust and calling out with high-pitched yells. Then the riders, on their best horses, came up to the prayer hogan, made a tight circle around the little structure, and shots rang out. The spectators saw the riders point their rifles to the sky, but on this day they were stunned and terrified when they saw a little boy of five or six rush forward and fall on his face in the sand. Was the child struck by a stray bullet? The child lay still and the father rushed forward to kneel by the stricken boy, while the crowd suddenly became hushed, with some people uttering low moans of pain and sympathy. Jack rushed forward to see what he could do. Then the boy jumped to his feet.

"I was just playing cowboys and Indians," he chirped. "I was a cowboy and I got shot by the Indians!" Peals of laughter and sighs of relief rose from the crowd. The boy's father pulled the child back to where the crowd was standing to make room for the return of the horsemen. Three more times they came, and three more times they circled the hogan and fired into the air. Then they sped off to the cheers of the spectators. An old T'senjikinnie man said to Jack, "It was good to see so many horsemen. It was just like the old days."

"Thank you for letting me see all this," Jack said to Ida when the ceremony was over. "There was a little more excitement today than I bargained for, but it was great in every way." Ida smiled, a sign to Jack that healing had begun, and she pulled herself close to him on the way home.

CHAPTER THIRTEEN

❧

For the rest of the summer Jack and Ida sought every possible moment together. They had cookouts on the rocky slopes overlooking the valley. Ida showed him how to let the fire burn down to coals, how to set up a simple grill on four piles of flat stones. The steaks on the heated grill would sizzle and smoke, casting their aroma into the air. And when the fat dropped into the fire the flames and sputtering threw orange light into their faces. They clung to each other in the clear night air, gazing at the great star, Vega, as it rose in the east.

"That's Vega in the constellation of Lyra the lyre," Jack said. "It's the fifth brightest star. I'm sure the Navajos must know it. Do they have a name for it?"

"Yes, the medicine men have names for all the stars, but the names are kept secret. They are used only in holy prayers and ceremonies."

With the summer passing into autumn, Cygnus the swan followed, making its appearance earlier and earlier, rising on its side. Then, as night progressed, with its neck strained forward in flight, it pointed its head to the west and flew down the stream of the Milky Way.

When the days grew shorter and the lights of Fort Defiance came on earlier, the two would carry their Pendleton blankets, climb the hill overlooking the town, and lie together on the ground. They would not come down until the wind grew stronger and until they heard the sharp cries of the coyotes rising in the distance.

Ida no longer spoke of applying to college or going on to school, nor did Jack bring up the subject. Their love-making was their world, its setting the grand sweep of land and sky.

It was early November now, but warm days still lingered, lengthening the softness of autumn. On one such day Jack sat by himself on the stone steps of the sanatorium. Light from the west cast long shadows across the tree-lined main street of Fort Defiance. The street was alive with Navajos in family groups, visiting in the hospitals or coming to trade at the trading posts. They drove by in pickup trucks or in open, horse-drawn, green-painted Studebaker farm wagons. The brown-faced women sat quietly in the open backs of the pickups or alongside their men on the high seats of the wagons. The blouses they wore were adorned with silver buttons and pins and they wore their proud necklaces of turquoise and coral. The men, silent and serious, wore bluejeans, Western shirts, and cowboy hats.

This might be some foreign country, Jack thought. I've been here now over a year and I still can't get over how enchanting all this is. But I'll be leaving here in a few months to go back to New York. That was the plan I had when I came here, my original plan. But if I leave, could I leave without Ida? She is part of me now, but she is of *this* world. She has such pride in herself, such pride in her people, these people streaming by before me on this soft afternoon. Could I take her from here? Do I have the guts, the strength to take this girl who is of this other world, who is not Jewish, when I have been told all my life I must not do this? Today, with everything so beautiful, anything seems possible. But do I dare?

The weather changed quickly, and soon the wind blew, bearing on its cold breath the first taste of snow. There were light crusts of ice on the ground, the first light snow having melted and then frozen again. Jack heard the crunch of footsteps at his apartment door three nights later. Ida was standing there.

"Come in. What's wrong?" he asked when he saw her face clouded and worn. She'd dressed against the cold in the quilted jacket Richard had sent her from Korea, its silken outer shell embroidered with dragons. Instead of a skirt and penny-loafers she wore Levi's and heavy shoes.

"It's warm in here," Jack said and he pointed to the fire he'd just started in the stone fireplace. Some of the wavering firelight fell upon the ceiling and its heavy wood beams.

"I've missed you. Why haven't you come up to Red Lake?" she asked, her voice heavy with loneliness, with pleading. "You haven't talked about it for a long time, but I know you're thinking about it. Thinking about going back to New York. The summer's over and you're thinking about going back to New York."

She's been thinking about the same thing, he thought. What will happen to us? Could I take her with me?

"Yes, I've been thinking about New York," he said "But things have changed now." He looked steadily at her, knowing that she knew his meaning. "You're my wife." The words came quickly and easily. "I want you to come with me. We'll get married. You'll come back to New York with me and then we'll come back. I've only got one more year to go in New York. Then we'll come back."

He held her to his chest. She looked up into his face.

The world at large will accept a woman as beautiful as this, he thought. They will accept me and Ida as lovers. 'All the world loves a lover,' isn't that right? But then there are my folks. There's bound to be a fight, there will be their rejection of her. I'll just have to face that later.

"It will be all right," he said, saying nothing to her about his certain knowledge there would be a fight ahead.

Two nights later Jack sat on the edge of a bed in the hogan of Ida's parents. The room was dimly lit with a kerosene lantern whose glass chimney was dark with soot. Jack spoke this re-hearsed speech to her father:

"In a few months I must return to New York, but I cannot leave without your daughter. I'm here to ask your permission to marry her and to take her with me. I know how attached Ida is to you and to the Navajo people. I know how much she loves this valley. I won't keep her away for very long because after a year we'll return to this part of the country. We'll settle in Albu-querque and she can come to visit with you as often as she wishes."

Jack half-listened to himself as he spoke these words and he thought, This was some fine speech.

Ida sat in the shadows giggling, more from release of ten-sion than from amusement. She and Jack had planned this family meeting and she was pleased that Jack was carrying out his part of the bargain. It was going well. She admitted to herself she'd been a little afraid he might lack the courage to go through with it. Then she translated for her mother. Ida's father turned to his daughter and asked her in a formal way if this was all right with her. Ida giggled again and said Yes, it was all right with her. She turned to her mother and said something in Navajo. Jack sought the woman's face in the shadows. He saw her smile and then she said, "Ha ko *sheenh.*" Then Ida's father faced Jack and said, "Well, I guess that will be all right."

Now Jack had to get on the phone to call his mother.

Chapter Fourteen

Jack decided he would make his telephone call to New York that same evening from his apartment in Fort Defiance.

"Getting married out there? When? To whom?" were the questions shot out over two thousand miles of telephone lines by Cecile Berkowitz.

"To Ida Bird, a Navajo girl I've fallen in love with."

"Why are you doing this?" Cecile asked, her voiced strained with anguish and disbelief. "You know you were raised in a Jewish home. You know we've given you a Jewish education. You know we've lost our Six Million in the Holocaust. We can't afford to lose any more."

"You're not going to lose me, Mom."

"Maybe not you, son, but when you marry outside of our religion, your children and their children will not be Jewish."

"Look, Ma," Jack said after a strained silence, "I've known Ida for over a year. She's a wonderful woman. We're very much in love. When people are in love things can always be worked out. On Thursday there will be a ceremony in the Navajo Way. It will be held out here. Her people have had their own centuries of tradition and I respect that tradition as I respect our own. Come out to our wedding. You'll see how beautiful their Way is.

I'll send you the tickets and you and Pop can fly out here from New York."

There was long silence on the other end of the line and then a click. Jack called back an instant later.

"I can't believe this, Jack. You must be out of your *mind*. Think it over. And if you go ahead with this, your father and I won't be there."

Jack lay there on the bed where he'd prepared himself for the call and his head swam. He had the sensation he was falling. He felt he had to grab on to some connection with his former self. His spirits brightened as he thought of what to do next. He called his brothers.

"We're happy for you. We're behind you. Just let us know and we'll be there." It was his brother, Elihu, only seventeen months older than himself.

"Mazel Tov!" Howard, Jack's oldest brother said. Jack sprang from the bed, and, still holding the phone, rattled off his invitation and his plan for his brothers.

"The Navajo wedding will be on Thursday night on the Reservation. I know it will be hard for you to get up here on such short notice, but we can meet in Albuquerque on Friday and all go up together for the civil ceremony in Santa Fe the next day."

Mazel Tov! Howard had said. Jack did himself a little turn on his way to the kitchen and poured himself a shot of Haig and Haig scotch.

Ida and Jack were to be married in a traditional Navajo wedding four days after Mr. Bird gave his approval. Preparations began immediately. Ida's brother, Thomas, and his friends built a new hogan in that short period of time. Fresh lumber from the sawmill breathed its piney scent since there was not enough time to paint the inside.

"I know that in the traditional Navajo way the bridegroom is supposed to bring presents, horses, to the brides's father," Jack said to his secretary, Mrs. Bullis, on Monday morning. "Frankly, though, I think something more practical makes more sense, like sheep. Ewes. That way they can count on an increase of the value of the gift in future years. Would six sheep be all right?" Mrs. Bullis laughed. She knew of no one who had ever given sheep before.

"O.K., I can sell you some sheep. I can have them trucked from my mother's flock down near Sanders." Jack was pleased and they made a deal, fifteen dollars a head. Jack had bought himself a bride.

On Thursday morning the day turned dark and wet, some sleet mixed with rain. Jack and Ida were on their way to Gallup to buy the wedding rings.

"I hope it doesn't get too muddy. You don't know how bad the roads can get sometimes," Ida said. In Gallup, people hurried about with their heads down into their coats as the wind blew colder. But as they came out of Zale's jewelry store, somewhat flushed with the pair of gold bands they'd bought, the wind had died down. The rest of the day, though cloud-covered and cold, remained dry.

They arrived at Red Lake in the late afternoon. Jack toured the newly-built hogan. As he circled the interior on the beaten earth floor he looked up and marveled at the way it was put together. Six two-by-fours which framed the roof rose from the six corners of the structure toward the center. There they met a small hexagonal frame about eighteen inches across that left an opening for the stovepipe to pass through the roof to the outside. The hogan had no windows. The door was an opening, covered with a blanket, that faced to the east.

Nellie, Ida's sister, working with a treadle-operated sewing machine, had just finished making Jack a new, purple velveteen blouse. Jack tried it on, and Nellie, smiling that it fit, sewed on silver buttons for the front opening and for the cuffs of the sleeves.

"Here," she said with a little laugh, tying a traditional colorful bandana around Jack's head. "The knot goes on the right side."

Ida, meanwhile, was getting dressed in the richest Navajo style. She wore a bright red velveteen blouse with silver points on the collar. Her necklace was of turquoise nuggets with a pendant of white clamshell. Her ankle-length, three-tiered "squaw-skirt" was of a shimmering blue material with a woven-in pattern. Her yucca-washed hair, black and shining, was tied in a "tsi-yeh," a bun tied with a skein of white wool. Large turquoise nuggets hung from her pierced ears and silver and turquoise bracelets graced her wrists. When she drew her skirts up to walk around the hogan Jack saw that the mocassins she wore were of deer-hide and the wrap-around upper portion went to just below her knees.

The ceremony was about to begin. Jack and Ida were led to the place of honor, their backs against the west wall of the hogan that had been draped against the cold with hangings of rich and colorful Pendleton blankets. They were seated, for further comfort, on additional folded Pendleton robes. From that position they watched as the guests began to arrive.

"I'm happy to have this real Navajo wedding," Ida whispered to Jack. "There hasn't been a traditional Navajo wedding in this part of the country for many years." Many of the Navajos working at the Indian Hospital at Fort Defiance and at the sanatorium came out of curiosity because they had never seen such a wedding. Jack's medical colleagues at the hospital, several of them Jewish, and their wives, came out of respect for Jack and out of respect for the Navajo tradition.

"Where are all these people going to sit? There won't be enough room now for my own family. And how are we going to feed all these people?" Ida whispered as the crowd continued to pour in through the east-facing hogan door.

For Jack, the show was great fun. In spite of the crowding everyone was excited. The crowd was hushed as elders of Ida's T'senjikinnie clan, her mother's brothers and uncles, began the ceremony with quiet dignity offering the new couple advice. Chick San Juan, a member of the Tribal council and a relative on her father's side, provided translation into English.

"The man and wife are to get along with one another in harmony," began Hosteen Curley. A tall, slender man from Ganado, impeccably dressed in tan Western gabardine trousers, polished cowboy boots, and a red plaid shirt, he was himself a medicine man. "They are to treat one another with respect. The children, growing up in such an atmosphere would then learn courtesy and respect."

"The man and wife must share the work. But each may have his own possessions. The wife may have her own sheep or cattle to do with as she likes," was the advice of Winslow Shirley. He had come down from his ranch at Tsaile, near the Canyon de Chelly.

Meanwhile, Lorenzo Yazzie, Ida's mother's youngest brother, circulated as quietly as possible taking Polaroid pictures of the marriage couple and of the distinguished guests. Nobody seemed to mind the popping of the flashbulbs; this was an important event.

As part of the ceremony, Jack and Ida were handed a woven basket filled with blue cornmeal mush. After they washed their hands in water, Ida dipped her finger into the blue corn and fed Jack, then Jack fed Ida. This brought a murmur of approval from the crowd. Then the basket was passed around for everybody to share in the symbolic meal. The basket completed its circuit around the hogan and was emptied.

"If your mother were here," Ida whispered to Jack, "she would be given the basket to keep. That's our tradition." Jack had not told Ida the reason that his mother was not present. He tried to conceal his emptiness but Ida could see that Jack's expression of jollity had disappeared.

"I'll tell you what we can do," Jack answered after he'd thought about it for a while. "Do you see Joan Shine sitting over there? She's Jewish and married to Dr. Shine, the eye doctor from Fort Defiance. We can give the basket to her. Sort of substitute Jewish mother."

That night Jack took Ida to bed in his apartment in Fort Defiance. She was his wife now in the Navajo way. He touched her shoulder, as he had imagined more than a year before, and he felt its softness through her flannel nightgown.

Jack's two brothers, Howard with his wife, Basha, and Elihu with his wife, Betty, flew into Albuquerque the next day.

He arranged for them to stay at the rambling, porticoed, Spanish tile-roofed Alvarado Hotel near the railroad station. Ida, always discreet, would spend the night with her friend Marian, on the campus of the University of New Mexico where Marian was a student.

The little wedding party dined that night in the restaurant of the old hotel. The electric lights of the chandelier, turned down to a dim glow, produced a subdued atmosphere, and the dull gray walls added no brightness. There were only a few other guests in the dining room.

"I'm so glad you guys are here," Jack said. "I know it was such short notice, but it's too bad you couldn't have been up at Ida's home, met her family, and for the Navajo ceremony. You would have seen some color there." Jack turned to Ida and smiled, but she remained quiet, more than usually subdued. Well, that's all right, Jack thought. I don't expect Ida to do any entertaining tonight.

Ida turned her head in Marian's direction from time to time. Marian was more animated, and smiled, sensing Ida's shyness, giving her friend moral support. Marian had huge brown eyes and a perfect face. She was shorter and less angular than Ida, and full-breasted, a perfect Navajo beauty in her own right. Jack's brother, Elihu, began an instant flirtation with Marian. He'd always been a flirt. It didn't matter to him that his wife was right there. He flirted for the pleasure flirting gave him, and also because it was his way of teasing his wife. Betty said nothing, but she held her mouth in a vice-like tightness of disapproval. Jack knew that Betty would make him suffer for it later.

Jack's brother Howard contributed by telling a story: "Two great bulls are out in the pasture on a cold and snowy night. 'Brrrr,' says the first bull. 'Brrrr,' responds the second. Then the first bull says, 'I think I'll go into the barn and slip into a Jersey.'"

"I thought nice white men weren't supposed to tell dirty jokes," Ida whispered to Marian in Navajo. "It isn't that we haven't heard dirty jokes before. You know we've heard plenty of them told by Navajos. This story was actually pretty funny, though." At this point she began to laugh a little. "I just didn't expect to hear one from a polite white man who is also my brother-in-law."

The next day was sunny for the drive to Santa Fe, but the sun's slanting rays were unmistakably those of autumn. Jack and Ida completed their last-minute shopping: a new brown suit for Jack and a pair of high-heel, blue, patent leather shoes to match her wedding outfit for Ida.

"I'm getting married today," Jack said to the clerk at Stromberg's on Central Avenue. The clerk responded with a smile.

"Well, in that case Stromberg's offers you its congratulations. Pick yourself a tie."

Ida had been late finding just the right shoes but everybody's spirits were high as the family crowded into Jack's convertible for the drive north. He convinced the passengers to leave the top down so they could enjoy the views of the Rio Grande valley and of the Jemez mountains. Before long, however, the chill air and the wind became too much and the top went back up.

In his chambers behind City Hall, Magistrate Joe Baca was drunk. The front of his shirt was stained with tobacco juice from the cigar that never left his mouth. He managed somehow to read through the printed form that lay before him.

"By the authority vested in me by the County of Santa Fe in the State of New Mexico," he concluded, "I declare this marriage legally binding." A clerk brought in a certificate for his signature and the civil ceremony was over. Elihu took a picture of Jack and Ida standing at the desk outside the magistrate's room signing the register. That was it.

Poor Ida, Jack thought. She dressed so smartly to look her best. She wore the heavy blue woolen coat her father had just bought for her, a patterned blue dress of drapery material, and a little Juliet cap, also of blue. Yet the picture showed her face worn and dark.

Jack shepherded the party to Salazar's Mexican Café for the wedding luncheon. "This place is a Santa Fe tradition," Jack announced to his brothers and their wives, playing host and tour guide. The simple dining room with whitewashed walls, adorned with ristras of red chile, was near empty since it was late for the usual noontime crowd and too early for dinner.

"I would recommend huevos rancheros on blue corn tortillas," Jack recommended and they all took his advice. When the steaming plates were served with their soft, yellow eggs mounted on a bed of tortillas and with refried beans and Spanish rice smothered with red chile and melted cheddar, appetites returned, jaws ached in anticipation, and the afternoon was saved. With the main dish came baskets full of delicately puffed, air-filled, golden sopapillas. "Here," Jack instructed, "tear off the corner of one of these, fill it with rice and beans, and breathe in the aroma of the chile." Dry red wine was served. Spirits rose higher.

"Now for desert: another sopapilla, this time filled to the brim with honey." Jack felt himself the impressario. More tangy wine was served. Even Ida was smiling now. Jack felt a sensation of warmth rising to his face.

"'La panza llena, contento el corazon,'" he announced.

"To the bride, to the groom!" was Elihu's toast.

The late-afternoon sun began its descent early and the light faded behind a veil of clouds. Howard and Elihu looked at their watches as they calculated the time needed to return to Albuquerque to catch their planes at the airport. The wedding party dispersed with kisses and best wishes. With slowed steps and with overcoats drawn up to their necks against the cold, Ida and Jack dropped heavily into the front seat of the car.

"It got cheerful there for a while, didn't it, Ida?" Jack said before turning on the engine.

"But it's so lonesome now again. It's so dark all of a sudden. Are you sure you know the way?"

"It shouldn't be hard to find. You go north on the Old Taos road, up the hill and out of Santa Fe, and then down toward Tesuque. The Bishop's Lodge is about three miles down that road, on the right side, Dr. Schwartzman said."

Bishop Lamy's old retreat was now a resort and becoming more popular, though now in November, it was nearly deserted. The main lodge and dining room, a comfortable three-story building with a gabled roof, had a terrace that looked out onto a tennis court and a swimming pool to the north. Beyond, and up on a little hill, lay a series of cottage suites connected by a covered walkway.

"I hope you'll be comfortable here," the bellman said as he led Ida and Jack into the large sitting room of a suite where a bright fire was already blazing. Heavy, warm-looking, green drapes covered the tall, ceiling-to-floor windows. Light from two tablelamps provided a soft glow to the room. Each lamp-lit table had its own easy chair. A deep-piled, gray-green carpet covered the floor throughout.

"It's just perfect," Ida said thanking the young man as he left. "Oh, Jack, I feel better already." She came up to him, threw her arms around his neck and kissed him. Then she disappeared into the shower beyond the bedroom. Jack picked up a Gideon Bible from the drawer of the chair-side table in the sitting room where he waited. In the lamplight the pages fell open to the Old Testament, Jeremiah, chapter four, verses 23-26:

"I beheld the earth, and Lo! Disorder and confusion;
The heavens also, and there was no light.
I beheld the mountains, and Lo! they trembled;
And the hills also shook.
I beheld, and Lo! there was not a man.
And all the fowls of the heaven were fled.
I beheld and Lo! the fruitful field (was become) the desert;
And all its cities were thrown down,
Before the presence of Jehovah,
Before the fierce heat of his anger."

The wrath of the Lord, thought Jack. Mighty is the wrath of the Lord. My people, the ancient Hebrews. They really knew how to stick it to you! He continued to leaf through the pages and came to the Book of Ezra, chapter ten, verses 10 and 11:

"And Ezra the priest stood up and said unto them,
Ye have trespassed and have taken foreign wives,
To increase the trespass of Israel.
Now therefore make confession to the Lord God of
your fathers,
And do his pleasure
And separate yourselves from the land
And from the foreign wives."

The hair stood up on the back of Jack's neck. So the Hebrews of old also took Gentile wives and they were told they must divorce them! Jack heard the voices of his teachers and his rabbis and his parents: "You must not, you must *not* marry a 'shiksa.' The Jewish tradition must *not* be forsaken. Only by marrying a Jewish woman can you be certain the Jewish family and tradition will survive."

Just then Ida came out of the shower dressed in a light robe. She came through the bedroom and walked across the sitting room. She was twenty. Her shining, straight, black, perfumed hair trailed to her waist. The lines of tension and sadness were gone now from her face. She was untroubled by ancient taboos.

Ezra was wrong, Jack thought. That was then; this is now. Now the whole world knew that Ida was his wife. She was not a "foreign" wife. She was *his* wife and he would not separate himself from her.

CHAPTER FIFTEEN

❧

"Have you heard from your mother-in-law yet, Ida?" chirped Bernice Birnbaum. Bernice lived next door in the row of Fort Defiance apartments. She was tiny and blonde, the wife of Jack's friend, the dentist.

Why is she asking me that? Ida thought. She asked me the same question last week. Why is she bugging me? Does she know something I don't know?

"No I haven't," Ida replied trying to sound cheerful, imitating Bernice's sing-song. "But I expect to hear from her real soon," and with that she spun around, went back into the house, and let the screen door slam.

"Why did that nosy Bernice ask me if I heard from your mother?" Ida asked, zeroing in on Jack the minute he stepped into the front door. Jack realized the storm was already upon him. He had not told Ida anything of his mother's refusal to come to the wedding or of the conversation that had taken place.

"Well, Ida, it's going to take some time for my mother to get used to the fact that we're married now, that I married outside of the Jewish religion; and Bernice knows that."

"So I'm not good enough for your mother, is that it? Why didn't you tell me *before* we were married that my not being Jewish was such a big deal? Would someone like that Bernice have been O.K. for you to marry? Would she have been any better than me?" Her eyes now shone brightly with tears though none fell, and she turned to walk away into the kitchen,

Jack sat down on the living room couch and after a while, smoothing her apron, Ida sat down and joined him.

"You know, Jack," she was able to muster in a calmer tone, "At first I didn't even know you were Jewish. I knew you were different somehow from the usual 'Biligonnas,' the Anglos I knew as traders, the rednecks who lived on the Reservation and who worked for the Bureau of Indian Affairs. I knew the teachers and, of course, the missionaries, but it was not polite for me to ask questions. My parents always told me that it was enough to know that a person is a human being, one who has 'five fingers.'"

"But I did finally tell you that I was Jewish, didn't I? That I grew up in Brooklyn, and that it was a Jewish neighborhood?"

"You did, Jack, but I didn't even know what that meant. Actually, when you told me that, I was confused. I suppose I should have asked you more then. But when I was growing up on the Reservation I thought there weren't any more Jews on earth. The only ones I knew about were the ones in the Christmas plays who wore long robes and who came to admire the Infant Jesus."

"I think maybe the Catholics wanted to keep you in the dark," Jack said.

"Well, anyway, later I heard people say that there was a living Jew who owned a shoe store in Gallup. He went by a Navajo name which means, 'He Pulls You In.'"

"So whatever you knew about Jews wasn't too complimentary," he said with a little laugh. "But you liked me anyway! Look, Ida, the Jews have had a long, complicated, tragic history. A lot has happened between the time the Jews came to admire the Infant Jesus and the time that shoe store owner came to Gallup."

"But you shouldn't have kept me in the dark about all that. It makes me feel so stupid, and I get so angry."

Jack pulled her toward him when he saw the tears welling up again. "Look, Ida, I love you. We'll be leaving for New York in a few months. You'll meet a lot of Jews there. You'll learn a lot about us then."

"Why don't you start teaching me now? I'm willing to learn."

"Where do you want me to begin? O.K., I'll start with the story of the Jews as it is told in the 'Haggada,' the book that is read at the table on the Jewish holiday of Passover every year: 'We were slaves unto Pharaoh in Egypt and the Lord took us out from there with a mighty hand and an outstretched arm.'"

CHAPTER SIXTEEN

≈

In the spring, the cottonwoods along the main street of Fort Defiance and the Russian olives in Black Creek wash pushed out their fresh new leaves. The last traces of snow had long disappeared from north-facing walls of alcoves in the cliffs east of the valley. The fluttering crowds of juncos were gone and new pairs of mountain bluebirds wheeled about looking for nesting sites. In the shade under the piñons the breeze brought perfume of oozing sap and tree-gum.

At the sanatorium Miss Moss, after some persuasion, gave permission for the patients to dress in Navajo costume, rather than in robes and pajamas, for Jack's farewell. Mrs. Armijo made the presentation of a set of Navajo-crafted silver spoons and a Two Gray Hills rug. Ida's uncle, Lorenzo, organized the last family picnic among the ponderosas near Old Sawmill, and then it was time to go.

Jack and Ida loaded their belongings into his convertible. There were Ida's regular clothes, her Navajo costumes, her turquoise and silver jewelry, and a tiny, beaded leather pouch that contained a handful of corn pollen. Jack packed his albums of 33rpm, long-playing, high fidelity classical records and the steel-stringed guitar he had bought at a pawn shop.

They drove north on Highway 666, away from the Reservation on their way to New York. They were to take a belated honeymoon trip through the mountains of the West before turning east. The beginning of the trip was a joy for Jack, the fulfilment of a plan, but Ida was in tears.

"I thought you would like the idea of a great trip to see the rest of the country," Jack said. "And I thought you would love to have a chance to go to a live performance of the New York Philharmonic at Carnegie Hall."

Ida said nothing, her eyes becoming puffy with weeping as she watched the last vestiges of Navajo country, the volcanic peaks and pinnacles of Shiprock, fade from view.

"I know it's not easy for you to be so far from home," he continued. "Your folks are really so wonderful. And they've been wonderful to me, too, accepting me as a son. And it's especially hard to leave now when it's so beautiful on the Reservation. But we'll only be gone for a year. Just one year. Then we'll come back to the West again. And you'll be able to come home to visit any time you want."

Ida's tears stopped after they crossed the border into Colorado. She was comforted by the rich green of the irrigated valleys and by the massive and lofty gray, granite mountains. Their journey gave her a view of the triple peaks of the Maroon Bells above Aspen. The jagged uplift of the Grand Tetons above Jenny Lake in Jackson Hole, Wyoming, calmed her spirit. They drove into nearby Yellowstone Park where they joined the tourists waiting for the eruption of Old Faithful. They took pictures of Upper and Lower Yellowstone Falls as the waters tumbled between the yellow, volcanic tuff of the canyon walls. Then they headed east across Montana's green and yellow striped wheatlands, and into North Dakota. They drove late into the evening in pale, gray light that lingered after ten o'clock since they were so far north and the summer solstice was nearly upon them. Finally, through the dense pine forests of Michigan's northern peninsula, across the flat lands of Michigan, Indiana, Ohio, and then through the rounded, green mountains of Pennsylvania, Jack and Ida were approaching New York City.

"It will only be for a year," Jack said many times. But Ida's first words when they emerged on the Manhattan side of the

Lincoln Tunnel on a hot, steamy day in June were, "Why are all those people staring at me?" With the top of the convertible down, Ida did indeed see a thousand eyes looking at her. The exit plaza of the tunnel was lined on both sides by five-story New York tenements. On every floor windows were flung open on that hot and humid day, and every one of those windows had somebody leaning forward on pillows, peering down at the stream of cars and trucks below.

"They're not just looking at you," Jack explained over the roar of the traffic. "It's a hot day and people up there are just trying to catch a little breeze. And looking out of windows may be their only entertainment."

Ida became more comfortable only when, driving east across Manhattan, they left the tenements of the West Side, passed through the canyons of the garment district, and came out, at last, on Fifth Avenue. She breathed easier, finally, at the open spaces of Central Park.

"Will we live here, facing the park?"

"Only the very rich can afford to live facing the park. Of course, anybody can come and visit the park any time they want to. I know you will, and that you'll enjoy it. Right now, we've got to find a place closer to the hospital."

When they found an apartment, it was on the ground floor of an old-law, East Side tenement off York Avenue. One window faced the rear; the kitchen alcove, for it was only a one-room apartment, had a small window that looked out onto an air-shaft, a narrow space five floors down from the sky. When they finished their inspection, Ida choked away her tears. Jack opened the rear window only to be assaulted by the smell of urine. The little boys from the neighborhood knew their way through alleys and they came every day to piss on the concrete slab which was the back yard.

One day about a week later Ida came rushing out into the street to meet Jack crying, "What's that sour smell in the air? The sky is so yellow, and the air makes me choke, and little grains of black sand keep raining down!"

"You're right. It *is* pretty awful. I've never seen it like this before," Jack said. "And I've lived here most of my life." The Con Edison coal-burning electric power-generating station on the East River had just pumped tons of gas and ash into the air just six blocks away. He rushed her back into the apartment. Dingy, dark and stuffy as it was, the air was better inside than out. Ida wept and put her head against his shoulder. "Do you think all that bad air will harm the baby?" she asked, patting her belly which was, at that time, getting noticeably bigger. "I don't think so. But I tell you what. Let's go to the movies tonight. Movie theaters are always air-conditioned. It will make you feel better. And then maybe we can get an air-conditioner for the window."

Jacks' first hospital assignment was in the emergency room. But it gnawed at his conscience that while he was busy with his work, meeting new colleagues and friends, his wife spent many days alone in the miserable confines of the tiny apartment. They were in the same city as his parents. Now was the time, he felt, for a reconciliation with his family. His father had a weakness for women, and he knew his father would not be able to resist a girl as spirited and beautiful as Ida.

"You'll have to meet her, Pop," Jack said when they sat down to lunch at the Roosevelt Hotel downtown. "She wants to belong to this family."

"I'm not against it, son," Morris Berkowitz said with some softness. This was the first reunion with his youngest son in over a year. Morris was sixty-eight, but the smooth skin of his face and his nearly full head of hair made him look younger. Then, with a sterner expression he said, "But first you'll have to tell me *why* you married her."

"You'll know when you see her, " Jack replied. "And besides, there's a baby on the way."

Morris was silent for a while. Then his face softened and he said quietly, "We cannot reject life." He thought a while longer and then he said with a brighter tone, "Bring Ida up to the house this Friday evening. We'll have Shabbos together," and he took his son's hands in his.

Chapter Seventeen

~✐~

Morris and Cecile Berkowitz lived on the sixth floor of an apartment house on Fort Washington Avenue. The yellow brick, six story building stood on the corner of 162nd Street. It had a decorative cornice just below the roof line that gave it a fashionable look.

"I lived here for seven years," Jack said as they came around the corner. They had just walked from the subway station after the ride from downtown. "What do you think of it?"

"Pretty fancy," Ida said. "I didn't know you were that rich."

"Not really. This neighborhood was past its prime when we first moved here and it's even less fancy now, though not bad for Manhattan."

Just then Ida noticed a green, double-decker, Fifth Avenue bus drive by going south.

"I didn't know those buses came all the way up here."

"Yes, they do. On the way uptown they go up Broadway. We crossed Broadway on the way over here. On their way back they go down Fort Washington Avenue. That bus line made living here pretty nice. If you weren't in too much of a hurry to get downtown you could hop on the bus on that corner across the street. The bus goes down Riverside Drive for part of the way, and you can see the Hudson River for a while. Then it cuts across to Fifth

Avenue and then you get a view of Central Park. I used to take it on my way down to medical school when I still lived here at home."

"Well, then, you had a pleasant start to the day that way."

The entrance to the apartment building had an arched doorway bordered by tiers of molded concrete blocks that were designed to look like carved stone.

"Jack, this almost looks like the entrance to a church!"

"When you get inside you'll see a different effect." The apartment house lobby was decorated with heavy, carved wood, straight-back chairs that were stained the darkest brown. A fake fireplace stood against one wall. Sconces on the other wall held torch-like fixtures that leaned into the room and flame-shaped electric bulbs gave off the dimmest, flickering light.

"This looks like something out of the movies," Ida said. "Is it supposed to look this spooky?"

"Not intentionally. This is just the way they used to decorate the lobbies of these apartment houses."

The elevator was at the far end of the lobby. A short black man in a uniform operated the lift. When he pulled back the scissors gate Ida saw that he was missing his left arm. The man gave the couple a friendly smile and invited them into the cage.

"Sixth floor, please," Jack said.

They rose in silence, and after they stepped out at the sixth floor and the elevator started back down, Ida said, "It makes me a little uncomfortable to be waited on like that. I feel sorry for that little man, to live in a dark place, to have to take people up and down all day, to have to smile and be nice to them. It's almost like being a slave."

"You're right, it is a little sad. But with only one arm this is probably the only job he could get."

When they opened the apartment door, Jack and Ida were greeted by the aroma of pot roast of beef brisket stewing with onions and lima beans. Through the open door to the dining room they saw that the Sabbath candles were lit, casting a warm glow on the white tablecloth and on the twisted challah loaves.

Jack's mother stood in the doorway between the kitchen and the dining room. She was of medium height and slender. In spite of the Henna rinse that gave a superficial appearance of youthfulness, the crow's feet at the corners of her eyes betrayed the full extent of her sixty-three years. She wore a white apron trimmed with a ruffled edge and slippers open at the heels. Her smile, when Ida came forward to greet her, was only a fraction of a smile.

"So this is Ida," she said. "I'm glad to meet you at last. I'm glad you could come this evening. This our Sabbath, a special day for us."

"I'm glad to be here after such a long time," Ida said matching Cecile's coolness and formality.

Morris came forward extending both hands to Ida and he took her hands in his. He wanted to embrace her but Cecile was right there. "We've only had boys," he said, "but now we have you as one more daughter."

Ida saw something of Jack in the older man's face, some of that softness and merriment. She was a little surprised that Jack's father was so short, no taller than she was. And she had a little difficulty understanding his Polish-Yiddish accent. But the warmth was there. She knew she had him. It didn't matter that Cecile was so hard.

Ida stepped over to the dining room window to look at the riverscape before her, across the Hudson to the Palisades on the Jersey shore, up to the north, to the great George Washington Bridge.

"You have such a beautiful view from up here," she said. She had been closeted in the little apartment downtown for too long.

"It's time to come to the table now," Cecile commanded.

Morris handed Jack a black skullcap and he took one for himself. They placed the yarmulkes on their heads and stood together at the head of the table.

"Va ye'he erev, va ye'he voker, yom ha'shishi," they began in unison as they intoned in Hebrew the opening verses of the

Kiddush, the blessing before the Sabbath meal. "Va ye'chulu ha'shamayim ve ha'aretz v'chal tzva'am," they continued.

How does Jack know all that stuff? Ida thought. With his father it almost sounds like the medicine men singing in the hogan. And in her mind she was, for a moment, two thousand miles away in Arizona.

The chanting went on for several more minutes and ended with the blessing, over the wine, "Baruch Atoh Adonai, Elokainu Melech Ha'Olam, Boray Pree Ha'Gaffen." Jack and his father each raised a glass of sweet, red Mogen David Concord grape wine and drank.

"You take a sip from your glass, too, Ida" Jack said, and she tasted it. It was sweet and syrupy. She took some more. With her nervousness about meeting Jack's parents she had eaten almost nothing all day. And the pregnancy. She had forgotten how hungry that could make her. The wine produced a magical effect. She melted into the glow of the Sabbath candles. She wanted the effect to stay with her. She wanted the images of the smiling faces of her husband and her new-found father-in-law to remain with her. But the sweet taste of the wine sent her head spinning. The taste was that of the yellow Tokay, the Garden deLux Tokay that her brother, Thomas, had had her sample secretly from the pint flask he had sneaked home to the Reservation from the bootlegger outside of Gallup.

Cecile went back into the kitchen and produced a bread knife and a cutting board. Now was the time for the blessing over the bread. "Baruch Atoh Adonai, Elokainu Melech Ha'Olam Ha'Motzih Lechem min Ha'Aretz," Morris chanted. He then reached for the challah, the twisted Sabbath loaf glistening with its egg-yellow crust sprinkled with poppy seeds. He placed it on the cutting board and sliced inch-thick portions that he passed around. The fresh-baked, yeasty smell filled the air. The yellow color of the bread, the smooth and soft texture were new to Ida, and the unexpected sweetness of it delighted her.

The ceremonial Sabbath blessings and preliminaries were now over and Cecile got up to return to the kitchen. Ida pushed back her chair and started to get up to help.

"That's all right, Ida. You're our guest.. You stay where you are and I'll serve you with the men."

Only a guest, still not a member of the family, Ida thought. "O.K. Mrs. Berkowitz," Ida replied.

When Cecile lifted the heavy lid from the Dutch oven, the marvelous "meat-and-potato" aroma rushed into the air and out into the dining room. Jack felt that certain ache in his jaws. This was all too good to believe. All the things he wanted most in his life were coming together: the familiar aroma and the promise of the pot roast which was his favorite, the reassuring rituals of the Sabbath blessings, his father's acceptance of his bride, and the beautiful Ida herself right there with him. My cup runneth over, he thought, and he took another deep draught of the wine.

Jack looked across the table when his mother served the steaming plate of brisket of beef with its stewed potatoes, onions and lima beans. Then she set out side dishes of pale cole slaw and shimmering slices of cold, green, kosher dill pickles. Jack remembered an old family joke. He didn't think this was the time for it but he would tell it to Ida later: Mom, we learned in school that when you serve a meal you should always have a green vegetable, and Mom would say, Pickles by you is not a green vegetable?

Ida seemed to be searching about the table for something that was not there.

"Can I get you anything, Ida?" Jack offered.

"Yes, can I have a little butter for my bread?"

"We don't serve butter with meat," Cecile said sharply.

The color rose in Ida's face.

"My mother meant to explain," Jack interceded, "that in the Jewish dietary law we separate dairy products from meat dishes."

"Is there a reason for that?" Ida asked.

"Yes, Ida," Jack went on. "It's because in the Torah, the Bible, there is a commandment that says, 'Thou shalt not boil a kid in its mother's milk.' The rabbis tell us that this is just a way of saying a person should have compassion for other creatures, even animals."

Ida said, "We have feelings for animals, too. I was raised with sheep and goats. When we have to butcher one of them for food we always use the sharpest knife and we cut the neck as fast as possible."

Cecile's eyes lit up. "That's the way we do our kosher slaughtering, too. And we let the blood drain out."

"We do the same thing. But you know, it never occurred to us to boil a kid in its mother's milk."

Morris smiled at this and so did Jack. The tension was relieved a little. Cecile still looked a little grim-faced but then she relented and said, "Ida, if you like, we can give you a little chicken fat for your challah."

"Sure, Mrs. Berkowitz, I'd like to try that."

After he finished his first plate, Jack asked for second servings. "And heavy on those potatoes, stewed onions and lima beans, Mom." Ida thought it would not be lady-like, so she refused Cecile's offer for more in spite of her hunger.

For dessert Cecile served a compote of stewed prunes and dried peaches. The flavor and the still-chewy texture of the peaches took Ida back to the Canyon de Chelly. Every summer her father and her mother drove the wagon the two-day trip from Red Lake, over the mountain, to the home of her father's mother in the bottom of the canyon. There they would fill the bed of the wagon with peaches from her grandmother's peach orchard. The horses would have to strain to pull the heavier load over the sandy bottom on the way out. When they got home Ida's mother would pit and dry the peaches in the sun. Then she would stuff the dried peaches in a gunnysack and store them in the root cellar where Ida, her sister, and her brothers couldn't get at them. When the snows fell in winter, Ida's mother would order her to fill the pot with snow, and the dried peaches would be brought out from their hiding place. When they were stewed in the melted water over the fire the steam would rise and the hogan would be filled with the aroma of the peaches of summer.

The men were chanting again. Ida saw that Morris had brought out two little books with the strange Hebrew letters. Morris and his son were singing in unison the melodies of the "Birchat Ha'Mazone," the Grace After Meals. Jack sang loudest when he came to the closing stanzas. "Na'ar hy'iti, v'gam zakanti, v'lo ra'iti tsadik ne'ezav v'zar'oh m'vakesh lachem."

"Well, Ida, what did you think of them?" Jack asked the moment the apartment door had closed and as they walked down the hall to the elevator.

"They're still a little strange to me. I know I can get to like your father. It's just that it's a little hard for me to understand him, the way he talks. But your mother. I don't think we'll ever get along."

"Oh, just give it a little time. My mother, I admit, is a little bit stiff."

Stiff! Ida thought. That woman is cold as ice. She never accepted me and she never will.

They stepped out of the building and on to Fort Washington Avenue. A soft breeze blew in from the river. Ida had softer thoughts.

"That last song you sang at the table. You almost had tears in your eyes. What did the words mean?"

"It means that if a person does good and has faith, everything will turn out right."

Chapter Eighteen

❦

"Why you little *stinker!*" a voice said to Jack over the telephone. "Why didn't you tell anybody you were married? You know we've always been a close family!" It was Jack's cousin, Edith. She was the youngest in her family like Jack, and just two or three years older than he was. Her mother, Bessie, was Cecile's oldest sister. "And your mother! Why didn't *she* tell us about it? You'd think she was ashamed of something you did. We've got to meet your wife. I hear she's a real Indian princess. My kids are dying to meet her."

Color rose in Jack's face. He was glad Edith couldn't see him at that moment. "Well sure, Edith. Ida's a little lonesome here." His thoughts turned to his cousin. Edith had always been good to him. She was the one who welcomed him and hugged him when he was five or six when he would come to his aunt Bessie's house to spend the night. She was the one who would push three dining room chairs together to make a bed for him, and then she would fluff up pillows for him to sleep on. She was the one who taught him to ride a two-wheeler on her girl's bike that summer when he was thirteen. She let him use that bike until he was good enough to lean into the turns without fear of falling, and to ride fast enough so that he could feel the wind in his face.

"We'll come and pick you up on Sunday and we'll take you out to Long Island to meet the rest of the family," Edith said.

"I don't think I want to meet any more of your relatives," Ida said when Jack told her about Edith and about the family get-together. "From what I've seen of bitchy Jewish women, I don't think I can take any more of them."

"Which 'bitchy Jewish women' are you talking about?"

"You know, I told you about that Bernice in Fort Defiance. And then your mother. And then the wives of the Jewish doctors at the hospital. 'Oh *I* went to Wellesley when *my* husband was at Harvard.' '*I* was at Vassar when *my* husband was at Yale; Oh, you haven't seen *My Fair Lady* yet?'" she mimicked. "They think they're so high and mighty. I could tell they were looking down on me."

"Well, come on now, listen," Jack said. "Those people are not my friends and not their husbands either. My medical school class was different. They were older. Most of them had been in the war. And their wives were nicer, too. Let's forget that stuff you've heard. You'll see that my Aunt Bessie's girls are different. They didn't go to college either. Come on out with me Sunday and you'll see."

Ida dressed for the family meeting in a festive, white squaw dress with a multi-tiered skirt trimmed with blue rick-rack. She wore a silver concho belt and earrings of miniature conchos that matched those of her belt. Her necklace was of simple silver melon beads with a pendant silver disc that depicted the sun. On her feet she wore soft, high-topped, brown mocassins buttoned at the top with a silver button.

Edith's husband, Larry, a dental lab technician and a quiet fellow, was stunned into silence when he saw Ida step out of the dreary apartment building on East 74th Street. And he was silent as he drove, Jack with him in the front seat. The two women got off to a good start, chatting merrily together in the back seat. Edith's infectious laugh filled the car. As they drove down the East River Drive and then through the Queens-Midtown Tunnel, Jack listened to Edith's questions:

"When you say 'boarding school,' that sounds like a pretty fancy place. Am I right?"

"Heck no," Ida said. I don't know what it's like in the white world, but the Indian boarding school was like a prison camp. They served you in the school cafeteria on those cold metal trays with the depressions in them and they slopped the food into them. What was supposed to be hot was cold. But even if you liked it, you couldn't ask for more. You were always hungry. And you *had* to go to bed when they turned out the lights. And you *had* to go to church on Sundays, to the Protestant services if you were Protestant, or to the Catholic services if you were Catholic. I didn't think I was either so I tried to skip going to church as much as I could. Most of the time you were just lonesome for your family and they were so far away."

"How did you feel when you were picked 'Miss Navajo'?"

"I never thought I would make it. My brothers always teased me. When I herded sheep I was always dressed in overalls and high-topped, heavy shoes. And I always wore my hair in braids. My brothers said, 'You're just too ugly.' And when I won, they just had to shut up. And they didn't say anything either when I modeled clothes up in Santa Fe." She became silent then and her eyes filled with tears.

"What's the matter, Ida?" Edith asked seeing the sudden change in Ida's face.

"I just lost one of my brothers. He was killed in an auto accident a year ago. His name was Richard, and I just thought of him. I haven't gotten over it yet. I'm sorry."

Edith reached for Ida's hand. "It's O.K. It's all right to cry."

The car swept northward on the Grand Central Parkway, up past La Guardia Field where the sleek planes took off and landed, gleaming in the sun. Ida's mood brightened with the clear weather, with getting out of Manhattan, and with encouragement of bright-faced Edith to tell about her life. When they passed through Queens and arrived at Edith's house in Nassau County, the living room was filled with people, Edith's three sisters and their husbands, and Edith's two children, a boy and a younger girl.

Jack was proud that Ida maintained such a gracious cool with all this extended family, people she didn't know existed until

Edith's telephone call. For much of the afternoon Ida sat on the couch holding court. She looked earnestly into everyone's eye as he or she was introduced, and she memorized the face, the name, and the family connection: Florence and her husband, Cal, Alice and her husband, Ben, Esther and her husband, Sam. Edith's children were Michael and Karen.

"You know, in the Navajo way," she said to Edith, "you and your sisters are not just Jack's cousins, but his sisters. You are very close That's because Jack's mother and your mother are sisters. So you are all very important to me."

"Are you really an Indian princess?" asked eight-year-old Karen.

"No, Karen, there aren't any Indian princesses. That's all just movie stuff. But my great-uncle, Chee Young, was elected the first chairman of the Navajo Tribe. If you want to look at it that way," Ida said with a twinkle in her eye, "I guess you can say I *am* royalty." Karen stood there for a while and just stared. Her eyes roamed over Ida's silver concho earrings, her silver concho belt, her silver necklace with its silver pendant, and the silver buttons on her mocassins.

For a long time while Ida sat on the couch, her right hand dipped idly, automatically, and repeatedly into a large bowl of salted peanuts on the end-table beside her. The next morning she cried out with tears in her eyes, "Look, Jack! My ankles are swollen, and my hands. I can't even close my fists!" When she made her routine visit to the obstetrician that afternoon the nurses weighed her. She had gained fifteen pounds in two weeks.

CHAPTER NINETEEN

The disappointment of Ida's first days in New York now faded. She was a new celebrity in Jack's extended family. Jack was happier, too, that his fears of being cut off from his family were unfounded.

Ida became excited about her life in the city and she set out to explore as much of it as she could. She discovered Bloomingdale's on Lexington Avenue, and B. Altman, Saks Fifth Avenue, Bergdorf-Goodman, and Lord and Taylor on Fifth. She took the elevator to the top of the Empire State Building where she could see the city that lay before her, the bridges across the East River, Central Park, and the wide Hudson all the way up to the George Washington Bridge. With Jack on his days off she climbed the broad, stone stairway to the Metropolitan Museum of Art and stood before the brooding Rembrandt self-portrait and before the storm-tossed clouds of El Greco's "View of Toledo." And, most memorable of all, she sat with Jack on the parquet floor of Carnegie Hall with the New York Philharmonic Orchestra living and breathing before her as they played Beethoven's "Eroica" Symphony. Then she was content to wait for the arrival of their first baby.

Ida came about her decision slowly. No, nobody had spoken to her, or asked her, or put any pressure on her. She looked at her past, at the icy discipline she had been subjected to at St. Michael's in Arizona when she was eight or nine. She remembered the knuckle-rapping with hard rulers delivered by the hooded nuns for the slightest infraction of the rules, or simply for appearing inattentive, or just for daydreaming, lonesome for home. She remembered the cold flagstone of the dormitory floors she had to mop and the hours of washing, ironing, and starching the sisters' wimples. She remembered the fear engendered in her of mortal sin. She remembered being told she would even be condemned to eternal damnation for *thinking* "evil" thoughts though she had no idea what evil thoughts were. In contrast to that cold religion she had her first glimpse of the Jewish home at the Sabbath table.

"Jack, tell me what I have to do to become Jewish," was Ida's request. "I'm serious about this. It's not just to please you or your father or your mother. It's just that I find the Jewish religion so much like my own Navajo religion. I love the gathering around the table and the warm feeling it gives me."

Jack had been standing at the kitchen sink washing dishes. He turned around slowly. Then he knitted his brow as he sat down next to her.

"I can't tell you how happy this makes me, Ida. But you should know that it won't be easy. There is so much to learn. You will find it strange, even burdensome. So many Jews are giving up the religion, the tradition, the rules. They find it doesn't seem to matter in the modern world."

"Well, you're Jewish. Something in the religion made you the way you are and I love you."

Jack pulled her toward himself in an embrace that brought his face next to hers. When he was sure that she would not see him close to tears, he held her by the shoulders and looked into her face.

"I have an old friend, a Rabbi Norbert Friml," he said after a quick run-down in his head of how to proceed. "He was director of the Hillel Foundation at City College when I was there as a student many years ago. I'm sure he will help us."

On his next free Sunday Jack took the train to the Brighton Beach section of Brooklyn where he found Rabbi Friml had a congregation. Jack reached into his pocket and pulled out a yarmulke before entering the rabbi's study and put it on his head. The rabbi, a short, intense man with a high-pitched voice and a little black mustache hadn't changed at all in the years Jack had been away at medical school, in his post-graduate training in Boston, and on the Navajo Reservation. Jack was happy to see his old friend again, but he was not prepared for the rabbi's response.

"Jack," he said, "you're making a big mistake. It will never work. You would do better to get out of this marriage now." Jack felt the blood rush to his face and his scalp tingled. How could Friml say such a thing? He hadn't even *met* Ida. And a baby would soon be born. You can't abandon a baby! How could he throw this at me when we were such good friends before?

The rabbi saw Jack's eyes turn dull as Jack lowered his head in defiance. "All right, then," he said. "You know, *I* won't do this. It's against my principle. But if you want it, I'll refer you to another Orthodox rabbi who will."

Rabbi Melech Schiff lived in the Bronx. Ida set out alone to meet him because Jack was on duty at the hospital. She took the subway, the "E" train to the Concourse. The cold and dampness of the underground platform on which she waited for the train caused her to turn up the coat collar around her neck. She was alarmed at the increasing rattle and roar in the station as the square, lighted front of train sped toward her out of the tunnel. It hurtled down the track and into the station, pushing cold air and unfamiliar odors in front of it. She thought it would roar right by, but with a piercing screech it began to slow. A long string of brightly lit subway cars rolled in front of her and finally stopped. She stepped aside as the doors slid open and the passengers who'd been standing by the door pushed out. She hesitated. She thought there would be some signal, someone to tell her when to get on; suddenly the doors began to close. She looked down at the dark gap between the edge of the platform and the lighted floor of the car. She thought for an instant she wouldn't try it, but when the doors were halfway shut she propelled herself into the car. Still frightened, she held on dearly to the pole nearest the door. The train gathered speed and roared on into the darkness. She'd ridden the train from Gallup to Albuquerque where she could see the world about her, but this eerie darkness and noise caused her to tighten her grip on the pole till her fingers turned white. She was relieved at last to find the 167th Street station where she was to get off. She climbed the stairs into the mild air and daylight, and found the rabbi's house on a modest street of two-story houses.

"Come in, come in," said Mrs. Schiff, a heavy-set woman with a young face and a full head of stiff brown hair.

Is that a *wig*? Ida thought.

CHAPTER TWENTY

"Sit down, young lady, sit down and rest," Mrs. Schiff said. "You look tired. You've never been in New York before? You did very well to come here by the subway yourself and to find this place. I'll bring you a glass of tea. And have some dried figs and almonds."

She pointed to a red-tinted, blown glass bowl on a low coffee table and left the room. Ida's eyes swept about the room while she listened to Mrs. Schiff bustling about the kitchen. From the soft, overstuffed couch on which she sat, Ida looked at the heavy, brown drapes that covered the windows, and at a sideboard on which was placed a brass tray with two sets of brass Sabbath candlesticks. Framed pictures on the walls were enlarged photographs of bearded rabbis in black frock coats. They wore strange-looking hats, some that were shiny black and without brims that were worn on the back of the head; some large and flat with luxurious fur trim. In some of the pictures serious-faced women had high, stiff hairdos. Wigs also, Ida thought. Do all Jewish women wear wigs? Cecile Berkowitz doesn't. Would *I* have to wear a wig?

"Oh, you've never had tea in a glass before? The tea is hot. Hold the glass by the top and bottom rim like this." The rabbi's wife showed Ida how. "And here is a lump of sugar," she said, pointing to a bowl with the little white cubes in it.

Ida stood up when Rabbi Schiff walked into the room. He was a short man with a little beard. He was wearing a yarmulke on his head and soft, cloth slippers on his feet. "Sit, sit, Mrs. Berkowitz, finish your tea. And please, let me call you 'Ida.'" Ida blushed but she felt the comfort of the man's warmth. He reminded her a little bit of her new father-in-law, though he spoke without an accent.

"I understand your husband was a 'yeshiva bachur,' a Hebrew school student. I'm sure he'll be able to fill you in on a lot of details about the Jewish religion. But first, when you're finished with your tea, we'll talk about the history of the Jewish people."

The rabbi led Ida into his study, a room with a large wooden desk and shelves from floor to ceiling filled with books.

"Those tall books over there," the rabbi said, pointing to a shelf of folio-sized volumes with cracked leather bindings, "are the Talmud. My father brought them over here from Lithuania when he came here in 1906. You see, I'm already telling you some history. A very important part of Jewish history. The Jews always took their books with them whenever they could. Maybe you've heard the expression before, 'people of the book.' The Jews are 'people of the book.'"

The rabbi then skipped around in his telling of the story of the Jews, a little bit of the Jews of the Bible, of the Jews' revolt against the Seleucid Greeks and against the Romans, of the European Jews in the Holocaust and of the State of Israel. The hour went by swiftly. Ida imagined Jack's ancestors fleeing the Crusaders in Germany and settling in Poland; she pictured Jack's father and the rabbi's father leaving Europe, going down into the holds of steamships and crossing the stormy Atlantic.

"And next week, Ida, next week we'll study how to make the blessings over the Shabbos candles. Then later how to keep a Kosher home."

When she came home Ida recounted the details of her adventure on the "E" train and of the meeting with Rabbi Schiff and his wife.

"Why did that sweet lady wear a wig? And all the women in those old photographs wore wigs, too."

"With real Orthodox Jews," Jack explained, "it's a sign of modesty for married women to wear them. I don't see that you would ever want to, and I certainly wouldn't expect you to wear one of those things."

"You can never tell, Jack. I might surprise you," and she poked him in the ribs and laughed. Jack smiled and danced Ida around the room in a little waltz. He didn't tell her about his encounter with Rabbi Friml.

Ida made the trip to the Bronx once a week for nearly two months. She was pregnant and getting bigger all the time, but she persisted. She was learning something of Jewish prayers, and holidays. She came to this conclusion: "You know, Jack, the Jewish religion is just like the Navajo religion. You don't need priests or sacraments; you can pray directly to God." At the same time, on Friday afternoons on Washington Heights, Cecile Berkowitz was giving Ida lessons in Jewish cooking.

"The first thing you do with a brisket," Cecile explained as she was preparing the meat, "is to 'kasher' it. That means to make it Kosher. Any meat must be prepared this way, to remove the blood. First the meat, or even chicken, is soaked in plain water for forty-five minutes, the blood is washed off, and then it is placed on a wooden drain board. The meat is then sprinkled with coarse salt and this draws out more of the blood."

"It sounds complicated," Ida said.

"Just go through the steps with me. You'll find it easy to remember once you've done it even one time," and they did it together.

"The next thing you do with the brisket, once you've washed off the salt and the blood, is to brown the meat on all sides, put it in a covered pot with a little water and one quartered onion and cook it for two hours. Then you take it out on a board and slice the whole meat. Then you put it back in the pot, add tomato juice and lima beans, and cook on a low flame for two more hours."

"So that's how you did it that Friday night when I first came here. It was so good I'll never forget it."

Rabbi Schiff found Ida an enthusiastic student as well.

" I think you're ready now, Ida. Let me make arrangements for the final ceremony. According to Jewish law, the person being converted must step into the 'mikvah,' or ritual pool. This symbolizes the process of purification."

You mean like baptism? Ida thought. But she didn't ask or use the word. It sounded too Christian.

"I couldn't believe them when they told me I had to go into that pool *naked*!" Ida told Jack later. "All I had on was a white sheet over my shoulders. There were these three young rabbis with black, curly beards looking at me. I suppose there had to be witnesses. I nearly died when I stepped into the water and started down the steps. By the time I was in the water up to my neck, the sheet I was wearing floated on the surface and covered me. I was so glad those holy men didn't see my brown ass!"

CHAPTER TWENTY-ONE

Yanabah was the first Navajo infant born at the New York Lying-In Hospital. A brass plaque mounted to the right of the main entrance announced the founding of the hospital in 1771. In the nursery Yanabah's full head of black hair stood out among paler, pinker, balder heads. And Yanabah inherited her mother's "Mongolian spot," that purplish pigment on her back, a feature not seen on any of the other infants.

Jack's professor and mentor, Dr. McDivitt, honored Ida with bouquets of flowers and saw to it that Ida and the new infant would have a room in the VIP suite. Jack handed out cigars and brought his parents down from Washington Heights to welcome their new granddaughter. Cecile stepped into the doorway of the hospital room and then stopped. Ida noticed a change in Cecile's face, a lessening of firmness around the mouth and a new brightness in the older woman's eyes.

"Oh, what a beauty! What a perfect face! What a perfect baby!" Cecile cried, and with this she advanced quickly with her arms stretched forward. "Let me pick her up. Let me hold her."

"Please, not yet," and with an instinctive movement Ida turned away, toward the window, shielding the baby from her mother-in-law. Ida's face turned pale and she trembled that her response had been so swift. Slowly, she composed herself and settled back to the position she'd had before.

"Yanabah's just finished nursing and I'd like her to rest for a while," she said.

Cecile came up to the bedside and studied the baby more closely, noting the richness of the infant's color and the thickness of her hair.

"You know," she said turning to Ida, "She looks more like *your* people. Can I hold her now?" Ida handed the baby to Cecile, and the grandmother felt the weight of her granddaughter in her arms.

CHAPTER TWENTY-TWO

On one of those rare days in October in New York when the air pricked the skin with its freshness, when the sky was as blue as she'd remembered it in Arizona, Ida set out for the Plaza. She pushed the stroller with four month old Yanabah west along East Seventieth Street. She hurried to get past First, Second, and Third Avenues, broad north-south thoroughfares of the old part of the city that were lined with five-story tenements lined shoulder to shoulder. Launderettes, fruit-and-vegetable stands, hardware stores, butcher shops, barber shops, grocery stores, bars, and fish and seafood stores with their near-spoiled smells all lined the sidewalks at street level. Paper and litter were everywhere. She had to get past all this.

Ida's mood brightened as she approached and crossed Lexington and then Madison Avenues. Young trees were planted in openings in the concrete sidewalk near the curb. The shops were more genteel: boutiques, art galleries, fur salons, and little restaurants where the tables were covered with white tablecloths on which there were vases with real flowers in them. At last she came to Fifth Avenue and to the open air of Central Park. She took a deep breath. The smell was of freshly-fallen leaves beginning to dry in the sun. She looked out across the open lawns, still green, and to the trees, brilliant yellow against her blue sky of the West.

Ida hurried south along the park side of Fifth Avenue. She came to the entrance of the Central Park Zoo with its crowds of mothers and nannies, and children and babies, and strollers and carriages. She felt less alone. But she would not go into the zoo this day. She looked across the southeast corner of Central Park to the rounded corners and the light green, weathered copper trim of the Mansard roof of the Plaza Hotel. To the west, the Essex House sign marked the line of hotels and apartment houses of Central Park South. Ida crossed Fifty-ninth Street and reached the Park Plaza at last. In the center of the Plaza, its great stone fountain splashed in the sun. A gentle breeze from the north blew some of the spray onto the granite blocks of the Plaza pavement. The same breeze wafted the odor of horses and horse droppings to Ida's nostrils. Ida hadn't seen horses since she'd left Arizona, but there they were, lined up between the shafts of their open carriages, waiting on the south side of the Park with their liveried footmen. She wished Yanabah was old enough so she could teach the girl the name for horses in Navajo. She leaned down and whispered the name in the baby's ear anyway: "H'leenh!"

Ida allowed the wave of nostalgia to pass. She cast one last look at the magnificent front entrance of the Plaza. She wondered who were those magnificent people climbing the steps up to that magnificent portal, under that magnificent glass awning, ushered in by those magnificent doormen in those magnificent uniforms. Ida then wheeled the stroller with precious Yanabah to the south and headed down Fifth Avenue to those great palaces: Bergdorff-Goodman, Bonwit-Teller, and Lord and Taylor.

It was ten thirty-five in the morning. Ida had just crossed Fifty-fifth Street when, with flashing lights and wailing sirens, an ambulance careened around the corner. Loudspeakers from police cars boomed out warnings for everyone to stay away, to stand back. Fifty-fifth Street was cordoned off. Ida felt the terror, the tension in the air. She half-heard rumors she did not fully understand. She wheeled the stroller around and set out as fast as possible for home. She half-ran the five miles she had walked so joyously earlier, paying no attention to the fashionable boutiques on Madison Avenue or the squalor of the stores on Third, Second, and First Avenues.

Over the radio she learned that someone important had been shot just down the street from where she and the baby had been, and at the very same time she had been there. The terror of what might have been grew in her mind as further details emerged.

"You must promise me that we'll get out of this city as soon as possible," she pleaded with Jack as he walked in the door, and she told him of her close brush with disaster. "You've got to take us back to Albuquerque as you promised, as soon as your year is up."

Details of the shooting came to light in the next morning's paper. An infamous Mafia gangster, Albert Anastasia, had been shot in the head while he was getting a haircut in the Sheraton Hotel barber shop at Seventh Avenue and Fifty-fifth Street.

CHAPTER TWENTY-THREE

⬿

In March Jack opened the door to the apartment and pre-sented Ida with a bunch of fresh daffodils wrapped in green paper.

"Gosh, they're pretty. What's this all about?" Ida asked.

"Wonderful news. We're going to Denver."

"Denver! I thought we were going to live in Albuquerque."

"The trouble is that Albuquerque doesn't have a medical school. The job Dr. McDivitt lined up for me at Denver General Hospital has a connection with the University of Colorado School of Medicine. It will give me the chance to continue the kind of work I've been doing with the new drug treatments for tuberculosis."

"But that's not what you promised. You promised that after a year we would move back to Albuquerque. Now you've changed your mind. You didn't even come to tell me what was on your mind, about taking a job in Colorado. Denver is just too far from home," and tears filled her eyes.

"Denver is only six hundred miles from the Reservation," Jack said.

"Six hundred miles! How can I get home and back as often as I want when it's six hundred miles away?"

"Well, you can see your folks at least two or three times a year."

"That's not enough. And it's not what you promised. It's like lying. It's like when you lied to me about your mother and father not coming to our wedding."

"I didn't lie to you. I just didn't tell you at the time so I wouldn't hurt your feelings."

"That's just like you. Weaseling around. Not coming out with the truth right away. Now you're doing the same thing. 'Jack is for Jack.' Everything you do is for yourself and you don't have the guts to come out with it." With this, Ida reached into the crib, gathered up Yanabah, headed for the bedroom, and slammed the door.

"Look, Ida," Jack said with his face up against the closed door. "I said we would stay in New York for just one year, and we *are* leaving. At least we're getting out of this place. And I need to do the kind of work I need to do. I'm not saying that what comes out of my work will save the world, but it *is* important. And you can help me by being with me."

There was no answer from the other side of the door for a long time. When Ida did come out, carrying the baby, she showed no emotion.

"My vacation's coming soon," Jack went on. "Let's take the train out to Denver. You know it's a pretty city, so near the mountains. There we can look for a place to stay and I can look over the job firsthand. From there we can go on to Gallup. We can visit your folks and show them the baby."

Ida did not look at Jack but held the baby at arm's length and said to her, "Beh g'el *chee*, Beh g'el *chee*. Red Lake. Say that!"

Jack took the job at Denver General Hospital on their visit to Denver. That settled, they boarded a night train south to the junction at La Junta, Colorado, and there made the connection with the main line train of the Santa Fe from Chicago.

"Those mesas look like home," Ida said as the train climbed toward Glorieta Pass in New Mexico the next morning. The tops were covered with snow and they glowed pink in the slanting sunlight.

116

"You see, you're in the West again, getting closer to home," Jack said, smiling.

At Red Lake, Ida's mother held the baby, and examined Yanabah's round Navajo face, light complexion and brown hair.

"At'ed Pahe!" she exclaimed.

"What does that mean?" Jack asked.

"It means 'Tan Girl.' Just a nickname. Navajos have nicknames for everybody."

"That cabin over there is for you," Mr. Bird said to Jack, pointing to a square cabin of heavy, trimmed timber. It had one room, a door that faced east, and one window that faced north. A gnarled juniper tree that had hung on miraculously in the hard-packed, rocky earth provided decoration in the front. The room had a linoleum-covered floor, a made-up bed, a washstand, chair, and a large, new, square, brown-enameled woodstove.

"We'll have to go to Gallup tomorrow for a crib and a playpen," Ida said. When they had inspected the cabin and moved in their suitcases and the baby's things, Jack and Ida were called to dinner. The meal, the savory roasted ribs of a sheep slaughtered that morning, with flour tortillas, was prepared in the separate kitchen shed nearby and then served outside on a table under another twisted juniper.

"That's a beautiful little girl," Ida's sister, Nellie, said. She'd come over to visit the new arrivals and brought over her own family, three boys, aged ten, six, and four, and a two year old girl. "I'm really happy to see you back. How long will you stay?"

"We're just here for a short visit this time. We have to go back to New York for Jack to finish his time there. Then we'll move to Denver. It's not as close as Albuquerque, but I have to admit the mountains make it a beautiful place. We'll be back for a longer visit in the summer."

They settled in Denver in a two-bedroom garden apartment that faced a park and a set of tennis courts to the east. "This isn't bad, Jack said. "At least you can see some green and the sky." Ida, always with thoughts of the West, looked to the mountains. Every day when she hung out the wash she could see the mountains of the Front Range of the Rockies, snow-capped most of the year. She learned the names of the highest peaks: Long's Peak to the north, Mount Evans due west, and the famous Pike's Peak to the south. But this didn't satisfy her.

"Remember your promise, Jack. You said we could drive to Red Lake. When can we go?"

With Jack's first weekend off, Ida prepared a picnic of fried chicken to eat on the way, packed the car, and loaded Yanabah in the back seat. With the top down on a mild summer afternoon, she drove through the tall, wrought-iron gate that surrounded the cluster of red brick buildings of the old Denver General Hospital.

"Who's the beautiful girl in that convertible down there?" asked one of the nurses who'd been standing next to Jack looking down from a window on the third floor.

"That's my wife. And that's our baby down there," Jack said, his heart full.

Jack shared with Ida the joy of driving in the soft air on the mildest afternoon. The air cooled as they drove up into the green of the mountains, across the sweep of South Park, and then to the valley of the Arkansas River. The next morning the sun fell across the granite face of the President Range. As they lifted their eyes to those soaring peaks, so rose Jack's and Ida's spirits, less than a day now from home. Down across the San Luis Valley into New Mexico, Taos, Santa Fe, and Albuquerque swept by. West again into browner country, to Gallup, Window Rock, Fort Defiance, and, with gathering excitement, they drove into the valley of Red Lake.

"I want to stay," Ida said when they got there. "At least for two or three weeks. The last visit, when we had to rush back to New York, was much too short. I'm always lonesome when I'm away from here."

Jack knew this was coming. After all, he'd promised once they got to the West, Ida could visit as often and as long as she liked. This was one promise he *could* keep.

"O.K. You keep the car. You'll need it in case the baby gets sick and you have to take her to the hospital at Fort Defiance. I'll fly back to Denver and I'll come back down in a few weeks. Call me if you need me sooner."

And with that it was decided, not only for that first summer in the West, but for every summer, for the rest of their lives, no matter where they were to live, that Ida would spend her summers overlooking the valley, the cliffs and the mountains at Red Lake.

CHAPTER TWENTY-FOUR

In the garden apartment in Denver next door to the one where Jack and Ida lived, the toddler, Yanabah, had found a friend. He was John Trout, an Air Force pilot from nearby Lowry Field, who was recovering from the near-fatal crash of his jet a few months earlier. He was a bachelor, soft-spoken, and especially fond of Yanabah, who wandered frequently through his open door. Ida learned, when John's sister, Ruth, and her husband, Dick, came to visit, that John, though apparently recovering well from his injuries, was actually seriously ill. The cause of the crash was human error. John had a brain tumor. The tumor had impaired his ability to judge speed and distance.

"Will he die from that?" Ida asked Jack when she'd heard the news.

"It depends. If it's a malignant tumor he will die in less than a year," Jack replied.

The Hubners, Ruth and Dick, were from Milwaukee, open and friendly, absorbing Yanabah and Ida into their circle. Yanabah kept their spirits up while they waited for the results of John's brain surgery.

"Ride a cock horse
To Banberry Cross,
To see a fine lady

Upon a white horse," they would cue, and little Yanabah would respond,

"With rings on her *figgins*
And bells on her toes
She shall have *muggit*
Wherever she goes."

The news from surgery was bad. The tumor was malignant. The Hubners prepared to take John back with them, to Milwaukee and to the Veterans' Hospital there.

"Promise you will stay with us if you ever come to Milwaukee," Ruth said. It was the usual thing to say at parting. But to Ida, the bond that had formed with her new friends was very real. The cement of the bond was the sadness over the loss of a brother.

"Yes, we promise," Ida said.

After two years in Denver, with Ida home on the Reservation every summer, Jack's number came up in the doctor draft. The Cold War was on. Khruschev had ordered the blockade of Berlin. All physicians had a military service obligation.

"It won't be so bad," Jack said. "I think I might be able to arrange an assignment at Fitzsimmons Army Hospital. Fitzsimmons is a big army tuberculosis research center. I'll be able to continue my work and we won't even have to move."

But when the orders were cut, Jack's assignment was not to be at Fitzsimmons. He was going to Texas, to San Antonio, to the Brooke Army Medical Center.

"I'm not going," Ida said.

"What do you mean, you're 'not going'?"

"I'm not going. It's so hot down there I'll die. I finally made my peace with the idea of living in Denver even though it wasn't Albuquerque. And now you're thinking of dragging us further away? I'm not going."

"Yes you *are* going. You're my wife and you're going. And why do you keep on bringing up that same subject over and over: 'Albuquerque,' 'Albuquerque.' It's not my fault that I've been drafted and that we must go to Texas."

Ida bit her lip and started to look around the room, beginning an accounting in her mind of what they must take with them and what they must leave behind

Sadly, as if in slow motion, they vacated the apartment they'd lived in for two years and shipped the furniture to San Antonio. Ida took Yanabah and Alice, the new baby born the previous October, to the Reservation for the summer. Jack would call for them later when he completed basic training for medical officers.

CHAPTER TWENTY-FIVE

In September, Jack Berkowitz, Captain, U.S. Army Medical Corps, Reserve, began his tour of duty. He was Chief of the Infectious Disease Division, Medical Service, Brooke General Hospital, at the Brooke Army Medical Center, Fort Sam Houston, Texas. Ida, now with two little girls, Yanabah and Alice, joined him.

"Look at this letter that just came in the mail," Ida said. "We're here a week and they're on top of us already. They don't give us a minute to breathe." She handed the envelope to Jack.

"It's from the hospital, 'Department of Medicine,' but it's handwritten, 'Mrs. Adeline Sharpe,'" he read. "Colonel Sharpe is my chief so that must be his wife."

"Listen to what it says. It's the last part that really gets me," and Ida read the letter:

"'Dear Mrs. Berkowitz. You are invited to a luncheon to welcome wives of the newly-arrived medical officers at the Fort Sam Houston Officers' Club, Tuesday, October fifth at eleven-thirty A.M. If you are unable to attend, you must submit a letter of explanation in writing.'"

"Well, Ida, you'll just have to go. This is the Army, you know."

The Fort Sam Houston Officers' Club stood back from the broad parade grounds, with a well-tended lawn and a shaded porch which gave promise of a comfortably cool interior. A rambling, one-story building with a shake-shingle, ranch style roof, it was the first to be air-conditioned against the Texas summer heat.

Mrs. Sharpe, a stern-faced woman of fifty with short-cropped gray hair, waited in the Club lobby with Georgia Evers, wife of Lt. Colonel Walter Evers, Chief of Gastroenterology. Both ladies wore suits of subdued gray or tan, little, dark-colored straw hats, stockings, high heels, and white gloves. Mrs. Evers, taller, younger, in her late thirties, wore her long blond hair in a bun which projected behind the brim of her hat.

Ida had just come in from the bright light and she hesitated a while getting used to the dimness inside. She had confidence that she had dressed properly for the occasion. Her flowered print dress fit perfectly; her shoes, hat and purse were just the right color.

Those ladies over there must be the welcoming committee, she thought. She could see now how they were dressed. Just a little tacky, she said to herself.

"How do you do? I'm Georgia Evers," Georgia said. "You must be Ida Berkowitz. Welcome to the first luncheon meeting of the Medical Wives for the season. Come with me and I'll introduce you to Mrs. Sharpe. Then we'll go inside and meet the others."

Ida remembered to do the right thing. She took the glove off her right hand and shook Georgia's. As the wife of a division chief, Ida was asked to sit at the head table. Wives of the other captains, regular army medical officers who'd also just started at Brooke in Internal Medicine, most of them in their early thirties, sat at the smaller tables.

"What a day it was today, Jack," she told him later. There I was at the head table and I thought, 'What am I doing here? I'm just a sheepherder.' I bet all the other captains' wives must have been jealous of me."

"They *were* jealous of you, Ida," Jack said with a smile. "Not because you sat at the head table but because you're beautiful." With that Ida came over to him and kissed him.

The evening dinner dances at the Officers' Club were more exciting to Ida.

"I'll have to buy a set of dress blues," Jack said. "They don't give us a uniform allowance for that so it will have to come out of our own pockets."

"How much will it cost?"

"A hundred and fifty dollars."

"A hundred and fifty dollars! You're a reserve officer and you'll only be in for two years. How many times will you ever get to wear it, two or three times?"

"It's just one of the things I'll have to do, Ida."

On the evening of the first dance, Jack dressed in his new uniform.

"It's like the Army uniforms you see in movies of the Civil War," Ida said. The dark blue of the military blouse was set off with the brightest brass buttons. The insignia of rank, twin bars in Jack's case, were set off on curved boards on either shoulder.

"You would have worn a uniform like that if you were out in the West fighting the Indians," Ida said, laughing. She liked the color of the lighter blue trousers with the wide yellow stripe down the outside seam. And she liked the deep red band of the military cap on which the officers' shining eagle crest perched so smartly over the black leather visor.

"You are very handsome, Captain Berkowitz!" Ida said. "Almost as handsome as Colonel Sharpe," and she laughed again.

Yes, Jack thought. I have to admit Robert Sharpe *is* a handsome fellow. But more than that, he has that genuine Southern charm. Jack remembered walking into the Colonel's office for the first time to meet him.

"We're awfully glad to have you here, Doctor Berkowitz," Sharpe said, coming forward from behind his desk to shake Jack's hand. "I've read some of the work you've done with Dr. McDivitt's group on the treatment of patients with streptomycin-resistant tuberculosis," he said. "We don't have a lot of chronic tuberculosis at this hospital but we do have many cases of acute infectious lung disease, especially in young soldiers. With your knowledge of lung disease, I'm sure you'll be able to make a contribution here, too."

He's a doctor, treating me like another doctor. I like that, Jack thought. Jack looked about the room. There was Sharpe's academic pedigree, the diploma from the University of Mississippi. There was a black and white photograph of the football squad of which he'd been a member. He had the same kind face now, the same slender build. Jack couldn't help liking the man.

"He reminds me of Leslie Howard," Ida reported after she'd met him. The doctors' wives had been led on a tour of the hospital. "I loved Leslie Howard, that beautiful man, when I saw 'Gone With the Wind.' Colonel Sharpe is just like that. Remember I told you I saw 'Gone With the Wind' at the Kimo Theater on Central Avenue when we used to be taken there as a group from the Albuquerque Indian School."

"I'm glad you liked the Colonel because I liked him, too. The genuine article. But don't go overboard. Remember who you're married to."

By the end of October, especially in the evenings, the air in San Antonio had moderated to a delightful, dry coolness. Jack and Ida walked up to the entrance of the Officers' Club for the evening dinner-dance at the prescribed hour of eight o'clock. Ida wore a knee-length dress of pink chiffon that swished softly as she walked. She put her hair up in a bun held in place with a high, Spanish tortoise-shell comb, trained two wisps of hair in front of her ears as spit curls, and placed a scarlet rose over her left ear. And she placed drops of Chanel No. 5 perfume on her neck and wrists.

The Colonel in his dress blues, with the embroidered silver eagles of his rank on his shoulder boards, stood in the entryway of the club, Mrs. Sharpe at his side, welcoming the arriving guests.

"Doctor Berkowitz, and Ida, it gives us great pleasure to welcome you here this evening," he said, inclining his head ever so slightly, holding on to Ida's hand for an extra second.

"Yes it's a beautiful evening," Ida replied, lifting her face and looking up at him.

"It's a pleasure to meet you, Captain," Mrs. Sharpe said to Jack. I've met your wife on two occasions before. We hope you have a good tour here at Brooke." As she said this she gave Jack's hand a little tug to the side and looked over Jack's shoulder. The next couple to be greeted was waiting behind him.

"I didn't realize he was so *tall*," Ida said a little breathlessly as they walked into the ballroom. "Did you hear how he called me 'Ida' and said what a 'pleazhuh' it was to welcome us 'heyuh'?"

"Yeah," Jack said. "There's that real Southern charm for ya'. Gets 'em every time."

"I'm so glad you will be sitting next to us," Georgia Evers said, coming up to Jack and Ida, motioning for them to go toward the head table. "Ida, I'd like for you to meet my husband, Colonel Walter Evers," and she presented her husband, a slender, balding man in his late forties.

"I'm happy to meet you, Mrs. Berkowitz. Georgia tells me you're from Arizona, from the Navajo Reservation, is that right?"

"Yes, that's right. And this is my first time in Texas. But I notice there are no Indians in Texas. What happened to them?"

"I guess they got pushed out of East Texas by the Mexicans and the early white settlers. The Comanches went over to the West Texas plains and they made a lot of trouble there. But the Mexicans have some Indian blood in them," Evers said. "Now Oklahoma, that's where you have a lot of Indians. And they've got *oil*, lots of oil!"

Ida, showing a little color, pushed herself away and said nothing.

When the dinner ended, the tables were pushed back, the lights went down, and the music started. After the first waltz ended, Colonel Sharpe came over to Ida and extended his hand. He led her to the middle of the floor, faced her, and gave her the slightest gentlemanly bow. When the "Tennessee Waltz" began, he bent towards her, holding her waist at the length of his arm and led her with unerring grace across the floor. With "Moon River," he held her closer to himself. Other couples moved away, as if by prearranged signal, to give the Colonel and his new lady the middle of the floor. Some of the dancers simply walked slowly to the side of the room and stood and watched.

With the next waltz, Jack stood up and asked Adeline Sharpe to dance.

"Thank you, no," she said. "I have arthritis." Jack wondered a little if she objected to dancing with him because he was a Jew.

CHAPTER TWENTY-SIX

〜

Within a year after Jack and Ida arrived at Fort Sam Houston, Colonel Sharpe was promoted. The presentation ceremony for a promotion as important as elevation to the rank of General is always one of great excitement and joy, particularly when the officer is well-liked and respected. General Sharpe, with his usual grace and charm stood in the center of the room.

"I'm very happy for him," Ida said to Jack while they waited in line. "Aren't you?"

"Of course. There are certain people I've admired as my chiefs, like Gordon McKenzie in Denver, and Walsh McDivitt in New York. And now Robert Sharpe has his star. Yes, I'm very happy for him."

When Ida's turn came to offer her congratulations, the General held her hand in his and his eyes narrowed with a smile that lingered.

She's got him, Jack thought. Now she's got a *general* on her string.

Jack's work at the hospital, as his chief had predicted, led him to become familiar with a type of acute pneumonia in young soldiers that did not respond to penicillin and was called "atypical pneumonia."

"When we get back to Denver," he told Ida, "there is a new field I'd like to get into. I'd like to learn more about the agent or agents that cause this type of pneumonia and perhaps to find better ways of treating it."

"Whatever makes you happy," Ida said. "We've only got a few more months to go here in Texas."

Near the end of Jack's two years, he and Ida received an invitation to spend an evening with General and Mrs. Sharpe.

"What's up? What's this all about?" Ida asked.

"I don't know. It can't be anything bad. It may just be a way of being especially sociable since we'll be leaving soon."

The Sharpeses lived in an imposing mansion in an old section of Officers' Row that had been set aside for generals and other commanders of high rank. Although it only had two stories, the Victorian building looked much taller, the vertical rise of the house due to the high ceilings of the rooms within, a means of keeping a house cool in hot climates. The exterior of the building was graced with a steeply pitched Mansard roof and with ornate mullions and cornices.

The last of the fading light of the summer evening gave way to the twinkling light of fireflies. A mockingbird began what was to be his night-long song. The air was damp but it was beginning to cool. The General, now out of uniform, in an open-necked, green, knit sport shirt and tan slacks, set out reclining chairs on the lawn. He offered Jack and Ida drinks in tall, frosted glasses.

"Jack," he began, "You've done very well in your assignment as a reserve officer here at Brooke. I've heard nothing but good reports about your performance. I've invited you both here," he said, nodding to Ida, "to consider enlisting for a career in the regular Army Medical Corps." He looked at Jack now. "I can see a good future for you."

Jack remained quiet for a while, looking down into his glass. It was getting too dark now to show the faint blush he couldn't conceal. Jack was almost ready to accept General Sharpe's offer on the spot. He wanted so much to please "his" general. He knew this kind of support could be counted on for the rest of an army career. Jack wondered whether another reason was that the General did not want to let Ida out of his sight. When this last thought occurred to him he felt no jealousy, but he thought to glance in the direction of Mrs. Sharpe to see what her expression might be. Would there be a hint of sourness on her face? There was none. Adeline Sharpe had sat through countless recruiting pitches like this before. This was just routine. Her face was calm and supportive. She was a general's wife.

"Sir, I'm very flattered that you've made this offer. Ida and I will certainly give it a lot of thought."

Jack remembered his roots. What am I, a yeshiva boy, a graduate of the Talmudical Academy, doing here? I can see myself as a medical research scientist, a professor of medicine one day. But a medical officer in the regular army for the rest of my life?

A few days later, and before Jack and Ida had come to any decision or even given very much thought to an army career, Ida was invited to an eleven-thirty luncheon and card party at the Sharpe home. Ida rushed to bathe the two little girls, Yanabah, four, and Alice, two. She dressed them in summer cotton shorts and knit cotton sport shirts. She pulled on a white dress with large, printed roses, her nylon hose, her high-heeled, blue patent leather shoes and her light cotton gloves. She found the right straw hat, navy blue. She piled the children into the Chevrolet station wagon and drove them across the base to the Child Care Center. She rushed back to the station wagon and drove the short distance to the old Officer's Row. She would not be late.

Ida was the first to arrive. She parked the station wagon and walked up to the open front door. Card tables were set out in the tall-ceilinged living room, cool and dark beyond the foyer, but Mrs. Sharpe was nowhere in sight. Ida waited for a moment and then took a step or two into the foyer. It was quiet. Then, though she was not certain what it was at first, she heard a muffled sob. It was a girl's voice. Ida recognized it as Brenda's, the Sharpes' fifteen year old daughter. Then another, strident voice. It was Mrs. Sharpe.

"Why *aren't* you ready? I've told you to be presentable, you pimply-faced moron!"

Ida turned about as quickly as she could with her high heels, and on her tiptoes, stepped out of the foyer, out the door, and back down the walk to the station wagon. There she waited in the car for some of the other women to arrive.

That evening Ida told Jack the story.

"I don't think I can live in this kind of world. These people are *so* polite on the outside, but they are just mean, mean, mean on the inside. That poor little Brenda. It wasn't right. I know I wont be able to trust Mrs. Sharpe or any of those people again. Let's just get back to Denver as we planned."

"There's a complication I've been meaning to tell you about."

"What complication?"

"The University of Colorado no longer has its connection with Denver General Hospital."

"What difference does that make? Why can't you just go back to Denver General and forget the university connection?"

"I can't do that, Ida. I want to continue my research and teaching. I asked my division head if he could find a place for me at the Lung Research Institute, but he said he couldn't. I was very angry when I found out about it, but I didn't tell you at the time. He knew I'd done a good job at Denver General. Now I'm determined to look at some other offers I've had, and I've had two, one in Dallas and one in Milwaukee."

"Dallas! Milwaukee! How can you drag me and the children all over the country like that? Denver wasn't Albuquerque but at least it was in the West and not that far from home. But Dallas, Milwaukee! I won't *let* you take me so far from home any more."

"Look, Ida. Dallas has a really great medical school now. Mickey LeBlanc wrote to me last week and offered me a job as Assistant Professor of Medicine and head of the tuberculosis division."

"Who's Mickey LeBlanc?"

"Mickey was once Dr. McDivitt's Infectious Disease Fellow back in New York. Now he's Professor and Chairman of the Department of Medicine in Dallas. I remember him as a really great guy. He knows something of the work I've done on the Reservation. Let's just go up to Dallas and look at it while we're still close by. He made reservations for us at the Dallas Hilton. We can get a baby sitter for the kids and at least see something of the city. After all, we've been in Texas two years and have never been there. It'll be like a little second honeymoon."

"You can sweet-talk me into a nice trip, Jack, but I won't promise you anything."

CHAPTER TWENTY-SEVEN

~

North of San Antonio, Texas was green and pleasant in the early Spring morning. The farms around New Braunfels were perfectly tended. The newly plowed ground gave off its pleasant, rich odor and blossoming fruit orchards sprinkled the scene with color. In the morning sunlight one could pick out the farms at a distance because each had its own, tall, blue-enameled, AO Smith, glass-lined silo.

"This isn't like any part of Texas we've seen before," Ida remarked.

"Yes, it almost seems like the Middle West. German immigrants settled this part of the country in the nineteenth century and many people still speak German here."

The land became more forested and hilly as they drove north to San Marcos, green here with Texas live oak. Still further north the land became flat again, a little less green but rich with grazing cattle. They passed the famous landmark courthouse at Hillsborough and, later, signs pointing to a town called Waxahatchie.

"Ever hear a name like that before?" Jack asked. "I guess it's all part of Texas."

Beyond the broad valley of the Trinity River, skyscrapers rose into the sun, a great and vibrant city, with the gleaming, glass-fronted hotel at its center.

"This is luxury," Ida said as she threw herself backward onto one of the two queen-sized beds in the hotel room. "But let's not stay in here. Let's get out and see the town. Let's go to Nieman-Marcus."

They followed the directions given by the hotel clerk and found the original Nieman-Marcus store. It was still housed in an old, three-story commercial building, but the elegance displayed inside, the clothing, the furniture, the jewelry, gave evidence of what was said to Texans, "The very best is right here in Texas." That is when Ida got her first Nieman-Marcus credit card.

The next day Jack was taken on a tour of the old tuberculosis hospital where his work was to be.

"It's really a pretty sad, old, red brick pile," Jack said to Ida after he'd seen it. "They used to put patients outdoors on balconies for what they thought was a 'fresh air cure'. What's sad about it is that the 'cure' didn't work. A lot of people in the old days just lingered and died."

"Then why would you want to work in a place like that? It sounds so depressing."

"The place you work at isn't as important as the chance you get there to do really important work. It's the work that keeps your spirits up."

"I'm not sure I'll be able to keep *my* spirits up in a place like Dallas. Downtown Dallas was fun yesterday, but that's not what daily life here will be all about."

That evening Dr. LeBlanc took personal charge of the recruitment effort. They were to come to his home that evening. The LeBlancs lived in a collonnaded, plantation-style mansion in the old, but still prestigious, university section of Dallas. Sheila LeBlanc was an open-faced, friendly Midwestern girl, with short honey-brown hair and kindly gray eyes and only in her middle-thirties. Jack was pleased to see how quickly Sheila took Ida under her wing. He knew that Sheila did this not because she was the professor's wife, but because she was a genuine and kind person and Ida appealed to her.

Jack was giving serious thought now to accepting this job offer. Southwestern University Medical School had attracted many brilliant faculty members from all over the country. Texas is mainstream United States now, Jack thought. I'm ready to discard any prejudice I might have about living in the South or in Texas.

Back at the hotel Jack lost no time in getting to the heart of the matter. "Well, Ida, what do you think? I'm beginning to get warm about taking this job."

"You may feel warm about this place but I tell you it gives me a chill."

"What do you mean? You couldn't ask for nicer people than the LeBlancs. Sheila just about took you in as her sister."

"Look, Jack, Sheila or no Sheila, I just couldn't live in the South. Margie Ketso had a terrible time down here."

"Who's Margie Ketso?"

"You should remember her. She's a Navajo girl from Fort Defiance. She's kind of dark and she wears glasses. When she perms her hair it really gets kinky. She agreed to go down to Houston with Dr. Johnson's family to baby-sit for his kids when they left Fort Defiance. She made a contract for a year but she nearly died before the year was up. Everybody down there thought she was black. When she went downtown on her afternoon off they made her sit in the back of the bus. Navajos aren't used to being treated like that. To a Navajo every other person is a human being, one who has five fingers."

"But things aren't like that now," Jack said.

"Yes, they are. I've seen it. Didn't you see the mean looks on those white people when they were in their cars at the intersection? They were looking at the black people on the corner waiting for the bus like they were lower than dirt. No, Jack, I couldn't live down here."

It was with some sadness that Jack thanked Mickey LeBlanc for his kindness. He hoped Sheila would understand. Sheila had been transplanted to Texas herself.

At the end of Jack's army tour at Fort Sam Houston, Ida, breathing easier, helped load the kids into the station wagon. There was a job waiting for them in Milwaukee.

"You know I'm still angry that you won't consider going back to Denver. What do you need the University for?" she asked, though she had asked the same question before.

"You can't do research without a close connection with a university. There is a promising new drug for tuberculosis that just came out last year. But that drug may have some serious side effects. That and any new drug must be looked at carefully. In the end, that drug may help a lot of people. And then there's the research I want to do on atypical pneumonia."

"Research, research!" Ida said, her voice rising and tears beginning to form. "You should do some research to find out what will help your wife!" There was a long pause. Finally she said, "You know the only reason I consented to go to Milwaukee is because the Hubners are there. John Trout died last year and I know how his sister feels. I haven't gotten over Richard's death either. At least in Milwaukee, Ruth and I can be of some comfort to each other for a while. But remember, I want us back out of there in two years."

Milwaukee was even farther away from home than Dallas but at least it wasn't the South. They drove out of Texas in a summer rain and pointed the car north over the Oklahoma border.

CHAPTER TWENTY-EIGHT

＊

Four years later Jack Berkowitz was Assistant Professor of Medicine at Marquette Medical School in Milwaukee continuing research in new methods of treatment of tuberculosis. He also found a colleague, David Lipsky, who collaborated with him on new research on atypical pneumonia.

Ida was matron in a two-story brick colonial house built in the 1930s on an elm tree-lined street in a still-pleasant neighborhood, though not near the fashionable lake front. They had chosen that neighborhood because they had two girls, Yanabah and Alice, at the Hillel Academy Hebrew School just two blocks away. They had one small girl, Rose Rachel, who had been conceived in Texas and another baby on the way.

"Why must you join so *many* Jewish organizations," Jack asked Ida when he found that in addition to the Hillel Academy P.T.A., she had joined Hadassah (General Zionist), Pioneer Women (Labor Zionist) and Mizrachi Women (Religious Zionist).

"Jack, I find these Jewish women so different from the ones in New York. Many of them have such fascinating and really terrible stories to tell, like the ones who've been in concentration camps. Did you know that they still have numbers tattooed on their arms? And they have such good food at those Kafe Klatches, you know, strudels, madelbroit, rogolach, and taiglach."

"Sounds delicious. Just don't let yourself get fat eating that stuff."

"You know I must have made a terrible mistake the other day. I was at a Mizrachi Women's luncheon. When Mrs. Liebowitz, you know, the wife of our kosher butcher (she's one of those with a tattoo) set out a plate of almond macaroons that smelled so good, I was so excited, I called out, 'What wonderful chazerai!' You could hear a pin drop, the silence was so stunning. My face turned all colors of purple."

"Well now you know. 'Chazerai' is a word you use if the food set before you is treife, not kosher, made from pig meat. That's what you get for trying to be too Jewish all of a sudden."

"I'll be a little more careful next time," Ida promised. "But the women were very gentle and sweet with me."

Ida's fun and joy with Jewish organizations came to a sudden halt one day. Eight year-old Yanabah came home early from school, tears streaming down her face.

"Rabbi Schwachter at school made me cry."

"What did he say to you?"

"He said, 'Your father made a big sin when he married your mother.' What did he mean by that? I was so upset I just ran out of there."

Ida stormed back to Hillel Academy and confronted Rabbi Schwachter, a squat young man with a short, dark beard.

"What did you say to my daughter? I want to hear it from you! And what did you say about my husband? You know you hurt my beautiful, innocent child! Why did you do that? And who are you that *you* are so holy? You know you are on Indian land. You came over here and you stole this Indian land."

Ida took Yannabah out of the Jewish school that very day and enrolled her in the public school a few blocks away. It was a *fait accompli*. Nothing Jack could say to her would change her mind. She would not take Yannabah back to Hillel.

"You know, Ida, Jews have prejudices just like anybody else," Jack tried to explain. But Ida would hear nothing of this. The string had snapped. The spell was broken.

The fourth child was a boy. Jack's father and mother, who were now living in Houston because of the harshness of winters in New York, flew up for the "briss." Ida retained an attachment to a different rabbi, the kindly Chassidic Rabbi Tellman, and she was honored when that rabbi agreed to officiate at the circumcision. Unlike the young Rabbi Schwachter, the saintly Chassid had welcomed Ida to his congregation, his home, and his family.

On the dais where the circumcision was to take place, Jack touched the face of his eight day old son for the first time. How cool and sweaty, Jack thought. It's as if he knows he's about to enter the world of pain! Jack's throat swelled so that he could hardly speak, but he managed to announced the child's name to the world, "Joseph Benjamin Kee ben Yaakov."

The ladies from the Mizrachi Women provided honey cake and sponge cake, pickled herring and gefilte fish. Jack's parents provided the drinks, the Mogen David Concord grape wine and the scotch whiskey, Haig and Haig Pinch. Rabbi Ruel, the mohel, had been summoned to perform the circumcision.

"How much does Rabbi Ruel charge?" Ida had asked. One of the Mizrachi ladies who arranged these affairs answered, "The usual charge is one hundred-fifty dollars. But for 'shiksas' it will be more."

CHAPTER TWENTY-NINE

❧

Five years had now passed since the move to the Midwest. It was 1966. Ida had been making her annual summer trip to the Reservation. Jack would drive her and the children on the way out and then fly back to Milwaukee. He would busy himself in the laboratory until late in the evening, have a light supper out, and then return to the empty house.

What's that on the stairway? he asked himself one night when he saw a small object on the landing. It was a child's shoe, the little shoe of a young child. He felt his throat closing. It's all right. It's all right to be lonesome, he told himself, and he tumbled into bed.

For his annual summer vacation the last two weeks of August, Jack flew back to Arizona to be with the family, and they would drive back together over the Labor Day holiday.

"What's that cloud hanging over the city?" Ida asked as they came down out of the mountains on U.S. 285. Denver lay before them, the tops of its tall buildings blotted out.

"Smog," Jack answered.

"Smog! That's poisoned air! They're poisoning the air in Denver just like they did in New York City."

"You're right. It's pretty disappointing. It never was like this. It's probably from cars on the highways more than smoke-stack pollution."

"It's all the same. Whenever the white man gets his hands on anything he ruins it. Look what they've done to our beautiful Denver!"

"It may not be this bad all the time. It's probably just a temperature inversion, high pressure or something above trapping the air below."

"It doesn't matter. Bad air is bad air. And look how much the city has grown," Ida said pointing to several large tracts of new houses under construction on the road from the mountains. "The city's grown right up to the foothills." They remained silent for a while, stunned at the changes that had taken place on what they remembered as open, rolling, grass-covered hills. "And you know Jack, it's those real estate developers. Look at them gobbling up Indian land, getting rich on Indian land."

There was a new job waiting for Jack at the medical school in Milwaukee, a promotion of sorts, to assistant dean in charge of postgraduate medical education.

"That sounds pretty fancy," Ida said when she heard of the new appointment. "But how much longer are we now going to have to stay in Milwaukee?" That was always the question, How much longer must we stay so far away?

The answer came in less than a year. Jack found the routine of recruiting lecturers and the scheduling of conferences tedious. And he missed his contact with patients and with his research. Soon he heard from friends in Denver that the University of Colorado was now seeking to re-establish its connection with Denver General.

"It's beginning to sound exciting. There's a chance for us to get back to Denver," Jack announced. Ida threw her arms around his neck.

"Not so fast," he warned. "I'll have to find out more details. I don't want to make the mistake of taking on an administrative job that isn't for me. You know I get depressed when I'm away from patients."

"And you know *I* get depressed when I can't have you with me in the West."

A few weeks later Jack sat in the Denver living room of Dr. Gordon McKenzie, Professor and Chairman of the Department of Medicine. The warm glow of shaded lamps fell on oriental rugs in profusion, a camel saddle, and wall hangings from different parts of the world. Dr. McKenzie had played a major role in the World Health Organization's program to eradicate smallpox and in his development of a vaccine against influenza. His living room was a reflection of himself as a world citizen; to Jack he was a kindly, understanding, and generous mentor.

"How would you like to come back?" he asked.

"As what?"

"As Chief of Medicine at Denver General with the academic rank of Associate Professor."

On the telephone to Ida in Milwaukee Jack's voice rose with excitement. "Get ready, Ida. We have to be in Denver July first!"

CHAPTER THIRTY

The first summer the Berkowitzes returned to Denver, Ida and the children were back on the Reservation. The succession of days was Ida's delight, and she was especially reassured now that Red Lake was in easy reach once again. She breathed easily the thin, cool, morning air as she watched the sun come up over the sandstone cliffs across the valley. She savored the smell of burning wood in her mother's stove as the coffee brewed. She was again fluent in her native Navajo language and enjoyed the long conversations with her mother and her father.

Near ten o'clock on one such mid-August morning the sun bore down to heat the thin air at seven-thousand feet. She had allowed the children to sleep in late but it soon became too hot in the cabin. Yananbah, Alice, and Rose Rachel tumbled out of bed to seek some relief under the shade of the juniper tree.

"They won't have anything to do with us," Yanabah complained when her mother came out of the cooking shed. Joseph, following his mother, squinted in the sun as he kicked up dry dirt.

"Yeah, Mom, they never talk to us," Alice said. "They pretend they don't understand English but we know they do. We asked Junior and Roger to let us ride Speedy but they just galloped away and laughed at us."

"Well, you know they're just boys. And you're right. Of course they know English. They speak to *me* in English. They're on vacation, too, and they just want to have their own good time. They don't feel it's up to them to entertain you when we come down here. And besides, they're probably a little shy. So don't expect too much from them. They'll come over to you when they're ready."

Roy Junior was the oldest of all of Nellie's children. He was getting more muscular at sixteen. He was actually the shyest. Instead of saying anything, he would just crinkle up his eyes in a smile. He was beginning to be careful about his appearance. He was often at his grandmother's cabin borrowing her iron and ironing his cowboy shirts.

The next two boys, Roger and Alvin, Yanabah had to admit, did speak with the girls at times. Alvin even brought a baby goat one time and invited Rose Rachel to feed it. He showed her how to mix canned evaporated milk and water and how to hold the bottle with her fingers gripping the base of the nipple while the kid sucked.

Willie, the next boy after Alvin, avoided the girls altogether. He seemed angry all the time which scared the girls. He seemed never to have gotten over the time when he and Alice had had a scuffle when they were both about five, and when Alice threw a rock at him and hit him in the head.

"When Daddy gets here next weekend we'll go up to the Canyon de Chelly," Ida said, promising to give the girls a better time. "I'll show you Spring Canyon where Grandpa grew up."

When the weekend came the family piled into the car and drove north. The road took them up onto the ponderosa-covered Defiance Plateau where it was cool, then down across a sagebrush plain to the south rim of the Canyon de Chelly. Spring Canyon Overlook gave them a view of a narrow, box canyon which joined the main canyon from the south.

"From here you can see the little stone house where I remember visiting Grandpa's mother. Don't get so close to the edge now, Alice. There are still a few peach trees left in that little orchard over there. That's where we used to get our peaches in the fall."

Ida's voice trailed off here and Jack saw a look of sadness steal over her face.

"What's wrong?"

"You know I'm standing here trying to recreate the past," Ida said, "but there's something wrong here now."

"What is it?" Jack asked again.

"It's the sky. That's it. The sky isn't blue anymore. It should be bright blue on a sunny day like today but it isn't." She turned to the northeast. "That's it! It's coming from there." Jack followed her example and looked in that direction.

"It's coming from there," she said pointing at the sky to the north and east. "It's coming from those power plants in Farmington! It's pollution! They're polluting the air! And it's coming all the way over here. I never thought it would happen, here in the Southwest, here on the Reservation."

"You're right, Ida. I remember the sky was always blue on sunny days when I first came down here. In just a few years the air has changed."

"It's those greedy white men! First they strip-mine the land, rip up the piñon and juniper to get at the coal, then they burn it and poison the air!"

Jack drew her away from the canyon overlook. She was beginning to tremble. He thought of words to soothe her.

"You know I've heard they're trying to perfect scrubbers to reduce the pollution from those power plants. Maybe they'll be able to clean up the air in a few years."

"In a few years! They won't be in any hurry. Meanwhile they'll let the poor Indians choke. And Jack, it's not just the air they're poisoning. It's the water, too."

"How's that?" Jack asked.

"I heard from my friend Marian. She's working in the Tribal Office at Window Rock. They've been getting complaints from the Navajos who live below Black Mesa. The Navajos who live there say their sheep are dying. Since they started strip-mining up on the mesa the water that comes down from there is poisoning their sheep. The tribe sent out people to test the water and found there is too much acid in it. You see, the white man profits and the Indians get it in the neck."

"I can see you going into politics. You'll be Navajo Tribal Chairman one day."

"Don't joke. Just get me closer to the Reservation, to Albuquerque, like you promised."

CHAPTER THIRTY-ONE

❧

"C'mon kids, we're going to Gallup," Ida announced one day after Jack had gone back to Denver. Grandma needs some new shoes."

"Can we go swimming?" Alice asked.

"Can we go to a movie?" Yanabah asked.

"Can we get ice cream?" Rose Rachel asked.

"Can we take the kitten with us?" Joseph asked.

"I'll think about swimming, and movies, and ice cream, but no, Joseph, we can't take the kitten," Ida ruled.

They all piled into the station wagon with Grandma Bird in the back seat. If Ida took the dirt road north, past the Red Lake Chapter House and over to the new sawmill at Navajo, she could take the new, paved road to Fort Defiance. Instead she took the old road south for the twelve miles to the "Fort."

"This is the road your father used to take when he came up to Red Lake to take me out," Ida said turning to Yanabah. "Alvin was only four at the time. When he saw the blue convertible coming up the road, he used to run up to me as fast as he could and shout, 'It's the *doctor*! It's the *doctor*!' and I used to get so embarrassed."

"Aw, c'mon Ma, you used to love it," Yanabah said smiling, her eyes crinkling up in the corners.

"As *if*," Alice said. "As if you didn't *know* he was coming."

Grandma Bird, listening to this chatter though she didn't understand the words, smiled her broad smile.

Since the new road had been built across the valley, the old road was now hardly used. The road swept along the valley of the Black Creek Wash. One could almost see shallow water in the wash through the Russian olives and the cottonwoods. Some three miles south of the Bird place, the road climbed up out of the stream bottom and up a little hill where it ran through a clump of piñon trees. From there, framed by the trees, you could see clear across the valley to the line of the pink cliffs.

"Your father used to love this part of the road best of all," Ida said, slowing the car as it approached the blind spot at the top of the hill.

"Yeah," Alice said, "'The Royal Road to Romance.' I've heard him say that."

In spite of herself, Ida blushed. The kids saw the color in Ida's neck and laughed.

On the other side of the hill the road went down again to the level of the wash.

"Pretty soon we'll come to the place that always used to get flooded when the rains came. Water would come rushing down that gully on the right. We got stuck there one evening when your father was taking me into Gallup to meet some of his professor friends. I was all dressed up in a fresh blouse and a stiff skirt that I'd just ironed. It had a stiff petticoat that I ironed, too, to make the skirt flare out."

"Oh, I know what kind of a skirt that was," Yanabah said. "It was the kind they used to wear in the *fifties*," she giggled. "That's the kind of skirt girls used to wear with *bobby socks* and *saddle shoes*. Were you wearing bobby socks and saddle shoes then too?"

"Yes, I was," Ida said a little stiffly. How do these kids know all that stuff? she thought. "Well, anyway, I took off my bobby socks and my shoes and I got out and pushed."

They were passing that same low spot in the road, though now the road was baked and dry since there'd been no recent rain.

"You must have been strong, Mom, to push a car out when it was stuck in the mud," Rose Rachel said.

"Your father didn't believe I could do it. He said, 'You're crazy to try that.' I told him to start the engine and then get it into gear. He didn't know that all it takes is just one little push, so I gave it that push and the car went forward and out of the mud. I was embarrassed to get back into his nice clean car with my muddy feet. I also didn't want him to see how big my feet were. But he didn't seem to mind. I think he was proud of me. By the time we got to Gallup the mud on my feet had dried and caked off so I was able to put my socks and shoes back on again."

"Yeah, those *bobby* socks and those *saddle* shoes!" all the girls screamed out at once and laughed.

It was a bright summer Saturday, just around noon, the busiest of all times in Gallup. Navajos from all over the Reservation had arrived in cars and pickups. Ida pulled into the parking lot behind J.C. Penneys on Coal Avenue, a block south of U.S. Highway 66. Most of the pickups, having stopped at the supermarket first, were piled high with paper sacks full of groceries and cases of soda pop. Ida led her mother and the children into Penney's by the rear parking lot entrance, trying to get her little party in ahead of the crowd who were headed for the same entrance.

Once inside, they found the aisles of the store filled with Navajos wandering up and down between the racks of clothes and bins full of smaller items, socks, underwear, purses, and tennis shoes. Tennis shoes — that's what Grandma Bird had come to town for. She was still picking up and turning over different pairs of canvas shoes, low-quarter Keds and unnamed brands, when she whispered something to Ida in Navajo. Ida, who'd been bending over the bins helping her mother, stood up and looked about. She was looking for a clerk, and when she found one, she said, "My mother has to go to the bathroom. Can you tell me where the bathroom is?"

"We don't have a bathroom in the store," the clerk said.

"What do you mean, 'Don't have a bathroom'?" Ida's voice and her color rising together. "What do you expect people to do when they have to pee?" Yanabah and Alice came up quickly to their mother's side.

The clerk, a young Anglo woman with short hair, her uniform a red jacket with a J.C. Penney badge, replied in a tone lower than Ida's, "There is a bathroom," and then in a whisper, "But it's only for the staff. Your mother will have to go to the Chevron station on the corner."

"Do you mean she can't use the bathroom here? She's a customer here," Ida said in a still louder voice. "And the other Navajos are customers, too," she said with a sweeping gesture pointing to the large number of Navajos filling the store. "You mean you welcome all the Navajos to come here and shop," she said, her voice rising still higher, "You make your living taking money from the Navajos but you won't let them use the bathroom?"

The children came up closer to Ida and held on to her skirt. Yanabah began to pull her mother away, but Alice, tears beginning to form, stood firmly by her side.

"I want to talk to the manager," Ida demanded, and followed the clerk to the rear of the store. The manager, a middle-aged man with a little white mustache and wearing glasses said, "I'm sorry, Ma'am, it's company policy. We can't provide toilet facilities for everyone who comes in here. The city ought to provide for public toilets."

"*You're* the city," Ida flashed. "You make your money in this city. Why don't *you* do something about it? It's *your* responsibility as long as people come here to shop, for *you* to take care of your customers."

Ida wheeled about and called to her mother, "Ha *koh*, shi' mah." Grandma Bird stopped her browsing through the pairs of sneakers and came out of the store.

"They think we're dirty, don't they, Ma," Alice said with tears in her eyes.

"That's right. These dirty white people think *we're* dirty. Let's get out of here. And I know they won't let us use the bathroom at the Chevron station either unless we buy gas there. We'll go to Earls's café and have lunch. They treat us Navajos better. Where's Joseph? Yanabah, go back into the store and find him. He's forever wandering off, that little guy."

Grandma didn't get her sneakers in Gallup that day.

CHAPTER THIRTY-TWO

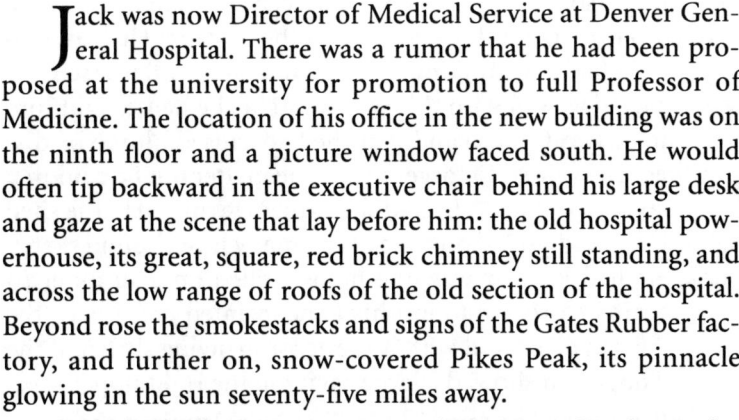

Jack was now Director of Medical Service at Denver General Hospital. There was a rumor that he had been proposed at the university for promotion to full Professor of Medicine. The location of his office in the new building was on the ninth floor and a picture window faced south. He would often tip backward in the executive chair behind his large desk and gaze at the scene that lay before him: the old hospital powerhouse, its great, square, red brick chimney still standing, and across the low range of roofs of the old section of the hospital. Beyond rose the smokestacks and signs of the Gates Rubber factory, and further on, snow-covered Pikes Peak, its pinnacle glowing in the sun seventy-five miles away.

"There's someone here to see you," announced Esther Mehr, Jack's secretary, interrupting his reverie. Mrs. Mehr was a soft-spoken, polite woman in her early fifties with graying hair and glasses. Jack looked up and saw a thin, dark-faced woman standing before him. She was one of those persons whose age it was not possible to guess; nevertheless, he had the impression from her face that she was quite old.

"I heard you were here," the woman said simply. "I just wanted to see you. I used to be one of your patients in Fort Defiance." To the puzzled expression on his face, she added, "I came to Denver, had surgery, and was cured here."

Jack remained silent. His face showed no sign he recognized her.

"I'm married now," she went on, "to a black man I met in the hospital. We have a child and we're living in Denver."

The woman grew silent. Jack could find no words to put her at ease. The face of the woman lacked mobility. If she felt sadness, her face did not show it. She gave Jack her maiden name but he did not recognize it. She waited a few moments for him to respond but he remained silent. Jack knew she was disappointed but little of it showed in her face.

"I just wanted to see you," she repeated. Then, drawing her coat around her straight, slender shoulders, she turned and walked out the door.

Jack was embarrassed that he failed so completely to recognize this person. He had been condescending. He hadn't even gotten up from behind his desk when she came in. He had been uncivil. He had been unkind. He was annoyed with himself. He was annoyed as well with this woman, that she had caught him so completely off-guard and that she had caused him to be discomfited. He wanted to forget the whole matter but he couldn't. Who was this person? Why had she come? He turned to the shelf behind him and pulled out one of the many little, bound sketch books he had kept. It was one he had filled on a summer so many years before. He found his hand-printed entry with the name she had given and with it the accompanying sketch of the X-ray. The sketch showed a large cavity in the right upper lobe.

"Ellen Bitsie!" he cried out loud as he recognized the name at last. That fresh, sad face, he thought, those quiet, slanted eyes, that soft gaze, that light-skinned forehead above the mask! How sad she is now, so drawn, so lifeless, so drained, so old!

Jack turned away from that sad moment. What more could he have done? He could have run out past the secretary, out into the hall. He could have caught up with her before she took the elevator down. He could have touched her hand as he never had, talked to her as he never had (she had been too shy), asked her about her child, her husband, her parents. He could have told her about his own life, about Ida, and about their four half-Navajo children. He could have told her that it was the sketch book that had brought back all the memories he had of her as a stoical, proud, beautiful girl of sixteen.

Pride, that's what it was all about. Had he used that poor girl, or had he used all of his Navajo patients, just to enhance his scientific reputation? Had he married a princess among the Navajo just to enhance his own vision of himself? Had all of his striving been so he could sit in his executive chair in his high perch and gaze down upon the city? Was it not pride that had stiffened him, blinded him to Ellen Bitsie? He turned away from this dark picture of himself. No, he had never used that girl. He had pitied her, admired her, loved her. And was it not love, or the memory of love, that led her so many years later to seek him out, to find him, to say simply that she "just wanted to see" him?

He had to get himself down off the ninth floor. The height had deceived him. He needed to feel himself in the proper relation to the ground, to the earth. He took the elevator down, avoiding eye-contact with any of the passengers. He rushed out through the ground floor lobby, past the emergency room doors, and out onto the street. He crossed the busy, one-way traffic on Speer Boulevard and on to the grassy, tree-lined strip along Cherry Creek. He could breathe easier now under the trees that each spring blew some white, some pink, some darker pink, the blossoms of pear, peach, and cherry. He cast a long look down and then up the shallow stream where the water moved sideways and then forward among the rocks, where the mallards raised their ducklings in the chill of March. Jack viewed in his mind the stream's sources on the high plains where the wheat farmers tried their luck against the drought, where before that the Kiowas rode against the buffalo. Then he pictured the stream in its downward course where it joined the South Platte, the river that flows north to Nebraska, then joins other waters to flow eastward as the Platte and then to the Missouri. The Indians were right. A man must be connected to the earth and to its waters that flow under the sky.

It was no longer right for him, he would no longer have joy sitting on his high perch on the ninth floor, behind the door whose sign announced him as "Director of Medical Service." That he might be promoted to full Professor of Medicine at the university no longer had meaning for him. For now he would walk more slowly, listen to people more intently, never let his mind wander when spoken to, try to reach others in pain, and to spend less time tilted back in his chair gazing upon the distant mountain.

CHAPTER THIRTY-THREE

The Berkowitzes lived in a split-level, five bedroom house in a new section of southeast Denver ten miles from the city's center. The house had a Spanish look with a white stucco exterior and a red tile roof. It had three fireplaces, three baths and a wet bar downstairs in the den. There was a sunken living room with a polished oak floor. Bright Navajo rugs were scattered about. A cathedral ceiling with exposed wooden beams soared above the living room. Facing the living room fireplace was a couch of genuine dark leather, and shaded lamps made for a warm touch.

On a raised platform behind a balustrade was the dining area. The dining room table and chairs were heavy, rough, dark-stained, provincial Mexican, and a tall Mexican armoire towered over the table. A great wood and wrought-iron chandelier with fake flame-like electric bulbs cast a dim light from above.

Ida had chosen the house for its Southwestern style and because the house was on the west side of the street. Its eight-foot high, double-front doors thus faced the east, as was proper for a home where a Navajo was to live.

"I'd like to take turns with the chiefs of medicine at the university and at the veterans hospitals and give some of the interns' parties here," Jack told Ida one day.

"That would be fine. You know we've got lots of room. We can have all your interns, residents, and staff, and I'll invite our Greek folk dance group."

Jack hesitated.

"That sounds like an odd mixture. How can you be sure all those people can have a good time together?"

"I know they can. I know by now that all people are the same. Throw them together with music, dancing, and something to drink and you'll see."

On the night of the first of what turned out to be many parties, Mrs. Karsiotis, wife of the owner of the Olympia Restaurant in Denver, brought dolmades for snacks and helped Ida set up the trays. Mr. Mavrides from the folk dance group and Dr. Phil Ernest from the neurology department at Denver General Hospital took up the Navajo rugs from the wood floors, pushed the leather couch and the lamp-tables aside. Yanabah set the eight-track tapes on the stereo player and the wild twang of bouzoukis began. The party warmed up with ouzo and retsina and the living-room floor soon bounced under the dancers' feet to the rhythm of the *sirto* and the *kalamatiano*. Professors of medicine danced in the circle with Greek sailors and housewives; interns danced with high school girls and dowagers.

"You were absolutely right, Ida," Jack said happily when the party was over and as the guests were leaving. "I never had such a good time in all my life as I did tonight."

"Trust me, Jack, just trust me."

The house in Denver with its Mexican-style dining area, was suitable for small dinner parties as well.

"Dave Lipsky is here in the States on a visit from Israel. You remember him, don't you? He was my partner in the work we did in Milwaukee on one of the agents that causes atypical pneumonia."

"Of course I remember him. You used to disappear with him entire weekends at a time in his lab with those germ-free mice."

"Don't knock it, Ida. It was good work we did. Six or eight research papers came out of that. I think there are some loose ends he'll want to discuss, perhaps worth one more paper for publication."

"O.K., but do your shop-talk before you bring him to dinner. You know how I hate shop-talk."

Dave appeared unchanged, perhaps a little heavier and more hard of hearing. His hair was almost all gray by now. With his shirt collar outside of his jacket and without a tie, he was beginning to look like a real Israeli.

"Is your family all with you now in Israel?" Ida asked.

"Yes, we're all together now. Beryl, our only son, finished at the University of Wisconsin and came over last year. Our oldest girl, Aviva, is married to a security officer after serving her time in the Israeli Defense Forces. Our two youngest girls will be going into the army soon also."

Jack remembered that his brother, Elihu, had gone to the same Zionist summer camp many years before. While Jack knew of Dave's Zionist leanings, he was nevertheless a little surprised when he learned that Dave and his family had made "aliyah," the permanent move to Israel, a few years before.

"You see," Dave began, "In spite of the pride and joy we have living there, building a nation again for the first time in two-thousand years, we still have the feeling we're living in a fortress. The country is only sixteen miles wide in places, and we're surrounded at all times by enemies ready to push us into the sea."

"Yes," Jack said. "That's certainly the down-side of it. Myself, I'm a man of peace. I know I couldn't live under the constant threat of violence like that."

"Jack, you must remember the old Hebrew proverb, 'Im ayn anee lee, mee lee?' which means, 'If I'm not for myself, who *will* be?' We have to look out for our own future. Jews and Jewish families must stand together. The children of Jews should marry Jewish men and women."

Ida was following Dave's discourse but when she heard that last remonstrance, she erupted, "Why is that so important? Who do you think you are that you look down on other people? I'd be happy if one of my children married a black, another an Oriental. After all, we're all people! And who are you to come and tell us that you are better than we are?"

The color rose in Jack's neck. Ida was right, of course, in her way. He gathered his thoughts for some kind of response.

"I suppose that in a perfect world all people could live in harmony. Dave, you can see how passionately Ida believes that that perfect world begins when two people are brave enough to make that world, one family at a time. That's what we've done. But Ida, when in the real world people feel threatened, as Jews in Israel feel, they have to find their strength in themselves."

Ida said nothing for a while. Jack went on, "I shouldn't have used the word, 'they.' It goes against my grain to separate myself from my own people. After all, Ida, we've raised our own children as Jews, sent them to Jewish schools, and you've made a Jewish home for us here. You've seen the beauty of Jewish life."

"But that doesn't make Jews any better than other people," Ida said.

"You're right," Jack replied. "Jews aren't better than other people. All people have their own beauty and character, as you've taught me by letting me see what Navajo life is like. But you shouldn't blame Jews or Navajos or anyone else for trying to preserve the best parts of themselves, their culture and their tradition. That's all David is trying to say, isn't that right, Dave?" Jack said turning to his old colleague.

"Why are you taking his side?" Ida shouted, flushed, and near tears. "You're *both* foreigners. And you are both shitting on Indian land!" With this she pushed herself away from the table, rose swiftly, and, leaving the room, snapped off the light from the wood and wrought-iron chandelier overhead.

CHAPTER THIRTY-FOUR

L iving in Denver and reasonably close to the Reservation, Ida found many reasons to go home. Jack found her one day in the garage preparing for a trip.

"You know, the drinking problem at home is getting worse and worse. I have a fight with my brother, Thomas, over his drinking every time I go home. Those white people have had the nerve, the *nerve*, to set up a liquor store right at the entrance to the Reservation. AIM is organizing a protest and I'm going to march with them," she said and started to pack the car.

"Better be careful, Ida. Those American Indian Movement crazies are just spoiling for a fight. And those redneck policemen have guns. Remember, when whites feel they have the law on their side, they'll use them against Indians just like they did at Wounded Knee," Jack said, more than a little frightened by the determined look on Ida's face.

"Look, Jack. Stay out of this. Alcohol is killing us. I can hardly get Thomas to stay sober two days at a time. Those people are poisoning us right at our doorstep. And do you know who owns that 'Navajo Inn' just outside of Window Rock? The richest man in Gallup."

"How do you think a handful of long-haired AIM members are going to accomplish anything when the Navajo Tribal Council hasn't been able to do anything for years? The 'Navajo Inn' is on state land and the Tribe has no jurisdiction there."

"You wait and see. It's not just Dennis Banks and a bunch of guys. There's going to be me. And my friend, Marian. And I'm taking two of the kids."

"You're *what!*"

"Yes, I'm taking Rose Rachel and Joseph. They wouldn't dare point their shotguns at us. Not when they see two little children with me," Ida said.

"No you're not. You can get your own head blown off if you want to but you're not going to put the life of our two little kids on the line."

But Ida had been one step ahead of him. She'd already sneaked the kids into the rear deck of the station wagon and covered them with a rug. With a swift movement she jumped into the driver's seat, slammed the door shut, fired up the engine, backed out of the garage, and spun off out of sight.

Jack stood there trembling. It would be too embarrassing to call the Denver police. It's a long way to the Reservation. She'll calm down before she gets there, he thought and went into the house.

The next day the New Mexico State Police, armed with shotguns, set up a road block just at the state line marker, within sight of the rounded sandstone hillocks called 'Tse Bonito,' the Beautiful Rocks. Reporters and photographers from the *Navajo Times*, the *Gallup Independent*, the *Albuquerque Journal*, Channel 7 TV, KOB Radio, the *Denver Post*, the *Arizona Republic,* and *Newsweek* magazine were there. The cameras were focused on Dennis Banks who was accompanied by twenty Lakota Sioux from the Pine Ridge Reservation. The other marchers were the local Fort Defiance AIM chapter president, four Navajo students from the University of New Mexico, Ida's brother, Thomas Bird, Marian Hubbel, Ida's friend who now worked as a special representative of the Tribal chairman, Ida Bird Berkowitz, with eight year-old Rose Rachel on her left, and four year-old Joseph on her right.

"You are now approaching a New Mexico State Police road-block," a voice boomed over the loudspeaker. "You are asked to stand aside. Only necessary vehicular traffic will be allowed through. Be advised we are only here for your safety."

"We are here for our safety, too," Ida shouted back. "We are here for the safety of the Navajo people. For the safety of my children here. We are here in peaceful demonstration to shut down the 'Navajo Inn.' The alcohol they are selling there is killing our people."

"You'll have to step out of the roadway, lady."

Ida moved forward. The TV cameras now pointed in Ida's direction; flashbulbs, still cameras, and microphones found Ida and the children at the head of the march. The captain of the uniformed state police found the cameras and the microphones pointed at himself as well. Instinctively, he lowered his shotgun. He came forward, not using the bullhorn this time.

"If you and the children will come this way, ma'am, we'll guide you through, but please keep to the side of the road."

Dennis Banks and the Lakotas now crowded behind Ida, marched past the flashing lights of the police vehicles and on to the Navajo Inn. The liquor store was closed by the New Mexico State Liquor Commission two weeks later.

Photographs of Ida, Rose Rachel, and Joseph appeared in all the western newspapers and *Newsweek* magazine, and were copied by the *New York Post*. "Navajo Woman Fights Alcoholism," was the caption. Jack's cousin, Edith, showed it to all her sisters on Long Island and in New York. Edith's daughter, Karen, said, "I told you she was a Navajo princess!"

Two years later the liquor store reopened ten miles down the road from the Reservation border. It was renamed, the 'Sagebrush Inn.' The Mayor of Gallup, in an interview with the *Gallup Independent*, said, "The new store serves the needs of the Navajo people. Its convenient location means that our Navajo friends don't have to travel the additional fifteen miles to town to make their purchases."

"It just makes me sick. *Sick!*" Ida exclaimed when she told Jack about the new liquor store. "Those white people always get their way when it comes to screwing the Indians. They've got a new sign on the highway right near the new store. It says, 'Watch Out for Pedestrians.' Pedestrians! 'A-glanis,' Drunks, is what the sign means. The sign might just as well say 'Watch Out for Our Poor Drunk Indians.' You see them sitting on the ground drinking right there, and then they try to cross the highway to get a ride somewhere. Doesn't that make you *sick*?"

CHAPTER THIRTY-FIVE

Ida sat on the leather couch in the living room, waiting by the phone, her face drawn and with dark circles beginning to form beneath her eyes. She heard the engine of Jack's car coming into the garage and got up to meet him in the kitchen.

"Have you heard any news?" Ida asked, though she knew by the lack of expression on Jack's face that there wasn't any.

"Nothing yet. I just notified the police this morning. You know they won't start a search until a child has been missing at least forty-eight hours."

"That's so *stupid*. A child could be raped, cut up into little pieces, and buried a million miles away by forty-eight hours!"

"Ida, try not to think the worst. Alice has got more sense than to allow herself to get into a dangerous situation. After all, she's fifteen years old."

"It's bad enough that our precious child has been missing for two days without your being so unconcerned."

"I'm not any more unconcerned than you are. It's just that there's nothing we can do that we haven't done already. We've contacted the D'Addarios and their Sherry is gone, too. That means Alice is not by herself. There's safety in numbers."

"You know I never trusted that wild little bitch, Sherry D'Addario. She's capable of doing just anything. I can't see how you can find any comfort that Alice is with *her*."

"Look. Ida, you've been sitting staring at that telephone all day long. Let's ask Yanabah to man the phone so we can take Rose Rachel and Joseph out to the park. The change will do us all good."

The soft, spring air in the early evening in Washington Park was filled with moths. Millions had been in the air for many days, an explosion of thistle moths such as had not been seen for years. The medium-sized, tan-gray moths were on the tree-trunks, on the grass, in the air in front of people's faces, almost up into their nostrils. Jack had seen them flying as high as his ninth floor window at Denver General Hospital. Yet they were harmless, just a distraction. Rose Rachel and Joseph ran about, chasing them, shooing them away, giggling, behaving like normal children, their minds turned away from the gloom that enveloped their parents.

Dr. John O'Connell, Jack's colleague at Denver General, Director of Pediatrics, came ambling along in his usual slow way down the park roadway that had been closed to traffic.

"What brings you out here this time of day, John?" Jack called out. "Are you out to catch a moth or two for your collection? Any of them get up your nose?"

"It's a rare phenomenon, these millions, maybe billions of moths," John said in his serious way, ignoring the jest. "One wonders where they come from, where they hibernate, where they pupate when they're not here."

"It certainly is one of nature's great mysteries. Ida and I are out here for a little distraction, to witness it. We've been so pre-occupied with our daughter's disappearance."

"Yes, we've heard about it. But perhaps you'll be surprised to find her home by the time you get there. That's what happened with our daughter, Jane. Just last year, when she was seventeen. You know Jane. She's a friend of Yanabah's. Jane is really a good girl. We don't know why she just got up and left. Came home four days later. Maybe it's just some primal urge to migrate, a mystery, like what seizes the moths."

"In Alice's case, though," Ida said, "I think she just got in with the wrong crowd. And she's just restless and impatient to begin with."

"Hadn't she gone through eight years of Hebrew school?" John asked. "I heard that through Yanabah and Jane."

"Yes, that's right," Ida said. "But things changed when she was about thirteen and started public school at Hamilton Middle School. When she got to Jefferson High School, and that's a pretty good school in a nice neighborhood, she just couldn't take it for some reason. She ended up going downtown to a special high school for kids with discipline or learning problems. But Alice is extremely bright. She has no problem learning anything. She reads at a college level. She taught herself to read when she was in kindergarten. We just don't understand why she's gone and put us through all this. I'm really so worried. But I thank you for your encouragement."

At nine o'clock that evening there was a telephone call. Jack jumped for the phone.

"Is this Doctor Berkowitz?"

"Yes, speaking."

"This is Officer Marantz from the San Diego Police, Beach Patrol."

"What's he saying? Is she all right?" and Ida ran to pick up the extension phone in the kitchen.

"Do you have a daughter named Alice?"

"Yes, yes. How is she?" Jack asked.

"We picked her up with about seven other kids on the beach where they camped out over night. They all hitch-hiked here, they said, in the back of a truck."

"But is she all *right*?" Jack asked again. Actually, he felt an enormous sense of relief because, from the officer's tone, he knew she was at least alive.

"Yes, she's all right. She looks tired and says she's hungry. What do you want us to do with her?"

"Take her to the airport. There'll be a ticket for her to fly home to Denver. And thanks. Thank you, officer."

At the airport arrival gate at Stapleton, where Jack decided he would pick her up by himself, Alice walked through with an air of complete nonchalance, as if nothing had happened. Her tangled hair was down to her shoulders, her T-shirt, blue jeans, and sneakers dirty.

"Is Mom pretty mad?"

"Not mad anymore. Just distraught. It's been a rough couple of days. We're glad you're O.K."

"Yes, I'm O.K."

"I know you're hungry. Let's go on home and get something to eat."

CHAPTER THIRTY-SIX

It was now October. For some weeks Ida had felt that curious feeling of emptiness, that ill-defined sadness that told her it was time to get back home. These sensations might occur at any time, in the quiet afternoons when the children were away at school, or even in the commotion of family meal-times. But the cure for her unease came with a collect call from her sister, Nellie, from the pay phone outside the sawmill office at Navajo.

"Our sister, Irene, hasn't been feeling well. The family had a conference. We went to a crystal gazer who said she needed a Yei B'chei ceremony. It will be held at Crystal next week. The Ganado branch of the T'senjikinnie clan are all coming. Also our uncle from Tsaile. We want you to come, too. And bring your family if you can."

"Jack and I will be there."

It was only a one-day trip from Denver. The winter route they took to the Reservation ran down Interstate 25 to Walsenberg, over the Front Range of the Rockies at La Veta pass, down through the San Luis valley to Taos, then to Santa Fe, Albuquerque and home. While they were on their way, Ida's brother, Thomas, shot a doe at the summer sheep camp.

"I thought you weren't supposed to shoot does, only bucks," Jack said.

"Look, Jack, don't interfere," Ida said. "We do it our own way. Besides, Thomas shot it on our own land."

Jack wasn't a hunter. He'd never shot an animal and he knew he never would, especially one as large and beautiful as a deer. But if there had to be hunters, he'd accept them. And as for Thomas, he'd always been fond of the man.

Thomas was older than Ida by five years, a ranchhand, railroad worker, and carpenter. He was always a willing worker around the place, the collection of small wooden houses, a corral, a summer cook shed and two hogans on a rocky slope above the valley. He was a loner, having gone through two wives because of his drinking, his fights, and his stays in jail. When he was at his wildest, just out of his teens, they'd kept him in the older jail at Fort Defiance, but in more recent years, in the new one at Window Rock. He still did some heavy drinking, and it frightened the children to hear his bellowing, his shouting "Goddamit!" up on the hill when the family came to visit.

He was tall and slender, tight-muscled in his bluejeans, Western straw hat and cowboy shirts. He had a saddle nose and large, rough hands with fingers stubby and clumsy-looking from his carpentry, which Ida had always complained was too fast and sloppy. But there was goodness about him, too. He always came down the hill to Ida's house by the road to welcome her and the family when they came from the city for a visit. He had taught Jack how to use a post-hole digger and how to tighten barbed wire with the wire-stretcher in the Spring when it was time to repair the fences. And he taught Jack how to use the fencing tool to pry the rusted horseshoe nails from the old cedar fenceposts. When the two of them worked together their hammers would ring in a series of rising notes as they drove the nails and the tightened wire into the posts. When there were reports of deer running in the high, ponderosa country in the Fall, Thomas took his father's thirty-ought-six and brought down the meat to Ida.

"Now I'll show you how I'll handle this hindquarter," she said to Jack as she prepared to go to work on the venison. "And

I know you're going to like it when it's done." She soaked the meat in cold water, washed off the blood, then salted the meat with course salt, placing it on a drainboard to remove more of the blood. Then she washed it thoroughly one more time. "I'm doing it just like your mother taught me, to 'kasher' the meat," she said to Jack with a wink. Then she splashed dark red wine over it and completed the marinade with aromatic spices, bay leaves, and garlic. "And now it's ready for the Yei B'chei tomorrow night."

The ceremony and the chanting had been going on for seven days. Late on Friday afternoon the Yeis appeared in their masks for the first time. Everybody wanted to see them. Different family groups had already begun to take their places and to build their own small campfire sites along the sides of the quadrangle in front of the hogan. Once each family staked out its place, as long as there was somebody to hold it, that place would be theirs for the final night on Saturday.

The blue masks of the Yeis, with eyes, nose, and mouth cut out, were their only costume for this, their afternoon appearance. The rest of the their clothes were the usual Navajo dress of bluejeans and Western shirts. Their appearance was brief, a foreshadowing of what was to come. The clown among them kept things lighthearted. The children shrank away in mock terror and then laughed and giggled as the clown picked out one group of children and then another feigning an attack, and then whooping away appearing to be wounded. Then there was laughter as mothers and grandmothers joined with hollering and cat-calling, shooing the clown away.

"That was fun," some of the children shouted. "Will the clown Yei be back?"

"Not anymore today," one mother said. "But they'll be back tomorrow night."

On Saturday afternoon Jack stood outside the hogan listening to the singing going on inside. He was happy just to stand there. The singing *belonged* where it was. The perfume of the piñons, the gracious shadows of the ponderosas on the nearby rounded, pink sandstone hills, and the steep cliffs of the mountains in the distance all blended to become part of the scene.

Men, and now and then some women, pushed aside the blanket that covered the east-facing opening of the hogan. The sound of the singing became louder when the blanket was pulled away. There seemed to be no hurry, no urgency. Some of the people entered, some left. They smiled and they greeted one another as they came and went. The women were bringing in enamel-ware pots of steaming coffee that had been prepared in the brush-covered cooking shed behind the hogan. The cooking fires were always going as the T'senjikinnie family served coffee, fried bread and mutton stew to all who came. The crackle of the fires and the thump of axes wielded by men and boys splitting wood was always heard. The pleasing smell of burning piñon and cedar was always there. Occasionally there was the tinkle of a sheep-bell from pens behind the cooking shed. The mutton served to the guests was always fresh.

As Jack stood outside the hogan listening to the chanting, a Navajo woman wearing a velveteen blouse, an ankle-length cotton skirt and a kerchief over her head came up to him.

"Don't you remember me? I'm Sarah Goldtooth, Ida's cousin from Sawmill. I remember you from twenty years ago when you used to be a doctor at Fort Defiance. I worked at the cafeteria at the main hospital but we used to deliver food to the sanatorium. Yat'eh *Doctor*!" "Yat'eh," Jack replied. "Well, it's nice to see you again," she said and she moved on.

Jack didn't remember her, but he felt better that somebody knew him. At least I'm recognized as an in-law, he thought. At least I belong here in some way.

A Navajo man of middle age wearing a sport jacket and glasses spoke to him.

"Why don't you go inside?" he asked, speaking perfect English. Jack didn't really feel comfortable going inside. This was *their* ceremony, their most solemn and important religious rite. If he were to go inside his being there might disrupt it. In a way, his being there, like a tourist, might cheapen it. He knew

Navajos resent being gawked at, studied. In spite of the friendly greetings and invitations, Jack knew he was still a white man, a stranger, an outsider. He was content to stand outside, to wander about, to just listen, to feel the magic and the power of it.

"The medicine man says it's all right," Ida said coming up to him from inside the hogan. "I asked him and he said it's all right for you to come in." Ida took him by the hand, pushed aside the blanket, and he was inside.

He stepped to the left in order not to block the doorway. The medicine man had his back to the opposite wall facing the doorway. Young men assisting him sat on either side. Jack knew the etiquette of entering a hogan. He stepped quietly to the left where the men sat and found a place for himself on the floor with his back against the south wall.

The center of the hogan was cleared of its usual wood stove. The medicine man's assistants were working quietly on the sandpainting on the smooth floor of the hogan under the light coming through the smoke hole since the stove and the stove-pipe had been removed.

The medicine man was dressed casually like the rest of the Navajos in bluejeans and Western shirt but he wore a colorful red bandana tied around his head. He was about fifty-five years old with much thick, iron-gray hair cut short in modern style, and he had the rounded belly of a well-fed man. He wore a heavy turquoise necklace, a large silver concho belt, and many silver and turquoise rings. At his side, his medicine bundle of soft leather lay open. Its contents, a number of tiny leather pouches, stones of different colors, and the feathers of birds large and small were laid out. Farther away were little bowls of different colored sands: pure white, black, red, yellow, blue, and green.

The medicine man directed the work of the young men who were his helpers. They did the work of creating the colored figures on the smooth, light-brown sand of the background. The young men would take a pinch of color from one of the bowls and, with great skill and patience, roll the pigment out from between their thumb and forefinger. They would draw a straight black line here, a yellow line right next to it there, a green corn stalk and a green, angled corn leaf next to it. The medicine man was giving his directions in soft, measured tones. Occasionally he would ask a young helper to make a correction or to lengthen a line. Only now and then would he lean forward, get on his knees, take a pinch of colored sand and do some of the work of creating or correcting the sandpainting himself.

Jack felt privileged to be able to observe the process. The medicine man knew that Jack had sat down in the shadows. He looked in Jack's direction and he nodded his head ever so slightly. That was enough for Jack. He felt he had been given permission to be there and he relaxed a little more.

There were four assistants. Two of them had long hair tied behind their head in the old Navajo way. One of the two with long hair bent over and whispered something in the medicine man's ear. Jack knew he was being talked about because, a moment before, that same young man had looked in his direction.

Uh, oh, this looks like it might be trouble, Jack thought.

He watched intently as the medicine man touched the young man on the shoulder, nodded his head, and smiled a little in Jack's direction. I guess that means he's telling him its O.K. for me to be here, Jack thought. But still, maybe it's *not* all right for me to stay. I don't want to be the cause of any doubt about my being here. Ida told me in the past that the least little disturbance or interruption in a ceremony can break the magic of it. It then might have to be done all over again. All the expense, all the time and effort of so many people might end up being wasted.

Jack had been in the hogan for about half an hour. He got up quietly, stepped very carefully around the outstretched legs of the men and boys on the south side of the hogan, pushed aside the blanket, and was out again into the fresh air.

It was Saturday night. Electric light bulbs had been strung on lines between poles that ranged along the outside of the quadrangle. Gasoline-powered generators made a steady, muffled roar, but Jack soon got used to the sound and heard it less. Loudspeakers mounted on the roof of the Tribal police van boomed out announcements. Some of the elders made speeches which Ida translated for him.

"We want you young people to respect this ceremony," they said. "We don't want you to get drunk or get into fights." Then they went on to acknowledge the gifts that had been brought. "We understand that Joe Yazzie is the one who trucked in the full tank of water. Ah-shay-hay. Thank you, Joe Yazzie. And Jim Begay, we thank you and your boys for bringing in the wood. Stay around. We may need some more. And Albert Shorty. Can you hear me? Thank you for bringing in those fat sheep from Ganado."

Ida held on to a spot close to the hogan, just to the right of the hogan door. She set down several folding chairs around her little fire, one of them for her father who was now past eighty-five. She brought the venison rump and started to roast it on a grill fashioned with a long handle. The grill had four short feet that held it over the coals. She set the marinated meat on the heated grill and the juice began to sizzle and bubble. Steam rose from the surface of the meat as it began to cook. Then the outer layers began to brown. Drippings from the marinade fell onto the grill and exploded into more aroma-filled steam. She turned the roast slowly using a long-handled fork. When the meat began to smoke, the aroma of the roasting venison drifted toward families sitting by their own fires down the line. There was something different, exciting, tantalizing and delicious in that smoke.

"What's that you're cooking?" they asked as they came over in small groups. Ida took a sharp knife and sliced off the outer layer and gave a portion of meat to each of the neighboring families.

The meat just exposed was pink. When she turned the roast and cooked the pink part of the meat, this side, in turn, sizzled and smoked. The wind shifted. A rising column of smoke now drifted toward the hogan. The medicine man and the others were still singing inside. Each time the blanket was pushed aside and the door opened, the smoke from Ida's roasting venison floated inside.

It had been dark now for several hours. The dancing would not begin until shortly before midnight. Everybody was getting hungry. Behind, and off to the side of the quadrangle, some people were selling coffee, hamburgers, and fried bread from little booths or off the backs of pickup trucks. But the aroma of Ida's venison drew more and more people to her fire. She continued to slice thin portions from the smoking outer layers and to offer these slices to all who came. They ate with their fingers and they smacked the juice. Ida knew these people. They were relatives, neighbors, and old friends from Red Lake, Sawmill, or Fort Defiance. There was much visiting and chatting and laughing. Ida had now become the center of attraction and she continued to slice and to turn and to offer from the goodness of the deer meat that Thomas had brought down from the mountain.

With things well in hand, and Ida holding court, Jack slipped away into the darkness on his way to one of the privies. When he returned, threading his way again in a narrow space between two parked trucks, he saw the silhouette of a man lounging a little unsteadily against the side of one of the trucks.

"Excuse me," Jack said. "I'd like to get through." The man turned around. "What are you doin' here?" the man demanded. The light from the fires and from the electric light bulbs fell on Jack's glasses and on his face. "I'd just like to get through."

"We don' want you here," the man said, coming closer until Jack could smell his breath. Jack started to back away, to find his way around the rear of the parked trucks when the man started to swing his fist up toward Jack's face. "Owuuh!" the man shouted, suddenly in pain. His fist had struck the side mirror of the cab of the truck.

"Get outta here, a-glani, you drunk!" another voice shouted. "Don't you start making trouble around here." It was Mrs. Goldtooth from Sawmill, who had been resting in the cab of the truck. "This man," she said to the man and pointing to Jack, "is ni' hi' cha' da' *nih* (our in-law)!" She got out of the truck and, with a threatening gesture, shooed the man away. "It didn't use to be this way," she said to Jack, some sadness in her voice.

"Thanks," Jack said. He had the same feeling again, that he shouldn't be there. He went back to Ida's fire and crouched down next to her. He wouldn't tell her about the incident until later. He knew how mad she would get. She would have gone after the man with her long-handled meat fork.

Aroma of the venison now reached the inside of the hogan. At first, some of the singers, and then the medicine man himself came out. He squatted on his haunches in front of Ida's fire. Ida was now wreathed in smiles. It was the most distinguished guest of all who had come.

"Yat' eh, si zaydeh (hello, my cousin)," he said. Ida basked in the light of the important man. She now gave him a special honor. She handed him the knife and he cut his own perfect piece and he chewed it right off the knife.

"A-shay-hay. D'li kon at eh. Thank you. It was very good," he said warmly. Then he reached into his back pocket, pulled out a blue-and-white bandana, wiped his mouth, and went back into the hogan to sing. Those in the hogan noted that he sang with a new burst of energy for the rest of the night. The Yei B'chei was declared a success. Irene, Ida's clan sister, said she was feeling much better.

CHAPTER THIRTY-SEVEN

❧

"I just found out today that Gordon MacKenzie is planning to retire as Professor of Medicine at the university next year," Jack announced to Ida.

"Why is that important and what does that have to do with us?"

"When he leaves, the new professor should be free to pick his own man just as Gordon picked me. That means I will bow out, leave Denver General."

"Aren't you as good a person as any the new professor would pick?"

"Maybe I am. But you see, if I stay, the new chief might feel he *has* to keep me even though I may not be the person he really wants. It would get to be very uncomfortable for me, to think I was just there as an old hanger-on. I used to see older men in that position and I swore I would never let myself be found in such a spot, that younger men would pity me and put pressure on the boss to kick me out."

"You're too sensitive. Don't be so self-effacing. And you're not an old man. You're only fifty. Why should you give up so easily?"

"It's not a matter of giving up easily. You know ten years is a long time for anybody to be in one position. Did it occur to you

178

that I might feel I was getting stale? Or that even the Denver General people might even feel I've outlived my usefulness? You know I've been criticized already by the administration for not keeping my staff in line. The men in my department have been going over my head with their special requests, extra funding for this or that. And the staff have been grumbling because I don't do enough for them."

"Well then, what are you going to do? What are *we* going to do?"

"We'll leave."

"We'll leave? Where will we go?"

"To Albuquerque. There's a medical school there now. They've been looking for somebody to head a new division of General Internal Medicine. They've been under pressure, as have all medical schools, to de-emphasize the tendency of Internal Medicine departments to put out super-specialists. The world, it seems, wants more generalists. So it's Albuquerque. Don't you think it's time?"

"Yes, I think it's time. I've always thought it was time. It's a little late. Twenty years late. But it's still time," and she ran and hugged him and held on to him.

CHAPTER THIRTY-EIGHT

The lobby leading from the sanctuary of the B'nai Israel was suffused with light. The noontime sunlight that came through the glass front doors turned to a softer color as it reflected the bright yellow of the lacquered wood paneling. A reception line was just forming as the young rabbi, Irving Slotnik, and the Bar Mitzvah, smooth-cheeked, flushed, smiling Joseph Berkowitz, stationed themselves to greet the congregants after the Sabbath service had ended.

"That was a lovely speech, Joseph," said the first of the regular synagogue goers to emerge from the sanctuary. "Your parents must be very proud of you," and turning to Rabbi Slotnik, he greeted him with the traditional "Gut Shabbos, Rabbi."

"Gut Shabbos, Mr. Birnbaum. Yes, we're proud of Joseph, too."

Joseph, at thirteen, was five foot three, a fairly good height for his age. He was more round than angular. His hair was rich, black, and wavy though it had been straight when he was a baby. His shoulders were draped in an Israeli-made wool "tallis" whose stripes on a field of white were blue, purple, and pink. He wore a dark blue, velvet yarmulke embroidered with silver threads perched on the back of his head.

"A fine speech, Joseph," said Mrs. Goldstein, a stooped lady in her seventies. She wore a shining dress of ecru color, a long necklace of pearls, and her eyeglasses hung around her neck with a black ribbon.

"Thank you," Joseph said.

"I remember you as just a little boy when you first started to come to this synagogue with your father."

Then followed the full procession as the crowd filed out of the modern, tent-shaped sanctuary, and the rabbi and Joseph greeted them all. In the basement social hall, tables had been set for a traditional Bar Mitzvah Sabbath repast. Rabbi Slotnik raised his glass of wine and recited the blessings for the Sabbath "Ol Cain Bayrach Adonoi Es Yom Ha'Sahbbos Va'yekadshayhu" (Thus the Lord blessed the Sabbath Day and He made it Holy,) and for the wine, "Baruch Atoh Adonai, Elokainu Melech Ha'Olam, Boray Pree Ha'Gaffen" (Blessed are You, King of the Universe, Who Created the Fruit of the Vine.) Then he made a blessing over the challah, the signal for all to sit down and eat.

"Mom, Dad, Grandma, we all sit at the head table," Joseph said beckoning to them. Then, confident that his main Bar Mitzvah speech was behind him, he stood up and made this brief announcement: "I want to give special thanks to my parents, Doctor and Mrs. Berkowitz, and to my grandmother, Mrs. Cecile Berkowitz who sit beside me, and to all my uncles, aunts, and cousins who've come from the Navajo Reservation and from as far away as Washington, D.C., Salt Lake City, and San Francisco to be with me today."

"You're getting pretty good at speech-making, son," Jack whispered to him, while from the audience there came a round of applause.

Platters of thickly-sliced challah, pickled herring, tuna salad, kosher dill pickles, fresh cucumbers, celery, and raw carrots were passed around, and the meal was in full swing.

"Son," Jack whispered, "I didn't have a chance to tell you that your Bar Mitzvah speech was very moving. But you changed it from what I'd suggested. Yours was better and I *am* proud of you. I know it was spoken from the heart."

"Dad, the text from the Haftorah portion you picked for me was very learned, but I wanted to say something that was more meaningful to me. Alice helped me with some of the words but the thoughts were really mine."

"I know that, son. I have an idea that everyone who heard you will remember what you said."

"*I* certainly will," Ida said. She'd been leaning over listening to the conversation that had taken place, straining to hear over the noise in the social hall. "You know, Joseph, the people here all know what a good artist you've become. And when you said in your speech, 'Life is like a painting; it must be made of many colors,' everyone knew you were giving credit to your mother's Navajo heritage as well as to your father's."

The luncheon over, all of the guests came with more handshakes, more congratulations, and more goodbyes. Now Joseph could get on with his life. It had been hard for him to study, to get up to speak before a whole congregation in a synagogue, before an audience that would judge his performance, who would wonder that a boy whose mother was Navajo could become a Jew. He did it. He made it.

CHAPTER THIRTY-NINE

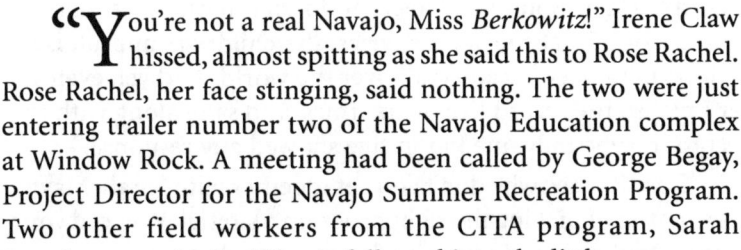

"You're not a real Navajo, Miss *Berkowitz!*" Irene Claw hissed, almost spitting as she said this to Rose Rachel. Rose Rachel, her face stinging, said nothing. The two were just entering trailer number two of the Navajo Education complex at Window Rock. A meeting had been called by George Begay, Project Director for the Navajo Summer Recreation Program. Two other field workers from the CITA program, Sarah Roanhorse, and Mimi Yazzie followed into the little room.

"I need everybody's input so I can prepare a progress report that's due next week," George began. "I want you to feel free to give me an honest opinion of how the program is really going. I don't just want you to give me the number of kids who showed up at the various locations, although numbers are important, too. What I want is your gut feeling of how the kids responded."

Rose Rachel, her voice strained and angry, unable to respond directly to Irene's unexpected assault, was the first to speak.

"George, I worked very hard so far the first part of the summer with the music and dance program. I have to tell you kids literally had to be dragged in. The posters we'd set up at the trading posts and at the convenience stores didn't do a thing. We only got kids to come when some active members of the chapters, who knew where all the families lived, went out and got them."

"Rose Rachel," George said in response, "that's the way it is with all social programs. It's always slow getting started. You've got to be patient. Give it a little time."

"What was discouraging to me, though, was that it was the same at the fourth week as it was at the first."

"Maybe it had to do with what you were trying to teach in your area," Sarah Roanhorse said. "I know you tried to teach them little dances, like 'Put your little foot, put your little foot, put your little foot right in,' but five- and eight-year olds from way out on the Rez, from places like Klagetoh and Steamboat Springs, just don't get it. That stuff is just too foreign to them."

"Sarah may be right," George said. "It's a big cultural gap you're trying to bridge."

"I also tried to get them to listen to good stuff. I played them records of 'The Sound of Music.' It doesn't matter what culture you're from. That music, the lyrics, the children's appeal, is so universal it's been accepted all over the world. And yet, even after I played the record five or six times, and sang along with the record, maybe only one kid in five showed any response."

"Rose Rachel, why don't you get together with Sarah. Maybe it's a matter of picking the right program material. We need your input. Don't think of giving up," George said.

Rose Rachel was depressed enough after the meeting. She didn't need that nasty blast from Irene Claw. She felt a little better after taking the quiet old road up to Red Lake. The late afternoon light falling across the valley onto the pink cliffs always brought her comfort.

This valley, this place is mine, too, she thought. I've come here every summer all my life.

"It's just jealousy," Ida said when she heard about what the Claw girl had said. "Nasty Navajo jealousy. That's all it is. Don't let that get you down. I know those Claws. They're the ugliest people. And Irene's mother. She was the biggest whore in Fort Defiance. You just sit out there on the porch and watch the sunset while I prepare dinner." But Rose Rachel just followed her mother into the kitchen.

"You know, Mom, I've been turning this Navajo thing over in my mind. Of course I'm Navajo. And a real Navajo. But I'm also something new. Something that couldn't have been if I hadn't lived in the other world. I've had the benefit of both worlds. And I can give something back to both worlds." Her eyes began to fill with tears as she said this.

"You're right. You're absolutely right," Ida said as she folded her daughter in her arms. Then Rose Rachel went out on the porch and saw that the three-quarter waxing moon was already up over the orange glow of the rocks.

CHAPTER FORTY

〜

September came and the cottonwood leaves, before they turned, just crackled a little in the dry wind. On the September of Yanabah's wedding, such were the leaves, and Jack's thoughts were always with Yanabah when he listened to the leaves rustle and whisper in the wind.

Yanabah looked more like her grandmother, Hasbah Bird, than her own mother, and she often had the same placid demeanor. But Yanabah was raised in a Jewish home. Candles were always lit on Friday nights and Jack chanted the "kiddush" over the Sabbath and the wine. On Saturday mornings before she was two, she walked with her father and mother to the synagogue in Denver. When her two sisters, Alice and Rose Rachel came along, the whole troop walked the twelve city blocks in Milwaukee to the synagogue of the saintly Chassidic Rabbi Tellman on Rosh Hashana and Yom Kippur.

When she was seven or eight, Yanabah asked her mother, "How is it you seem to be more Jewish than the mothers of some of my classmates?"

Then Ida said, "I didn't want to be halfway Jewish, like some of the women, including your father's cousin, Edith, who I met in New York. They used to take the ham and bacon out of their refrigerators when their mothers or grandmothers would come to visit. It's not that I had anything against them when they did that. You know how much I love Edith for the way she welcomed me when I first came to New York and met your father's family. But if I was to be Jewish, I wanted to do it just right. And still, you know, I am still Navajo. I feel comfortable being both Jewish and Navajo."

Yanabah started school at the Hillel Academy, Hebrew Day School. At the age of five she also started ballet. At home she learned that on Passover there were certain foods she must not eat.

"No, you may *not* have a cookie. It is *chumetz*," Jack said.

"But Daddy," she cried," I *love* chumetz!"

At the Hillel Academy she learned that even up to this day Jews are expected to know whether they belong to the priestly tribe, the "Kohanim," or to the "Levites," or to the general tribe of "Israelites."

"To which tribe do you belong?" the teacher asked one day. Yanabah stood up proudly, her dark eyes shining and her high cheekbones glowing and said, "Navajo!"

Yanabah became disillusioned with the strictness of Orthodox Jewishness after Rabbi Schwachter's mean-spirited attack on her father, when he'd said her father had made a big sin by marrying her mother. But she accepted for herself the strict discipline of the ballet.

"I want you to be sure you come to see me in 'Nutcracker,'" Yanabah said. "I'll be doing 'Maid' in the first act where I have to discipline all those nasty little children. And then I'll be one of the 'Snowflakes' in the second act."

"It's funny," Jack said to Ida, seeing Yanabah on stage. "I don't seem to see any other dancer but her."

Later, Yanabah had solo roles in "Nutcracker" as "Marzipan" and as "Spanish Dancer."

"Dark eyes, spit-curls, rose in her hair. What spirit, what fire! That's our daughter!" Ida said.

If her parents had their eyes fixed on this one dancer, theirs were not the only ones. Some years later, when Yanabah was twenty, Peter Beauchette saw her in Les Sylphides. The music of Chopin, the subdued lighting, the classic white skirts, the perfect body and arm movements of one of the magic sylphs captured the young man. Though he was self-confident in many ways, Peter lacked the courage to seek her out backstage.

Yanabah had started work as an electrocardiogram technician at the hospital. One night Peter, an emergency room physician, saw her as she answered a call at the E.R. wheeling her cart before her with that same erect, courtly grace he knew he had seen before.

"That's her! That's the one!" he exclaimed.

Then quickly, after his discovery, Peter reached out and made up for his earlier shyness. And Yanabah responded. Peter was Catholic. Now he and the half Jewish, half Navajo Yanabah would seek a way to marry.

"I'm not willing to give up my past and I know you aren't either," Yanabah said. "Why don't we have a combined religious ceremony with both a rabbi and a priest? People are more liberal these days; we should be able to work it out somehow."

"That's fine with me," Peter said with calmness that brought tears of gratitude to Yanabah. "I'll find the priest and you and your Dad can find the rabbi."

"Well, Ida," Jack asked, "what do you think about Yanabah marrying a non-Jew, a Catholic?"

"I've told you before that I don't care who our daughter marries. I feel more and more Navajo as time goes on. To the Navajo, every person is a human being, one who has five fingers. My family accepted you and they've loved you as I have all these years. We have four beautiful children. That's what counts. Now Yanabah has found someone she loves. We should just support her and give her all the help she needs."

Peter started to find a priest who would help in a combined ceremony. He asked Father Finnerty, Catholic chaplain in the hospital. Father Finnerty was an energetic Irishman of middle age with a large nose, a skin that showed signs of acne earlier in life, and glasses that magnified his gray, merry eyes. He was always ready with a cheerful greeting, a ready handshake, and a joke. Jack knew him and thought the chaplain would make a good choice.

"I've fallen in love with a girl who is not Catholic and I plan to marry her," Peter said in his meeting with Father Finnerty.

"Is she willing to convert to our Faith, to take instruction?"

"Well, you see, she is Jewish. Both she and her parents have strong feelings about being true to their own religion. I can't argue with that. What we propose is a ceremony with both Catholic and Jewish rituals in the service. Would you be willing to be the priest in such a combined ceremony?"

"My son, I know you. I've celebrated the Mass with you many times and I know you to be diligent in performing your religious duties. But I must tell you that the only wedding for a Catholic is a Catholic wedding. The Church will not recognize any other."

Peter thought he might find a more liberal priest in Father Al Sandoval at the Newman Center on the University campus. Father Al was about Peter's age, in his late thirties, tall, about six-three, with a pleasant smile and a comforting air. He was an intellectual and a scholar, and he'd studied medieval church manuscripts in Spain.

"I have no problem with a combined Catholic and Jewish ceremony. Find a rabbi and we'll try to work things out," he said.

Jack knew from the start that finding a rabbi would be a more difficult problem. Rabbis would demand religious conversion to Judaism or the intent to convert as prerequisites, and Peter's deep Catholic faith would not permit him to do this. So Jack did not even approach Rabbi Slotnik, the Conservative rabbi of the B'nai Israel Congregation, or the Reform rabbi in the community. He sought out, instead, a rabbi in a nearby city who had a more liberal reputation.

"I'm sorry, Dr. Berkowitz, I don't know you. While I love New Mexico and its diversity, I really cannot do this."

Now Jack regretted that he hadn't even tried to approach Rabbi Slotnik, in the congregation of which he was a member, where Joseph had had his Bar Mitzvah. Then he remembered that personal friendship with a rabbi was no guarantee that a rabbi would bend the rules. Jack flushed recalling the sting of rejection he'd experienced with Rabbi Friml years before.

Candles lit on Friday evening in the Berkowitz home continued to exert their comforting effect on the family. At the dinner table Ida came up with a plan.

"Yanabah, why don't you ask your father to do the Jewish part of the wedding? You were too little at the time to remember, but your father functioned as a rabbi when the Jewish chaplain at Fort Sam Houston was called away, the time we were stationed there. Jack, you even did the High Holy Day Services and I was so moved by how you conducted the singing and the prayers."

Jack remained silent. Yanabah's face brightened.

"Dad, I know you know enough Hebrew to do it. After all, I know you were a yeshiva boy at one time. Won't *you* be the rabbi for Peter and me?" Yanabah was too appealing.

"My darling, how can I say no? I can do it, but I'm not sure it will be entirely kosher. I'm not an ordained rabbi, you know. But yes, I will study up on it and I will do it."

Jack called his mother, Cecile, and invited her to the wedding.

"Yes, of course I'll come, son. Yanabah is precious to me. It seems only yesterday that I saw her for the first time, with that full head of black hair!"

Yanabah invited her Uncle Howard and her Aunt Basha. Basha Berkowitz was a librarian at a Hebrew Day school outside of Washington, and she had been active in Jewish affairs all her life. She was remarkably blond, wore her hair short, schoolmarmish style, and had blue eyes. She had a way of looking at you with those blue eyes and waiting for a while when addressed. Then, more often than not, she would laugh at some clever pun she'd just thought up. This time she didn't laugh. "I'll think about it," she said.

A few days later, Jack, Yanabah and Peter met with Father Al at the Newman Center to go over details of what would be a combined wedding ceremony.

"Could the ceremony be conducted under the traditional Jewish 'chupah,' the wedding canopy?" Yanabah asked.

"I don't see any objection to that," Father Al said.

"How about the words in Hebrew when the groom places the ring on the bride's finger and says, 'B'taba'at zu Aht m'kudeshet Li k'Dat Moshe v' Yisroel,' which means, 'With this ring you are consecrated to me according to the Faith of Moses and Israel?" Jack asked.

"No objection to that either."

Yanabah then asked, "Could you leave out the words 'Jesus Christ' from the Catholic Rite?"

"I'll have to ask my superiors. The marriage rite, you see, is a sacrament of the Church and the intervention of Jesus is a central aspect of any sacrament."

In the end, this potential conflict was resolved when Father Sandoval agree to address the groom and the bride separately. Facing Peter, he would ask Peter to affirm his vows "in the name of Jesus," and, facing Yanabah, he would ask her to affirm her vows "in the name of God." And Jack, at Father Al's suggestion, agreed that there not be two separate ceremonies, one after the other, but that the parts of the Jewish and the Catholic ceremonies be blended.

At the point when these lovely compromises were being worked our, Jack received this telephone call from his sister-in-law, Basha:

"Jack, I've thought it over. I will *not* attend Yanabah's wedding. My objection is that the ceremony is to be held in a public place. By playing the role of a rabbi, you will be toying too lightly with Jewish identity and Jewish tradition."

"I'm not sure I follow you," Jack said weakly.

"My concern is for no less than Jewish survival," she went on. "The history of the Jews is too full of individuals and of communities willing to die to preserve their Jewish identity. The modern history of the Jews is too full of individuals who have died to preserve the nation, Israel."

Jack was stung. I too, have struggled with my conscience, he thought. My family and I have come up with a solution which would declare my own identity as a Jew. At the same time this solution would present to the community the beauty of the Jewish tradition in my own life and in Yanabah's life. Finally, he found angry words to respond to Basha.

"I am just as good a Jew as you are! But as a physician, I see things in a different light. In every day that passes I see that life and disease and death know no religious boundaries. I know the history of the Jewish struggle for survival, yet that history covers a period of three or perhaps five thousand years. While that may seem to you a great period of time, my perspective covers the whole history of the human race."

"I've heard that argument before," snapped Basha, "and it is irrelevant."

For many days Jack was depressed because of this confrontation with his sister-in-law. Finally he hit upon an idea. Maybe, he thought, by introducing a third element into the ceremony, we might soften the heightened awareness of differences in identity.

"Ida, why don't we ask Aunt Tanabah to do a Navajo blessing at the wedding?

"That's a good idea. After all, Yanabah is Navajo too." Ida called Aunt Tanabah, Ida's maternal aunt and member of her own clan, the T'senjikinnies.

"Of course I'll come. Thank you for inviting me. I'll bless the children with the corn pollen."

The wedding now was just a day away. Wedding guests arrived from California, Colorado, Michigan and Washington. Cecile Berkowitz, white-haired, with pale eyes and calm face, was guest of honor. Morris, Jacks's father, had died twelve years before.

At a pre-wedding breakfast Basha Berkowitz appeared with her family. Jack, by this time, bore her no ill will.

"I have decided," she explained in a little speech, "to travel two-thousand miles to accompany my husband, Howard, and our children to be part of the family celebration. But I will adhere to my principles: I will not attend the ceremony."

On the mildest and calmest of early September days, the sun cast speckled shadows through the dry, but still green leaves of the cottonwood trees onto the lawn in front of the Memorial Chapel. Yanabah felt the excitement of the day as guests streamed through the heavy wooden doors and found their seats inside. Resplendent in her bridal gown, veil, and train, and carrying a bouquet of roses, she posed for photographs with her sisters, Alice and Rose Rachel, and with her mother.

"My prayer shawl is bigger than your prayer shawl," Jack teased Father Al. Jack was draped in the large, woolen, black striped "tallis" his father, Morris Berkowitz, had given him. Father Sandoval, in his white, priestly vestments, crucifix on his breast, wore only a thin, ribbon of a shawl around his neck. The good-natured priest laughed. Then the two marched out together onto the dais of the chapel and stood facing the assembled congregation.

Borne proudly on long, polished poles by young men appointed to the honor, the Jewish wedding canopy was marched down the aisle and then held open on the dais. The canopy now in place, the wedding principals, Yanabah and her mother, and Peter, guided by his father, marched down the aisle. Jack stepped forward.

"My friends," he began, using the famous salutation of Franklin Roosevelt, "this wedding ceremony, you will see, is a unique blend of traditions, symbolizing the union of our daughter, Yanabah Yonah, and Peter Beauchette, the fine young man she has chosen. This chapel is an appropriate setting for such a ceremony. Its long, narrow shape, and the transverse beams and corbels that support its roof are borrowed from the Pueblo Indians and their ancestors who inhabited the Rio Grande valley and the surrounding country for a thousand years.

"Its religious purpose as a chapel derives from the Spanish Christian tradition brought by the Spanish when they came to this valley four hundred years ago. The location of this chapel on the campus of the University of New Mexico is significant in several respects. The University represents, in part, that surge of energy called the 'Anglo' culture as it impacted into this territory one hundred-forty years ago, and, in a larger sense, a place appropriate for the expression of newer, larger, more liberal, more universal views.

"This blended ceremony comes out of the desire expressed by Yanabah and Peter to honor the traditions from which they come. Yanabah is respectful of the strength and character Peter derives from his Catholic home, school, and church, and Peter is respectful of Yanabah's sense of beauty and responsibility as the firstborn of her Navajo mother and her Jewish father."

In clear Hebrew Jack sang out the blessing over the wine and then provided the English translation. Peter then placed the betrothal ring on Yanabah's finger reciting, "With this ring you are consecrated to me according to the faith of Moses and Israel."

Then Father Sandoval, with the dignity of his vestments and his crucifix, conducted the Catholic Rite of Marriage, Peter affirming his vows "in the name of Jesus," and Yanabah "in the name of God."

Jack sang out the seven benedictions of the Jewish marriage service in Hebrew and then, so all could hear the ringing, exulting words in English, he raised his voice saying, "Blessed are You, Lord our God, King of the Universe, who created Joy and Gladness, Bridegroom and Bride, Mirth and Exaltation, Pleasure and Delight, Love, Brotherhood, Peace and Fellowship."

The wedding reached its high point when Aunt Tanabah, a woman in her seventies, stepped forward. She had a lined and leathery face, an aqualine nose, and small eyes that showed the blue-gray lines of age. She was dressed in the traditional Navajo velveteen blouse and a long skirt. She spoke to Yanabah first.

"Shi *yahzh*, my baby, I am going to bless you with the corn pollen." Then to Peter she said, "You too, my son, I am going to bless you with the corn pollen."

"Beauty before you,
Beauty behind you,
Beauty above you,
Beauty below you,
Beauty all around you."

Then there was the crunch of the wine glass and the claque that had been cued shouted, "Mazel Tov!" and it was over. The guests and the wedding party filed out of the chapel mingling and greeting one another. They spilled out and lingered in front of the doorway of the chapel and on to the front lawn. Jack listened to scraps of conversation, "So moving..." "What a good feeling..." "Most beautiful wedding..."

That night, at the reception, a Klezmer band played the strains of Yiddish music from Central and Eastern Europe. The music rose on the crisp, New Mexico air until it reached the foothills of the Sandia Mountains and echoed into the canyons.

For the next several days people continued to talk about the wedding. Basha's children had begged her to witness the service. They had succeeded in getting her to come as far as the chapel door. Someone reported that at the last minute she did relent and had come inside, but no one could be certain she actually had.

CHAPTER FORTY-ONE

Jack Berkowitz just finished seeing the videotape of himself dancing at the wedding of his daughter, Rose Rachel. It was plain to him now that *everyone* could see what he thought was his secret, what he saw in the mirror each morning in the bathroom. His face was wrinkled. His hair, gray at the temples, was thin at the top and just barely covered the bald area on the front of his head. Two thin, stringy folds of skin hung down from his neck. Ida calls this my "turkey neck," he thought. So what if everybody knows I am beginning to look my age? I can still dance to any music and I can fake the steps to anything that moves me. I can do the two-step, the waltz, the polka, the kalamatiano and the hora. Jack's left knee hurt for a few days after the wedding but that was getting better now.

Jack said to himself he really had nothing to complain about. The house he and Ida lived in was a one-story adobe on an acre-and-a-half in the Rio Grande bosque under the spreading branches of a two-hundred year-old tree. Corrales was an oasis of greenery, of irrigated fields and shade-giving cottonwoods in dry, brown, New Mexico.

When he handed the keys to Ida that day when they moved in fourteen years before, Jack started to say, "Use these in good health," but that cliché left him flat. Then he took a deep breath and something better came out.

"Baruch Atoh Adonoi Elokainu Melech Ha'Olam
Sheh' Hechiyanu, V'Kiyamanu, V'Higiyanu
La'Zman Ha'Zeh.
Blessed are You, Lord our God, King of the Universe,
That You've kept us alive, that You've sustained us,
And that You've brought us to this Happy Time."

Right after that, Ida stood up, serious and proud and beautiful as Jack remembered her as a young girl. She reached into a tiny, beaded leather pouch that she carried and brought out a pinch of perfect, yellow, golden corn pollen. She sprinkled some of this over the carved front door of the house. Then she raised her hand above her head and sprinkled the corn pollen in the first of four directions saying something softly in a barely audible monotone in Navajo. Then she sprinkled the corn pollen in the other directions. Although Jack couldn't make out the words because he didn't know Navajo that well, he knew she was thankful and that she was praying and blessing the house and their future in her own way.

"Beauty before you,
Beauty behind you,
Beauty above you,
Beauty below you,
Beauty all around you."

In this manner, Jack finally fulfilled the promise he made to Ida's father and to Ida, not after one year, but after *twenty* years. All during those years away, while they lived in New York, in Denver, in San Antonio, in Milwaukee, and in Denver again, where Jack worked to get ahead in a career in medical schools in teaching and in research, and while Ida gave birth to their four children, he thought of his unfulfilled promise. With some irony, when he reflected upon it, he thought of his promise as "Another of white man's treaties with the Indians shattered and broken!"

The children were now grown. Yanabah and her husband Peter had three sons, Alice had two children and had graduated from law school, Rose Rachel was office manager for a physician in Albuquerque, and Joseph was an artist, a sculptor, and a chef.

Ida's father, Mr. Joe Bird, reached the age of one-hundred and two and he lived to see Jack's belated promise fulfilled.

Ida often drives to visit her people. Jack usually watches her as she leaves the house, the one under the great cottonwood tree. He follows her with his eyes as she disappears down the road leading away from the bosque. He thinks of her driving across the treeless plain west of Albuquerque, down into the valley of the Rio Puerco, up again past the whitewashed church at Laguna, up under the mesas and past the base of bald-topped Mount Taylor, into the country of red sandstone cliffs, over the piñon-covered Continental Divide, past Gallup and then home at last. Then Jack pictures her as she enters the valley that lies between pink sandstone cliffs on the east and ponderosa-covered mountains on the west.

Jack knows that Ida's happiness depends on her knowing that she is free, free to live with Jack in his world, and free to live in her own world when she wishes. He is happy for her. When he can, he joins her in the evening when the light of the setting sun strikes the pink cliffs transmuting them to gold. They watch the flutter of sage sparrows, juncos, titmice, nuthatches, mountain bluebirds, and piñon jays under the trees. He listens with her as the valley comes alive with frog-song in the summer night after the rains. He sits by the fire with her savoring the smell of piñon smoke when winter storms outside fill the air with ice-crystals and when the snows weigh down the boughs of piñon, cedar, and ponderosa. At these times Ida will chant,

"Beauty before you,
Beauty behind you,
Beauty above you,
Beauty below you,
Beauty all around you."

and Jack will say in Hebrew,

"Sheh' Hechiyanu, V'Kiyamanu, V'Higiyanu La'Zman Ha'Zeh."

FOUR SHORT STORIES

TWINS

❧

I.

(New York Times, June 22, 1985, Sao Paulo, Brazil)
SCIENTISTS DECIDE BRAZIL SKELETON IS JOSEPH MENGELE'S

INQUIRY RULES OUT A HOAX

EXPERTS FROM U.S. AND TWO OTHER COUNTRIES
SAY THEY HAVE "ABSOLUTELY NO DOUBT"

II.

The Nazi doctor Joseph Mengele used to take personal charge as he picked out the twins among the crowds of Jews and gypsies coming off the trains at Birkenau and Auschwitz. Their forearms would be branded "Z" for "*zwillings*," their bodies would be measured in every detail, and, when one would die, the other would be killed by an injection of phenol so that their organs could be measured at autopsy.

III.

My wife, Ida, who is Navajo, tells me that among her people twins are at special risk of becoming harmed by witches. Such harm is forestalled by separating the twins at birth and by having them raised in different households. She tells of how Florence Shorty, a member of her clan, the T'senjekinnie clan, and her husband Albert had a set of identical twin girls in 1946. The babies, Lottie and Laura, were strikingly light-skinned, and, as Ida told me, each had a head of thick, blond hair, so different from the usual head of black hair of Indian infants. Because they were doubly conspicuous, twins and blond, Florence gave Laura, the younger twin to Nettie Begay, a T'senjekinnie clan sister, to be raised in Nettie's family near Crystal, New Mexico. Florence and kept Lottie and raised her at Ganado, Arizona.

Ida tells me that when the girls were four or five, they learned they were twins.

"When can I go to play with my little sister," cried Lottie. "Why can't we be together?"

"Ee-yah!" replied her mother. "We can't let the *Ya n'elgloshi* see you."

The child shuddered at the mention of the evil ones, and she remained silent for a while. But she continued to ask, and her mother just as regularly refused her.

IV.

When the Sabbath services at the B'nai Israel Congregation were over, we joined the rabbi in the traditional Kiddush. A simple table was set out in the social hall with several bottles of Mogen David kosher grape wine, a bottle of whiskey, a shimmering platter of cold pickled herring, and a braided challah sliced on a wooden board. It was a small but a jolly group. There were no more than thirty gathered; attendance was small at Saturday morning services on a weekend that was not a Jewish holiday, and especially when there was no celebration of a Bar or Bat Mitzvah.

The rabbi, a genial young man with a full head of prematurely grey hair, was given the honor, as is the tradition, of being first to raise his cup filled with wine, and he did so with the words, Ol Cain Bayrach Adonai Es Yom Ha'Shabbos

Va'Yekadshayhu. Baruch Atoh Adonai, Elokainu Melech Ha'Olam, Boray Pree Ha'Geffen."

Thus the Lord blessed the Sabbath day and He made it Holy. Blessed are You, Lord King of the Universe, Who created the fruit of the vine.

My preference was for the whiskey. A single straight shot of scotch or bourbon is quick to enter my blood, and it is all I need to raise the keenness of my perception. I recited the blessing over whiskey. "Baruch Atoh Adonai, Elokaynu Melech Ha'Olam, Sheh Ha'kol Ni'hiyeh Bi'dvaroh."

Blessed are You Lord, King of the Universe, that everything is created according to Your command.

Ahh! The amount of whiskey in the tiny cup was not enough to cause any griping in my empty stomach. Just enough to sharpen my vision. My eyes found in that gathering of older, greying men and women, two strikingly beautiful girls of seventeen or so. I'd never seen them before; they must have been out-of-town guests of one of the synagogue members. They were dressed alike in powder-blue, full-length dresses. Tiny white flowers of the pattern were set off with large fringes of white lace at the neck and collar, at the edges of the quarter-length sleeves, and at the hem. Their honey-brown hair fell in loose curls at their shoulders. Their skin was exquisitely clear, their cheekbones prominent and slightly blushed, and their eyes a perfect blue. They moved about the small gathering with absolute grace and pleasing smiles, speaking softly with the older congregants. I watched them for several minutes when, in one movement, they both turned their faces to me. They were clearly and unmistakably identical twins.

I was stunned with their flawless beauty, the girls now at the peak of their freshness and youth. But more than that, what struck me was the sudden and certain knowledge that these girls could not have been created by accident, by the chance falling together of gene particles. Otherwise, how could each be so perfectly reproduced? There must be some design, some carefully executed plan. I had never been so powerfully moved; I was face-to-face with the force of heredity, of biology, of creation. The words of my forefathers swept before me: Etzbah Elohim He. Sheh Ha'kol Ni'hiyeh Bi'dvoroh.

It is the finger of the Lord. That everything is created according to Your command.

V.

On a bright day in September, with the heat of the summer just past and with the freshness, the color, and the excitement of the tribal fair at Window Rock tangible in the air, Ida and I mingled with the crowds approaching the grandstand for the afternoon rodeo. Ida was resplendent in her Navajo costume, returning to the scene where, just the year before, she had been crowned Miss Navajo.

The fair was always a magnet that drew Navajos from all over the Reservation to come to see the rodeos, to see the night performances of Indian dances, and to renew old friendships. The fair was also a chance for some families to set up stands for selling fried bread and mutton stew to earn some extra cash.

We passed between the rows of booths where Navajos in great numbers waited their turn to have their fill of food before the rodeo began. The men were dressed in jeans, Western shirts, and cowboy hats; the women dressed in long skirts and richly colored velveteen blouses. All wore silver and turquoise.

The booths were not fancy, just roughly put-together boards with canvas tarps above for shade and a wooden counter where the women brought bowls of pungent, thin mutton stew. Behind the counter, others were busy pulling dough into soft discs, laying them carefully into the hot, clear lard in black, cast-iron skillets heating on Coleman stoves. The magic of the dough and the hot lard combined to produce the miracle of the rising, brown, softly puffed Navajo fried bread.

In front of one of these booths, two little girls of about eight caught our eye. They were in most respects like all other Navajo children, dressed in long, cotton skirts and velveteen blouses, adorned with bits of silver ornaments, brooches, pins, and buttons. Their cheeks were tanned, smudged, and crusted, and they seemed especially happy, chattering merrily in Navajo. The hair of each child was in long braids, but, surprisingly, these little girls were blondes. Sandy blondes, to be sure, but striking in comparison to the jet black hair of other Navajo children. Though not dressed exactly alike, their faces, their smiles, and their pale, hazel eyes were the same. They had to be the twins of Florence and Albert Shorty.

Lottie and Laura had found one another. The booths of their families were but a short distance apart. They were playing together for the first time, each seeing the mirror image of herself. There was nothing that Florence or Nettie could do. It would be cruel to separate them now that chance had brought them together. It would be all right for them to be with one another for a little while.

But if *we* had seen the twins and had taken such delight in the little girls, who else might have spied them?

Two days later, in the Shorty's corral outside of Ganado, a sheep lay dead, its belly cut open and its entrails spilled out on the ground, the shining membranes partly covered with dirt and flies. The same day, Nettie, outside of her hogan in Crystal, found a bone wrapped in canvas wedged among the branches of a juniper tree.

" The Ya n'elgloshi have found where the girls live," Ida said. "It didn't take them very long. They probably used their crystal gazers to find the places."

Word of these evil omens spread quickly among the T'senjikinnies. Hosteen Tso was summoned to perform a Blessingway ceremony to protect the twins.

In the Shorty's hogan that evening with only kerosene lamps and light from the fire in the wood stove illuminating our faces, we waited for Hosteen Tso's arrival.

"Why do the Ya n'elgloshi pick out twins for their nasty business?" I asked Ida's father. A kindly, soft-spoken man, Mr. Bird paused for a long time and then replied slowly in English: "Twins are very special. The twin gods, Monster Slayer and Child-of-the-Water, were given the job of killing the monsters and getting rid of all the bad people in the worlds below so that man could come up into this world and live in peace and harmony. But the twins, even though they were very powerful, did not get rid of all the evil in the world. The evil ones are still around here."

"When I was a young man," he went on, "A friend of mine actually saw some of them. He told me this story: 'I was out on the lower slopes of Fuzzy Mountain near Red Lake looking for some lost sheep. I went down into an arroyo, and I followed the arroyo for a while until I came to a place where a log had fallen across. There, in the bank of the arroyo, there was a blanket stretched across what turned out to be the entrance to a cave. I pulled the blanket aside and found a passageway leading to another blanket. Pulling that blanket aside, I found another passageway leading to yet another blanket. In the dim light coming from somewhere inside, I found a fourth blanket. I was very careful now because I could hear singing going on inside and I could see the light was coming from there. I pulled that fourth blanket just enough to see a circle of men sitting around a campfire. They were singing and praying to a medicine bundle near the fire. Each man was sitting on the folded-up skin of some animal. Some had wolf skins, some had coyote skins, and some had bear skins. The men had red color painted on their chins, then a stripe of black over their cheeks, then a stripe of yellow across their eyes and then white on their forehead. Then the singing stopped and the chief witch stood up and called something into a cave that connected with his. Two skulls came rolling out, the skulls of a pair of twins they had killed, and the skulls started to roll around and around the campfire.

"'Then the men got up, and they vomited, and pissed, and shat on the skulls. When they finished with that, and when they were getting ready to go out, they all leaned forward and were pulling their skins over their heads. At that moment I dashed in from behind the blanket, I grabbed their medicine bundle, and I started to run as fast as I could down the passageway that I had entered through, past the two inner blankets, past the last blanket, and out into the arroyo again. I could hear them shouting and running after me, but I kept on going. I was faster than they were, and I kept on running until I came to my hogan. I stopped there and I turned around. They were still coming after me in their skins. With a stick I drew four lines in the dirt in front of my hogan, and they couldn't cross the lines. I had taken their medicine away from them. Four days later, I found out they were all dead.'

"Witches go after twins," Mr. Bird went on in his explanation, "and they try to kill them. They try to take the whorls from the fingers of the twins or the whorls of hair from the back of the twins' heads. They keep the skulls for their bad medicine. They make a powder out of the fingertips or out of the hair of the twins they kill. They take the powder, and they blow it into the smoke holes on top of the hogans to witch the people inside. Or else they put it on their hands, and they trick you when they shake hands with you."

Hosteen Tso sang the Blessingway over the twins, one at Ganado and one at Crystal. The Shortys were never sure Hosteen Tso's singing would keep the girls safe, so they moved and took Lottie to Phoenix. Nettie and her husband took their children and Laura and moved to Denver. They are very cautious when they come back to the Reservation. They never let the girls be seen together, and they are very careful not to shake hands with anybody they don't know.

VI.

I came away from that Saturday morning worship powerfully moved. It was not so much by the ritual of the service, or by the trappings of the sanctuary, or by the pleasant association with fellow Jews, but by the feeling of elation at having seen, much as Michelangelo had envisioned, "the finger of the Lord." I understood more than ever that little else so powers human emotions as the presence of twins: reverence, fascination, or compulsion to penetrate their meaning. But that fascination with twins can trigger not only reverence for creation, but also evil's imagination.

VII.

You are dead now, Dr. Mengele! You will never see and you will never touch the twin beauties with the honey-colored hair.

Ya n'elgloshi, I hope you will never find Lottie and Laura, the ones with the sandy-colored braids. But I know those twins will have to be very, very careful.

SQUIRREL'S EARS

~

We moved Grandpa Bird to the Red Rocks Nursing Home in Gallup last year. He'd not been happy in the nursing home in Rio Rancho even though Ida was faithful in driving up the hill from Corrales to see him nearly every day. I was faithful myself in taking him out every Saturday morning, helping him from the wheelchair to the front seat of the car, then driving him down the hill to our place in Corrales for the day. There he could talk to Ida and there he could see some of his grandchildren and great-grandchildren.

"Now, in Gallup, at least he's closer to the Reservation," I said to Ida. "Almost all of the nurses and aids are Navajo and he has someone to talk to in Navajo whenever he wants to." I didn't have to tell Ida, because she knew as well as I, that most of the residents in the nursing home were Navajo too. But most of them were so far gone, so demented, that they were no company for him. It was no comfort for him to see those old shriveled faces and those blank, staring eyes. But Grandpa's mind and his memory were still good, as they are to this very day.

"I know I am going to live to one hundred and four," Grandpa has said many times. He's probably right.

From the large, east-facing window of his room he can see the cars and trucks on Highway 66 and the Santa Fe trains rolling in and out of Gallup. A little to the north of that he can see the continuous flow of traffic on the Interstate which runs in the new cut in the hogback.

His ability to see all this came about just within the last year, when he was ninety-eight. Dr. Arthur Weinstein took out the cataracts he had in both eyes and replaced those old, clouded lenses with new, plastic implants.

So he's closer to home now, being in Gallup. When Ida takes him out for an afternoon or for an overnight pass, as she will at corn-planting time, she can take him home to Red Lake. That's where his home has been for nearly sixty years. From the front porch of his cabin he can look down upon the valley to see the fields he had fenced and irrigated, and he can look across the valley to the pink sandstone cliffs that turn to gold at the end of the day.

Grandpa has said that he would live to be a hundred and four. He was still herding sheep when he was eighty. I had difficulty keeping up with him then when I was forty-five.

Of course, things happen to a man in the course of a long lifetime. Grandpa had his gallbladder taken out at the Indian Hospital at Fort Defiance when he was seventy-five. He did just fine. I took care of him when he had a very painful case of the "shingles" when he was in his eighties and I had to give him injections of Demerol. Another time I admitted him to the hospital under my own care when he had a case of severe inflammation of the face. I thought it was a case of erysipelas which required intravenous antibiotics. Then, when he was having repeated infections of his urinary bladder, we arranged for him to have prostate surgery. Again, his strong constitution helped him through.

But he was getting older. In the winter of his ninety-seventh year he became ill with cough and weakness. I brought him to my office where an X-ray showed that he had pneumonia and where an electrocardiogram showed a rapid, irregular heartbeat. I treated him with antibiotics and with digitalis to slow down his rapid heart rate and to strengthen his heart. Again he recovered.

This time we knew we would have to keep Grandpa Bird with us. He was getting too old and too weak to stay by himself in his cabin at Red Lake. This was especially true for the wintertime. He had only a wood stove for heat and the cabin would get cold if the fire went out or if he ran out of wood or coal. And then he might trip or fall on the ice and snow on the way to the privy. Often there was no food in the house and nobody to cook for him.

So we brought Grandpa to stay with us in Corrales. He had a room of his own, the bathroom was just down the hall, and when the weather was warm he could sit out on the patio and sun himself.

"Dad, come here!" our son, Joseph, called to me with some urgency one Sunday morning. "Grandpa asked me to help him but he can't get up." I rushed in to see what was wrong.

"Something happened to my leg," Grandpa said. "It's cold and I have no feeling in it." I felt his legs and his feet. The left foot was cold and it had no pulse in it.

"Phil," I said on the phone to my friend, Dr. Jacob, a vascular surgeon. "It looks like my father-in-law has thrown an embolus to his left leg."

"Get him down here to the hospital right away. I'll have my technician meet you there and I'll see him right after that." We found a wheelbarrow to get Grandpa out of the house and into the car to the hospital. Dr. Jacob took him to the operating room and he saved Grandpa's leg that day.

So now Grandpa is comfortable and safe in the nursing home in Gallup. Even his eyes are better. And he can get home now and then, and at the end of the day he can see the cliffs across the valley when they turn to gold.

Grandpa is half Hopi but neither he nor anybody has any stories about his Hopi father, or how that Hopi man happened to meet his mother, a Navajo of the T'a chini clan from Canyon de Chelly. Ida remembers her grandmother's peach orchard in what is called "Spring Canyon," a box canyon that opens into the Canyon de Chelly from the south, and the wagon trips from Red Lake each summer. Grandpa would drive the wagon up past Old Sawmill, through the ponderosa forest, past Fluted Rock, then down to Chinle at the mouth of the Canyon. From there he drove back up into the Canyon on its sandy bottom, past White House ruin, to his mother's place. They would return with the wagon bed full of peaches. Ida's mother would then pit them, dry them in the sun under a cheese cloth and store them in a gunny sack in the root cellar for the winter.

Grandpa used to tell his own story.

"I didn't start school or learn English until I was fifteen. The only boarding school was at Fort Defiance then and it was more than sixty miles away from Canyon de Chelly where I was born. The 'silah-o,' the Navajo policemen, used to round up the children to send them to school, but I didn't want to go to school. I just wanted to stay in the canyon and to be able to go when I felt like it to all the places I liked and that I knew so well.

"I knew of special places in the big canyon and in the little side canyons. I knew where all the springs were and where the grass grew damp and rich. The spring I liked best was back in Spring Canyon where my mother had her hogan and a peach orchard. When I would get to the spot I would spread the tall grass aside and there was the cool water coming up from the ground at the base of the cliff. I would brush away the water striders and the dead leaves from the surface of the water and I would put my whole head in it. How cool and fresh the water was after a hot climb to that place! I would feel the cool water soak right through my hair and it would feel so good trickling down the back of my neck. After that I would climb the slope a little way and I would lie on my back while the sheep came to drink and to eat the grass. I would let my eyes climb up the red cliffs that rose straight up to the sky.

"I would find the place where my mother and I used to climb up the trail to the top when we wanted to get out of the canyon. It was a very steep trail, almost straight up a big crack in the canyon wall. There were toe-holds and hand-holds that were cut into the rock by the Anasazis, the 'Old People,' when they lived in the canyon. Half way up there was a place where my uncle propped up a log and where he had cut notches so you could climb straight up.

"But most of the time I just wanted to stay down in the canyon. I wanted to feel the sun on my back and to feel its heat on my face. Some of the side-canyons were cool and narrow. If you looked straight up to the sky in one of those narrow canyons you could see the moon in the middle of the day.

"I loved the quiet of the canyon, but if you listened carefully, you could always hear something. There was the sound of the sheep bells and the bleating of my own sheep. You could also hear the sound of a neighbor's sheep in the distance. Sometimes you could hear the strange sound of the braying of a donkey as it echoed off the cliff walls even if the donkey was far away. The grasshoppers and the cicadas would fill the canyon floor with their humming and thrumming. From somewhere up the side of the cliff, the canyon wrens would call, their high notes followed by a trickle down of lower notes. In the air high above, the black crows would circle and make their sound, 'Gah-gee!' and that's what we Navajos use as their name. And then 'Tsip-tsip-tsip!' would be the short cries of the swifts as they make their crazy turns and dives in the air.

"I also began to explore the caves and the houses of the Anasazi, the Old People, even though I knew I wasn't really supposed to go into those places. I'll tell you more about how I started to go into those caves later. But those caves were just the right places to hide in because I knew the Navajo policemen wouldn't go there to look for me. I used to hide in my secret places in one or another of the Anasazi caves, never the same one each time. The 'silah-o' came back one time and said they had caught Grey Eyes, and they had sent him off. They said if my mother wouldn't hand me over, they would send *her* off, to the jail at Chinle.

"So they caught Grey Eyes! He had been to Fort Defiance before and he said he would never go back. It looked like things were getting pretty serious. Grey Eyes wasn't the kind of boy who could be caught very easily. Let me tell you about him.

"Grey Eyes was my cousin, about a year younger than me, and a little shorter, and not as strong as I was. He was related to me through my mother's side of the family. He was the son of my mother's brother, so he was not of my clan, the T'a chini clan. He belonged to my uncle's *wife's* clan, so he was of the Black Goat clan.

"Anyway, besides being my cousin, Grey Eyes was my best friend. He was just a little bit crazy, but that's why he was so much fun. He was always thinking up crazy things to do. I would usually go along with him, but sometimes I had to say, 'Look, sik'ess, my friend, that's enough!' Then he would listen to me because I was older.

"He didn't really have grey eyes. He got his English name when he was sent to boarding school at Fort Defiance the first time. He was sent to school by my uncle's wife's brother.

"'You're just growing up wild,' Hosteen Black Rock told him. 'I've heard about the crazy things you've been doing with your ropes and lassoes. Just because I taught you to weave a rope and how to throw it doesn't mean you have to have yourself killed. It's a lucky thing your cousin Joe Bird was with you when you tried to lasso that mountain lion. Now you're almost thirteen,' Hosteen Black Rock went on. 'You've got to learn English so you can help your mother. That way, when she goes to the trading post you'll be able to speak for her. Those white traders don't always understand Navajo. And sometimes they'll try to trick you if they think you don't understand English.'

"Well, the first day Grey Eyes got to the boarding school the head of the boys' dormitory asked him his name.

"'B'nah t'lpahe,' my friend said.

"That white man thought he knew Navajo but he really didn't. He thought 'B'nah t'lpahe' meant 'His Eyes are Grey.' Us Navajos use the same word, 't'lapahe,' for both light brown or tan and also for grey. So that's how my friend got the name 'Grey Eyes.'

"He used that name until he was an old man and he died with that name. But when he was a boy his eyes, those crazy eyes, were really light tan, almost yellow, like a cat's.

"But do you know what? When he was beginning to get real old, like I said, and he lived to be ninety, he began to get that grey ring around his eyes the way old people get. Pretty soon that grey ring got thicker and thicker and it covered up all the tan color. So all the white people who got to know him when he was an old man thought 'Grey Eyes' was the right name for him.

"Grey Eyes hated the boarding school from the very first day. He told me about it later.

"'The teachers talk *mean* to you. They make you get up in front of the room and they *yell* at you. They tell you to say a word over and over again. If you keep on getting it wrong, all the girls, and even some of the boys, laugh at you. They make you wear those stiff shoes that hurt your ankles and they make you tie the strings so tight. They hit you if they hear you talking Navajo to your friends. And they make you go to church. You have to sing all those songs about Jesus.

"'Anyway, I figured out a way to get out of that place. One of the janitors in the dormitory, Kee Tsosie, was a member my clan, the Black Goat clan. I told him that the pillow they gave me was too hard and that I wanted to stuff it with yucca leaves. I told him to get me a whole pile of yucca leaves and to hide them in my foot locker when I went to class. That night, after the lights went out, I started to weave a rope like my uncle Hosteen Black Rock taught me. But there wasn't enough. I stuffed some of the yucca leaves in my pillow so Kee Tsosie would think I was really using the yucca for pillow stuffing. The next day I told him some of the other boys wanted yucca for their pillows and I told him to bring me some more. So he kept on bringing more and every night I kept on weaving my rope. Finally, on the fourth night I had enough.

"'When it got real still, and when I didn't hear any more footsteps in the hall or any sound of horses in the street, I tied the rope to the head of my iron bed. Then I let myself down out the window. I hid in the shadows until I was sure nobody was still up or walking around. Nobody saw me. They didn't see the rope until the next morning.

"'I headed west through Bonito Canyon and I ran until it got light. I hid under a juniper bush all day. In the afternoon I heard the sound of slow hoof beats. It was Hosteen Yazzie, an old man I knew from Chinle. He was taking some goods on a string of burros and he was leading them from Fort Defiance to the trading post at Chinle. I told him my mother was sick and that I would go back to school as soon as I got a medicine man for her. I would even help with the burros if he would take me with him.

"'So that's how I got away from Fort Defiance. If I can help it, I will never go back there again.'

"Now I'll tell the story of how Grey Eyes tried to rope the mountain lion.

"Grey Eyes' mother had a burro and she let Grey Eyes herd the sheep and goats that belonged to her. In the fall and winter Grey Eyes' family lived on the north rim of Canyon del Muerto. But with a burro you can travel long distances. Grey Eyes would ride his mother's burro all around Chinle, at the mouth of the Canyon de Chelly (that's what 'Chinle' means: 'the mouth of the canyon') and then come up on the south rim to where my mother had our winter sheep camp.

"I was always happy to see Grey Eyes come around the canyon that way. Both of us could ride on the back of the burro together and we would ride all over. The south rim of the Canyon de Chelly is covered with tall sage brushes and they have big, knotty roots. On the burro you don't have to worry about getting your feet caught in those roots. And you can go farther and faster.

"Well, one day Grey Eyes and I were riding the burro on the south rim. He was helping me find a mother goat and her kid that were missing. We searched for the lost goats all afternoon and we had gone many miles to the south and east, almost to the foot of the mountain. The wind was starting to come up from the east. The burro was starting to walk slower and slower. We could tell he was getting tired so we let him rest in the shade of a cedar tree while we just sat on his back. The sun was getting lower and, at that time of the year, it cast long shadows on the ground. We knew we would have to be getting back soon. My mother would be disappointed that we couldn't find her goats.

"Just then we heard a loud scream, 'EEEEeeee!' just like a little boy crying. The hair stood up on the back of my neck. Just then the burro pointed his ears straight ahead. We didn't see anything at first, but when a burro points his ears, you know something is in that direction. My heart was pounding. Grey Eyes, who was sitting in front of me, began to fidget, and I could see him reaching down to grab his rope.

"She came around from behind one of the big sage brushes, very slowly, a long, tan, smooth mountain lion. We saw her head first. She was carrying the dead, white, fluffy kid in her mouth like a limp rag. She didn't see us because the sun was throwing its long rays into her yellow eyes and because we were standing still in the shadow of the cedar tree. She couldn't smell us either because the wind was coming from her direction.

"The big cat kept on moving slowly. More and more of her body kept on coming out from behind the sage brush. The burro kept absolutely still all this time and his ears just kept pointing straight ahead like two arrows. Pretty soon we saw the rest of the lion, first her big, floppy, front paws, then her shoulders rippling up and down as she walked. Then we saw the curve of her back, and then her haunches, and then her rear paws. Then, like in slow motion, hanging down at first and then curving up near the end, we saw that long, thick, tan tail, just as long as her body.

"I held my breath. The lion didn't even know we were looking at her. We were lucky so far. I was waiting for the lion to keep on going her way. I was just beginning to breathe a little easier when I saw Grey Eyes reach down and grab his rope. Then, with his rope in his hand, he raised his arm and started to swing it slowly in a smooth, steady motion.

"'Ch'indi!' I hissed, just loud enough, I thought, for Grey Eyes to hear. 'What the devil do you think you're doing! Don't even *think* about it.

"The lion must have seen the movement of Grey Eyes' arm or maybe she heard the sound I made. She turned away from us and, in a flash, her hind end and her tail rose up in the air, and she bounded away. We heard the crash of dried, broken twigs as the lion disappeared behind the thick sagebrushes and then she was gone. Finally we could only hear the rising moan of the wind coming down from the mountain.

"'Crazy, crazy, crazy!' I kept on yelling at Grey Eyes and I kept on yelling because I was still so scared. 'You can't just try to rope a lion like that. Don't you have any *sense*? You need a *gun* and *dogs*! You've got to know what you're *doing*!

"Grey Eyes slunk down a little bit. 'I was just going to lasso her to a tree,' he said. He knew he almost did a stupid thing.

"The burro was glad we turned around. We headed back into the setting sun with the cold, pine-scented wind behind us, back to my mother's winter sheep camp.

"Navajos aren't supposed to touch dead people or anything that belonged to dead people. Us Navajos who live in the canyon in the summertime know that all around us, in the caves in the cliffs, or in some places right on the ground, there are the square stone houses of the Anasazi, the Old People. They used to live in those places but they are now all dead. So we herd our sheep, we grow our corn, we plant our peach trees, and we build our hogans on the soft, level ground in the bottom of the canyon. Navajos never go up into the places where the Old People once lived. *Most* Navajos, that is. But every now and then some Navajos do climb up into those ruins. I was one of them.

"Right across Canyon de Chelly from Spring Canyon, there's a cave with a tumbled down ruin in it. And on the ceiling of that cave, the Old People painted the sky and the moon and the stars. You could see the dark blue paint from far away, but if you got closer, as I did when I herded sheep that way, you could see the moon and some stars in it. I wanted to get a closer look at the painting, but when I was little, my mother warned me not to go up in there. It would have been easy to climb up to that cave because of the tumbled down rocks at the base of the cliff.

"One time when I got older, one of our goats started climbing up the slope that led to the entrance of the cave. I followed the goat and I tried to chase it down. Before I knew it I was standing right on the floor of the cave. I was panting from the climb and I was a little scared to be there. I was careful not to touch anything. But when I looked up at the ceiling I saw what I never saw from below. The big, round, white ball in the middle of the dark blue ceiling was the moon, all right, and the smaller white spots were the stars. But the stars were scattered here and there. I tried to make out any of the constellations I knew, but the painting didn't seem to be a very good picture of the sky at night. But deeper into the cave, where the ceiling sloped down to meet the back wall, there I saw it, a cluster of many stars together. It was a painting of the 'Dilye'eh,' the Pleiades. The Old People really *did* know the stars. They knew the 'Dilye'eh' just like us Navajos know the 'Dilye'eh.'

"There, in that quiet cave, the long dead Anasazi were talking to me. They were saying, 'We, too, knew the Dilye'eh. Those are the stars that come up in the east before the sun in the late summer, that are high in the sky in the middle of the night in the winter, and that go down in the west right after the sun in the very early spring.'

"I didn't tell my mother that time that I was up in that cave. I didn't want her to worry about me. I was a little worried myself that something might happen to me because I stood there with the ghosts of the Old People. Pretty soon I realized that I was still all right, that nothing happened to me. So I wasn't afraid anymore. Maybe the ghosts of the Old People couldn't hurt you after all. But I still wasn't going to do anything foolish either.

"I was beginning to get interested in what the white men were finding in the caves and ruins around Canyon de Chelly. And I was becoming less and less afraid to go into those ruins. But it was Grey Eyes who helped me with my greatest adventure.

"A number of miles south of where the Canyon de Chelly opens into the plain to the west, there is another small and narrow canyon. It runs in the same direction as the Canyon de Chelly, from east to west, and it makes a cut in the same plateau. But it widens out in the west so that people traveling from Ganado in the south going to Chinle hardly notice it.

"Grey Eyes used to hang around Chinle a lot and that's is where he heard there was a ruin in that canyon called 'Tra Trahzi B'kin' or 'Three Turkey House' ruin.

"'It's very hard to find the mouth of the canyon,' Grey Eyes told me, 'But if you trust me, I'll show you how you can get into the ruin from the top and I'll help you.'

"It sounded like it would be great fun and I wanted to hear more about it. As I told you, Grey Eyes was a little crazy, but if you didn't let him get too far, you would be able to do things you never thought could be done, and yet you could get away with it.

"Grey Eyes was getting better at weaving the strongest ropes. He really thought his rope was strong enough to hold that lion that time. It probably *was* strong enough. I didn't let him that time because he didn't plan for it right. This time he seemed to know what he was doing.

"'I checked out all the bushes at the rim of Three Turkey Canyon just above where the ruin is. None of those bushes is strong enough to hold you. But about thirty feet back, there's an old piñon tree about a foot and a half thick. That's where I'll tie the rope. From there I'll run the rope to the rim and then I'll lower you down.'

"I knew I could trust Grey Eyes to weave a good strong rope but I didn't know how much of an overhang there was. I didn't know if I would be able to swing into the cave once I was lowered down. I might be left hanging in the middle of the air with yet another drop to the bottom of the narrow canyon. But I knew I was going to try it.

"After Grey Eyes tied the rope to the piñon tree, he tied it to my waist and he started to lower me down. After I was let down about forty feet I was able to look into the biggest cave I had ever seen. The ceiling of the cave was smooth and curved. It was about seventy feet from the ceiling to the floor of the cave and it was more than a hundred feet wide. Inside the cave were many, many small houses, maybe ten or fifteen of them. I had never seen so many houses all in one cave like that. It was like a little town. Yet there was nobody there.

"When Grey Eyes lowered me to the level of the floor of the cave, I found I was hanging in mid-air about eight feet away from the rim of the cave. There was no way I could get my foot on solid ground and no way I could climb in.

"So the straight drop to the cave that way wouldn't work. I signaled to Grey Eyes to hoist me back up. But nothing happened! Then I realized that Grey Eyes just wasn't strong enough to do that.

"'I shouldn't have listened to that crazy Grey Eyes,' I thought. 'Now it's too late!'

"Just then I looked down and I saw the branch of a juniper tree that was growing out from a ledge of rock about six feet below where I was hanging. I hollered to Grey Eyes to lower me down another little bit. I could tell he was scared too, but he let me down until my feet reached the branch. Then I kicked the branch and I started to swing, first away from, and then back to the branch. I kept on kicking and I kept on swinging closer and closer to the rock. I hollered to Grey Eyes to let me down another few feet so I could grab the branch with my hands. He followed my directions and soon I was hanging on to the tree. It bent under my weight and I thought it would break but it didn't. I just hung there for a while my heart pounded and while I tried to figure out what to do next. For a long time I didn't dare to look down. Finally I did look down and saw that, while I still held onto the branch, I could get my feet on the ledge just below where my feet were. I leaned forward and was able to touch the rock with one of my hands and I held on long enough to know I could lean forward and that I would not fall. I was able to let go of the branch now and I crept along the ledge holding on to the rock with my bare hands. A few feet away there was a crack that led up to the cave. I inched along the ledge until I reached the crack, and from there it was an easy climb into the cave. When I got to the level floor of the cave I just stayed on my hands and knees for a long time. I wasn't afraid to touch the dust of the cave where the ghosts of the Old People might be. All I knew was that I was safe.

"I just rested there for a while until I my heart slowed and I could calm down. When I looked up, I saw what I hadn't seen before. Way at the back of the cave there was one large house, larger than all the others, and it had three turkeys painted on the front of it. I had plenty of time to take a good look at how the Old People painted those turkeys. The turkeys had small heads and long necks, and long tails that hung down. Two of the turkeys had white heads, necks and breasts with brown bodies and tails, and one had a brown head, neck and breast with a white body and tail.

"Before I could spend any more time looking at the ruins I had to figure out a way to get out of there and to get home. I looked over the edge of the cave and I tried to guess haw far down it was to the bottom of the canyon. It was pretty far, maybe about a hundred feet, but there was a rocky slope about halfway down. I knew Grey Eyes had a long enough length of rope for me to reach that rocky slope. I called to Grey Eyes to release the rope so I could use it. I pulled the rope into the cave and I told Grey Eyes to wait for me at the mouth of the canyon.

"I was still shaking from the scary struggle I had. It's a good thing I didn't look all the way down when I was creeping along that ledge.

"When I looked around I realized that the white men hadn't started digging in this cave yet. I had it all to myself. It was quiet except for the wind and the 'tsip-tsip-tsip' of the swifts and for the fluttering of their wings as they flew in and out of the cave.

"I started to explore a room in the first of the stone houses. When I walked inside, my feet stirred up the dry dust that lay on the floor and the dry dust stung my nostrils. The light was dim inside the room but I could see that the walls in one corner of the room were black and there was some burned-out wood in the corner. A large clay pot with a pointed, black bottom stood almost upright in the middle of what had been a fire. It was as if the Anasazi had just got up and left, and they left the stew pot just where it had always been. I thought they might be back any minute and find me there and say 'What are you doing here in our house?'

"There was a smaller room that I had to crawl to get into. Inside there were some large, clay jars with stones on top of them. When I looked inside one of the jars there were ears of dried corn, but the ears were tiny, no bigger than my thumb. In another jar I found the dried seeds of either pumpkin or squash.

"I took handful of these and I stuck them in my pocket.

"It was getting late. The wind began to pick up and it made a moaning sound that was a little scary. I figured it was time for me to get out Three Turkey House ruin and get home. I tied Grey Eyes' rope to a corner of the stone house that was closest to the front of the cave. I looped it through the open door, through one of the open windows and then back to the door where I tied a good, strong knot. Then I started to let myself down off the front ledge of the cave. For the first fifty feet or more I dangled and I swayed a little in the wind. Finally my feet reached the steep slope with many large boulders, and I let go of the rope. My feet started slipping and I set many large rocks loose. Soon, some of the rocks that I loosened on my way down began to roll after me. One big boulder went whizzing by and just missed me. A smaller rock hit me on the ankle. I kept slipping and sliding. The canyon was getting darker and darker and it was harder for me to see where I was going. What a relief it was when I got my feet on the sandy bottom!

" I still had to pick my way around boulders and dead trees that were scattered here and there on the canyon floor. I tripped a few times and landed on my hands but I felt happy to feel the smooth, solid ground under me.

"It was almost night when I reached the mouth of the canyon. Many miles across the valley I could barely see the dim outline of Black Mesa set off by the last glow red glow of the setting sun. I whistled for Grey Eyes and he whistled back. I suppose he was glad to see me and that I was safe. I thought he would begin to ask me how I got into the cave, what I found there, and how I managed to get out. But all he asked me was, 'Did you bring back my rope?'

"The next spring my mother planted the pumpkin seeds. The seeds sprouted, first the little round seed leaves, then the large pointy leaves. I was excited to see the vines start to grow out over the ground. Soon the blossoms came out, large and fresh and yellow. But the pumpkins that came after the flowers hardly grew and the fruit had no flavor or sweetness. It was if the ghosts of the Anasazi were saying. 'You stole into our storehouse and took what didn't belong to you. Now we'll take away some of the pleasure you thought you would have from us Old People.'

"The 'silah-o' came back another time saying they'd found my friend, Grey Eyes, and they had sent him off to school again. They said if my mother wouldn't hand me over, they would send *her* off, to the jail at Chinle.

"That time I stayed away for two days and two nights. When I came back my mother was crying, 'I thought you fell down somewhere, that maybe you'd broken a leg.'

"I felt sorry for her, that she'd worried so much about me. I felt bad that I was so stubborn, that she might have to go to jail because of me. 'The last wagon-load of children left for Fort Defiance two days ago,' she went on. 'I know the 'silah-o' will be coming for me soon. I would have asked your uncle to take you there on his horse but he's away in Utah and and won't be back until next month. Now there's no way to get you to school even if you wanted to go.'

"I felt a lump growing in my throat but I wouldn't cry. 'All right, shi mah,' I said. I really want to stay here in the canyon with you. I know how hard it will be for you if I go. But it looks like I can't stay. So I'll tell you what I'll do. I'll *walk* to Fort Defiance.'

"'Shi yahzh!' she cried. 'It's over sixty miles to Fort Defiance. And it's dangerous to walk through the forest.'

"'I'll do it,' I said. My mother knew I'd made up my mind. She didn't argue any further.

"That evening, my mother made up a big batch of corn tortillas and she threw them into a sack with some peaches from her trees. She took her little pouch of white cornmeal for herself and a pouch of yellow corn pollen for me. We hiked up toward the head of Spring Canyon, but we stopped on the way to fill a clay jug of water from the spring. At the head of the canyon we rested for a while and we looked straight up the steep trail that went to the top. I wondered how we would manage the climb with the extra load of food and water, but she just slung the load in the shawl on her back, tied a knot in front, and she started up step by step. 'Be sure you don't look down or look back,' she warned me. Then up we went with hands and toes in hand-holds and toe-holds, all the way to the top.

"We rested there on the rim until our hearts stopped pounding and until we caught our breath. I looked down for a last time at my beautiful canyon, now deep in the shadows. I could still see my mother's hogan and the peach trees and the sheep corral. They all looked so tiny, so far down and so far away.

"It was nearly dark now and we camped for the night. 'What are you going to do now, shi mah?' I called after her when I saw her wandering off toward a clump of cedar trees. She said nothing but she started to strip bark off some of the trees. When she had an armful of bark she sat down and quickly wove the bark into two pairs of sandals for my feet. 'It's a long and rough road to Fort Defiance,' she said, 'And you'll need these.' When the stars came out we could see the Swan coming up on its side. Later in the night the Swan began to turn and to head down to the west. Still later, before the first light in the east, we could see the 'Dil-yeh-eh,' the Pleiades, rise above the horizon. 'The summer's nearly over, shi yahzh,' my mother said, pointing to the cluster of stars with her chin.

"Early the next morning, before the sun was up, my mother stood up and sprinkled the white corn meal in the four directions and said her prayer for me. I hugged her goodbye, and I started out at a run, south and east across the sagebrush-covered plateau. I headed in the direction of the dark green mountain, but it was over twenty miles away. I sang my morning song as I ran and I felt the cool, morning breezes in my face. I turned back now and then to be sure of my direction. Black Rock rose out of the plain on the other side of the Canyon de Chelly to the north. Way off to the west, the sun's rays were beginning to light up the sides of Black Mesa on the other side of the Chinle Wash.

"But I couldn't just keep looking all around. My foot almost got caught on the roots of one of the giant sagebrushes and the ground was getting rocky. It was getting hot on the open plain when the sun rose higher, but I kept on going. After a while the going got even tougher. I entered into an arroyo that I knew would lead me up to the mountain. But I had to be careful to avoid the boulders and the branches of trees that had been washed down by the rains and that were all over the floor of the arroyo.

"I followed the arroyo for a long way, going uphill all the time. Sometimes the arroyo was so deep I couldn't see over the top of it. One time, when my head was level with the ground above the arroyo, I saw a shadow moving along and following me. I tried to see what it was but it kept on ducking behind the sagebrush that was thick along the way. Finally I saw that it was running on four legs and that it was covered with fur. A 'Ya n'elgloshi!', a Skinwalker! I could feel the hairs stand up on the back of my neck. I grabbed a rock and I threw it with all my might. I was good at throwing rocks; with my first rock I hit him. I heard the rock go 'thump' on his chest. He let out a howl and then I saw him run off with his tail between his legs. It was just a 'mah-ee yahzha,' a coyote, but a big one. I was happy that I got a good look at him and that he was just a coyote and not a witch in an animal's skin. I was also glad that I saw him run off to the side and that he didn't cross in front of me. That would have been almost as much bad luck as if he'd been a real skinwalker witching me.

"Finally I got to where the forest began. First the piñon trees gave me a little shade here and there on the lower slopes of the mountain. The air was fresher with the smell of the piñon. Later, the air became cooler also from the breezes blowing downhill from the shade of the tall ponderosas.

"My heart was pounding now after the brush with the coyote and with the hard running I'd been doing for nearly four hours. I rested at the foot of one of those great ponderosas and I took my first bite of food. How good my mother's corn tortilla tasted! The peach was hot from the sun and its sweet, sticky juice ran down between my fingers but I didn't care. I took a long drink from the water that had come from the spring in my canyon. I was warm, too, but its taste was pure and it reminded me of home.

"I looked off to the north. Now that I was higher, I could see in the midday haze the red cliffs at the base of the Lukachukai mountains, and on top of them, the gray peaks of the Lukachukais themselves. And off to the northwest, the light fell on Round Rock, that big, round, flat-topped rock that stands in the broad valley of the Chinle Wash.

"I must have fallen asleep for a while, because when I woke up, the sun had swung around to the west. I got up then, stretched, and started out again at a trot south and east into the ponderosa forest. The floor was covered with pine needles and that made it much easier on my feet. I ran along in the cool shade and I felt the cooling breeze in my face once again. Overhead, I heard the wind coming up in the treetops.

"It was all so peaceful, running along like that when, suddenly, I heard a crash behind me. Then there was another crash beyond the trees to my left. I was frightened. I began to think that maybe the animal I had seen near the arroyo *was* a 'Ya n'elgloshi' after all, and that maybe he and his friends, once they got me in the forest, would try to get even with me. Maybe they were throwing their witching bones at me. But after a while I saw that the crashing noises were just from the big pine cones coming down from those tall, tall trees.

"It was pretty easy heading south and east along the forest floor. I could see where I was going because the forest floor was flat and because there were no large boulders or thick underbrush to block the way. Every now and then there was a clump of oak trees I would have to go around.

"As long as there was enough daylight I was able to keep right on going, but when it was beginning to get dark, I knew I had to find me a safe place to camp. By this time I had been running or walking about fourteen hours. I hadn't seen another person (except maybe that skinwalker, if it *was* a skinwalker) all that time. My feet were getting sore. I'd almost worn out the first pair of cedar-bark sandals my mother had made me but I figured they might last another half-day.

"I found a nice place to lie down. It was in one of those clumps of oak trees. It was a real protected place. Any animal or person or skinwalker couldn't get in without making a noise. It didn't take me long to fall asleep. You can imagine how tired I was. Even when the wind was blowing in the trees making a sound like a person moaning or sighing, it didn't scare me or keep me awake.

"I was stiff and sore all over when I woke up. It was barely light then. I stepped out of my hiding place and I took out my corn pollen to pray. 'Beauty before you, beauty behind you, beauty above you, beauty below you, beauty all around you.' Just as I was raising my arm to sprinkle the corn pollen all around me, I saw somebody standing there about a hundred feet away on the other side of a little grassy meadow. I the dim light I could see he was tall and heavy and that he was wearing something dark.

"'Yat'eh, sik'ess,' (Hello my friend), I called out to him. 'Chad ish ahn b'ana nah.' (What are you doing here?).

"He didn't answer. He turned his head. In the dim light I could see there was something funny about his head. It was too small for his body. He didn't have any neck, and his nose and his chin all came together in a point.

"'EE yah!' I shouted in alarm. '*Shash* at eh!' (It's a *bear*!) When I yelled like that, the bear let out a kind of yell of his own, his front paws flew up and he fell right on his back. Then he scrambled to his feet, let out a big shit, ran off on all fours, and disappeared into the darkness.

"It took me a long time to get over my fright. I was relieved that the bear was frightened, too, and that I didn't run into him again.

"When it became lighter I could see that the light was coming from the east and I was more sure of my direction. I headed off again to the south and east. I made as much time as I could while it was still cool. After I ran for a few hours I came to a place where the forest floor dropped off to a lower level and I crossed a large, open meadow. When I looked back over my shoulder, I saw a tall, gray cliff that had ridges on its face from top to bottom. The Navajos call that cliff 'Dsilth dah sah ahn,' and the white men call it 'Fluted Rock.' I knew from what my uncle used to say, that if you see that rock, you know you're more than half-way to Fort Defiance.

"I camped out again in an oak tree grove that second night. My first pair of cedar-bark sandals was completely in shreds. I was thankful that my mother had made me a second pair for the rest of my journey.

"When I started out the next day I noticed that the land was sloping down. The tall ponderosas were giving way to piñon, cedar and juniper, but it was still a high plateau. I came to place where, through the trees, I could see a deep, open valley that lay to the east of the plateau I'd been traveling on. A line of pink sandstone cliffs ran along the east side of that valley and the valley ran for many miles from north to south. There were some places where black rocks came up from the floor of the valley. My uncle said one time that the white men told him that those black rocks were once hot liquid that came out of the earth and then cooled and turned hard. Where there was a line of black rock like a wall that ran from east to west, my uncle told me, and where I would see a small canyon with red rock walls where it cuts through the mountain, there I would find Fort Defiance.

"At last I came to the place where I saw that wall of black rock and that red rock canyon. That's where I came down from the mountain. In a narrow valley near the opening of the red rock canyon, I found a two-story building made of red sandstone. Many, many small children were out playing in front of the building. The little girls wore short, cotton dresses, and the little boys wore short pants and long stockings and high-topped shoes. I suppose they were white man's clothes.

"Among the little boys there was a tall boy about my age. It was Grey Eyes! I ran up to him and we threw our arms around each other and we jumped up and down and we laughed. It wouldn't be so lonesome for me after all. Now I was at school at last. I would learn English and my mother wouldn't have to go to jail. As it turned out later, I stayed at Fort Defiance for many years, until I was a fully-grown young man.

"Later I worked for Lorenzo Hubbell at his trading post at Ganado. I hear it's a famous place now, but at that time it was just a little trading post like many others on the Reservation. I was pretty good with horses and mules at that time and that came in handy because we were sent to pick up supplies in Gallup with a wagon drawn by a team of four mules. The roads weren't good enough for the trucks they had in those days so we took the team. It took us two days to get to Gallup and, of course, we had to camp out on the way. Coming back, with the wagon loaded with flour, sugar, coffee, canned goods and hardware it was real hard work going back over the divide. It took us an extra day for the trip back.

"When they were building the new dam at Red Lake, I went to work with the white men from the Bureau of Indian Affairs. We had to level the land below the dam and we had to set out the plan and dig the irrigation ditches. Then we had to distribute the land to different families. The Clevelands, who used to have the whole valley for their sheep, didn't like to have newcomers taking some of their land. They didn't like the T'senjikinnies. They said the T'senjikinnies had plenty of land of their own to the north, at Star Mountain, and to the south and west, at Ganado. But they went along with the project when they were told they would get some of the irrigated land, too. They even made me president of the Red Lake Chapter even though I was married to a T'senjikinnie. We had forty acres of irrigated land in the valley. We built our hogan and our cabin on the slopes above the valley and that's where we herded our sheep, too."

When Grandpa told that part of his story I had a question for him.

"When you fenced those forty acres, how did you dig the post-holes?" When Ida and I first came to Corrales about fifteen years ago, and when we were fencing the gardens behind out house, I learned to use a post-hole digger. With a post-hole digger you could dig a round hole straight down two and a half or more feet into the dirt.

"Grandpa, did you have a post-hole digger? (You see, though Brooklyn-born, I now considered myself something of an expert on life in the West.)

"No," said Grandpa, "We just used a crowbar and a spade. And we cut the cedar posts ourselves and we hauled them down from the mountain." Those fences with their sturdy cedar posts are still there and they mark the work that Grandpa had done nearly sixty years ago.

"I would be home at Red Lake in the spring for planting and irrigating, and in the fall for harvesting," Grandpa continued. "For a good part of the year I was away working on the railroad, the Santa Fe and the Union Pacific, as a section gang foreman. Most of the Navajos on the work gangs didn't speak English, but I would be able to help them and to explain how the work was to be done. The railroad work took me all over the West and the Southwest, from Wyoming to California and from Texas to Arizona."

Grandpa is ninety-nine years old now. He's seen the seasons change with the wheel of time, from the peach orchards and the Anasazi ruins in the Canyon de Chelly, from the ponderosa forests of the Defiance Plateau, from the irrigated fields below Red Lake, and from the grand sweep of the mountains and plains of the West. We still ask for his advice.

"Grandpa, when is time to plant the corn?"

Grandpa Bird always takes a little while but then he answers in his steady, measured way, "After the time when you can no longer see the 'Dilyeh'eh,' the Pleiades, go down in the west in the evening, and when the leaves on the cottonwood trees are the size of a squirrel's ears."

Fort Defiance Revisited

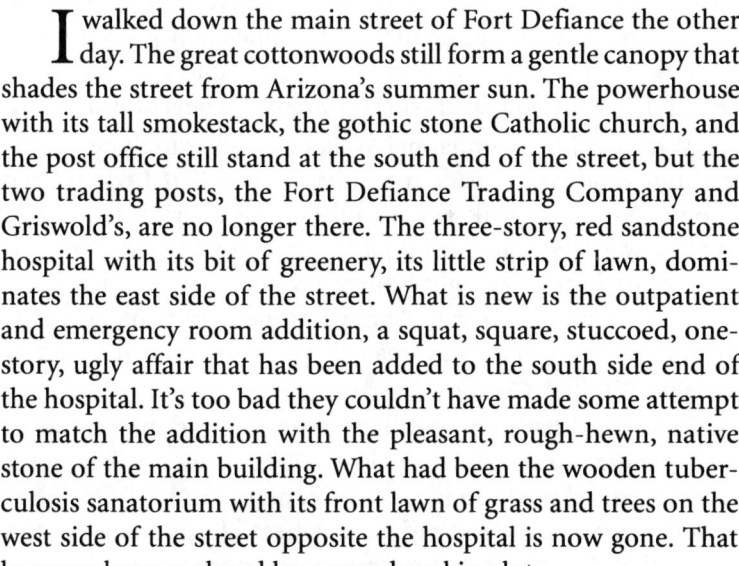

I walked down the main street of Fort Defiance the other day. The great cottonwoods still form a gentle canopy that shades the street from Arizona's summer sun. The powerhouse with its tall smokestack, the gothic stone Catholic church, and the post office still stand at the south end of the street, but the two trading posts, the Fort Defiance Trading Company and Griswold's, are no longer there. The three-story, red sandstone hospital with its bit of greenery, its little strip of lawn, dominates the east side of the street. What is new is the outpatient and emergency room addition, a squat, square, stuccoed, one-story, ugly affair that has been added to the south side end of the hospital. It's too bad they couldn't have made some attempt to match the addition with the pleasant, rough-hewn, native stone of the main building. What had been the wooden tuberculosis sanatorium with its front lawn of grass and trees on the west side of the street opposite the hospital is now gone. That has now been replaced by a paved parking lot.

Most days, in the middle of the day, and especially on weekends, the street is pretty quiet. A few Navajos are usually waiting to go into the hospital or driving down the street. The men still dress in blue jeans, Western shirts, and cowboy hats, and the women, especially the older ones, in traditional velveteen blouses and ankle-length skirts. But the younger women and girls may be seen in Levi's or shorts and wearing Nike jackets.

Chevy, Ford, and GMC pick-ups are still the principal vehicles, but these days minivans, conversion vans, and four-wheel drive, extended cab pick-ups cruise the street as well. The old, green, horse-drawn Studebaker farm wagons with their rubber-tired wheels and the people sitting on the driver's bench or in the bed of the wagon that used to be so colorful all disappeared a long time ago.

But the changes aren't that great considering that forty years have passed. Fort Defiance is still pretty much the same place. I had no difficulty recognizing it.

My assignment as pediatrician at the Fort Defiance Hospital was my first job, my first adventure after I finished my residency in Columbus. I was ready for the West, for a chance to see Indian country, for a chance to do some really good medical work where it was needed, and for a chance to get away from Ohio and the middle west where, frankly, I'd never been happy.

Why had I been unhappy? Well, being shy didn't help matters, but what really made me unhappy was that I was looked upon as a kind of freak. It wasn't that I was horrible to look at. My face was O.K.: plain, with glasses, but not ugly. My hair was dull-colored, straw, or light brown; my nose was acceptable, my eyes a nice mid-American, Anglo-European blue. What made me different was that I was small. Tiny. Four eleven and eighty-five pounds. Flat-chested.

"She must have an infantile uterus, or ovarian agenesis," I used to hear the smart-ass medical students say. Or, "She's just totally undeveloped; no life, no juice, no sex in her." Or, "She's hypothyroid; she doesn't radiate any heat." It just went on and on like that. Maybe I didn't really hear them say those things but I know that's what they thought.

They didn't know what was inside of me. It was just plain cruelty. It's true I didn't menstruate until I was seventeen, but I did menstruate, so it couldn't have been ovarian agenesis of anything like that. It is true I didn't have anything in the way of breasts, but I did have nipples, and I did have feelings in them.

I didn't wear make-up. I was just too angry. I wasn't going to do anything to please them. That's the way it was through high school, college, medical school, and hospital training. I was never asked out. No one ever made a pass at me. No one ever came on to me. I was never grabbed or held or kissed. I was cold in my virginity.

When I came to Fort Defiance it was the same thing.

"There's no *life* in her. She's dull. She's a *nothing*," the other doctors would say. There was a group of Jewish doctors in Fort Defiance at the time I came there. They were all specialists of one kind or another. The chief surgeon, Ben Kaplan, the chief pediatrician, Fred Schwartzman, the ophthalmologist, Sheldon Shine, the dentist, Martin Birnbaum were all married and formed their little clique. Jack Berkowitz was head of tuberculosis. He was single but he was busy sparking a Navajo girl (a beauty, actually, and a former Miss Navajo). I never got any feeling of warmth from any of them. And it *was* disappointing because I had expected more. After all I was a professional colleague.

But the Navajos, especially the patients, the children and their parents, were wonderful. They were the ones who radiated warmth, and they brought some warmth out of me. They had a name for me. Not out of derision, but out of love: 'Ason Yazzie,' (Little Woman).

In the summer of my second year James Kobiashi, a medical student from California, arrived in Fort Defiance to spend an externship, one month each on pediatrics and on surgery.

"Hi, I'm James, Dr. Bowman. I'll be your scut boy for the next month," he said when he showed up for duty on my floor.

"You won't have to do any scut work here. We have a pretty good lab. You won't even have to draw bloods," I said in my most professional manner. "But I do expect you to be on time for rounds with me every morning, to take the histories and to do the physical examinations, to write preliminary orders on all new admissions, and to take first call for pediatric emergencies on the nights I'm on call."

James Kobiashi was muscular, of medium height, (but, of course, taller than I) with a merriment about his black eyes that made it hard for me to maintain my official attitude for long. He radiated self-confidence, but he knew how not to be overbearing. There was richness in his voice and melody in his cultured speech. His appearance was as Japanese as his name, but he was refreshing, open, and enthusiastic.

Within a very few days of his arrival, he caught on to Navajo words of greeting. "Yat'eh ah'bin," (Good Morning) he would say every morning to all the little children on the ward.

The older girls would giggle and called back to him, "Yat'eh, azay-ich-inn" (Good morning, Doctor). He would tease the older boys and give them Navajo names, "Ashki de Jollie" or "Hosteen T'la pahe," if they were fat or lightly complected. They would tease him in return and call out to him familiarly, "Yat'eh sik'ess" (Hello, pal, or Hello, buddy).

Is it a wonder that Jim's skill in breaking down barriers worked on me, too?

"I've heard there's a great spot for a cookout called 'Natural Bridge,' just three or four miles from here. How about it? I'll get the steaks."

Just like that! The first invitation I'd had to anything since I'd come to Fort Defiance. It was easy to say yes. It was summertime. The daylight lasted until almost nine o'clock. The chance to get a way from the hospital for a change, to breathe the cool, piñon-scented air as the shadows lengthened, all these added to the appeal of Jim himself. Yes.

I was somehow completely at ease in spite of the newness of the situation for me. A man asking me out? He was just a boy. Jim was only twenty-three. I was twenty-eight, almost twenty-nine. I was his teacher. This wasn't a date. It was, as Jim said, just a cookout. Of course I would go. Nothing to it.

But there was a subtle change in myself. I would be gay, light-hearted. I washed my hair and I let it fluff out a bit. I didn't wear perfume, but the soap I showered with had a light, lavender scent. I put on a white, peasant-type blouse with short, puffy sleeves and a wide ruffle around the neck. I didn't care if I was flat. It was sick how those women used to worry about their boobs, how they used to pad their bras, how they subjected themselves to breast-augmentation surgery. Well, maybe I shouldn't be so hard on women for being vain, I said to myself, as I tried on a pair of silver and turquoise earrings I found in my top drawer. I'd bought them for my sister at the Navajo Arts and Crafts shop in Window Rock. They were pretty. I swept out of my room with a whoosh of my long, Navajo-type skirt, and I left my glasses behind.

Jim was right. It was just a short drive down along the valley of the Black Creek Wash on the old dirt road going south toward St. Michael's. About a mile past the black, volcanic dike that sticks up like a wall across the valley, Jim turned right and up about a quarter of a mile along an old wagon track. The track climbed the lower part of the gentle up-slope of the green Defiance Plateau. The sun had already dipped behind the brow of the mountain ahead and to the west, but looking back toward the east, the valley was flooded with soft, late-afternoon sunlight. Cottonwoods sprung up here and there along the meandering wash, and Navajo houses, hogans, little corrals and cornfields lay scattered about. Three miles across the valley a line of smooth, rounded, orange-pink sandstone caught the full sunlight, and beyond them, the clear brightness of the sky.

"You were right, Jim. It's absolutely beautiful here. I never knew there was so much loveliness so close to Fort Defiance."

Jim parked the car at the edge of a narrow arroyo that was all that was left of a small canyon that carried runoff from the plateau. A slab of flat, lichen-covered, gray rock about eighteen feet long and three feet thick lay across the top of the arroyo, deposited there by a flood that had come down the canyon some time in the past. The Navajos called it "Natural Bridge."

Jim set about gathering wood for the fire.

"Gather up some of those small flat rocks," he said. "We'll use them to support the grill."

Jim returned from a little excursion he made up the slope, out from under the branches of the juniper and the first of the piñon at that elevation, and he piled an armful of twigs and branches on the ground.

"Here. Make four flat piles of the flat stones in a square about a foot apart."

I did as he said and he lit the fire. The dried wood flashed up into flames in an instant. None of the damp, moldy sticks you find back in Ohio that smoulder and stink and never burn right, I thought. Wow! Look at that fire. I had to back away from the heat, but as I did so, I felt the cool air on my back. It was getting dark quickly in the shadow of the mountain.

The flame died down quickly. Jim was clever enough to use only small sticks and twigs at first, adding the larger chunks of wood later. He placed a flat steel grill he'd brought with him and he laid it across the stone supports I'd made for him. Then he waited until the grill became hot from the glowing coals.

I leaned back and watched the shadow of the mountain behind us creep across the valley. The color of the sandstone cliffs grew a deeper orange, and then, as the light faded further, the rocks took on a phosphorescent glow.

"In some ways," Jim said, "the color of those cliffs reminds me of the last of the sunlight on the windows of Oakland when you see them from San Francisco. The open valley here is a little like the open space of San Francisco Bay."

"You sound like you're lonesome for home," I said.

"Not a bit. It's just the space and the light. But the people, that's another matter. I'm glad to be away from there."

"I've heard that the West coast and San Francisco in particular is a very friendly place."

"Not if you're Japanese. When you're on the street, in a bus, or on a street car you can feel the eyes of Caucasians looking at you. You know they're tying to figure out what kind of an Oriental you are, Chinese or Japanese or Filipino or something else. Out here, very frankly, I feel much more comfortable. I guess I look enough like a Navajo that nobody thinks of trying to figure me out."

I felt a sudden rush of warmth for Jim. I'd thought he was so self-confident, so comfortable with himself. Here he'd opened himself up to me. I didn't say anything for a while. I didn't want to encourage him to go on bringing up painful memories. It was too lovely where we were.

Jim put on the steaks and the embers burst into flames and smoke when the fat dripped in the fire. He was in no hurry to turn the meat over. He liked the steaks with the fat black and crisp on the outside, just like I did. He stared into the fire for a while and then went on.

"They hauled my father right out of the Moffat, right out of his internship at the University of California Hospital. Can you imagine that? He was sent off with the rest of the Japanese to the internment camp in Idaho in 1942. They paid him twelve dollars a month to be one of the doctors in the camp."

The wind began to blow a little harder down the mountain. The smoke from the fire was getting into Jim's face, so he moved around to where I was sitting. He leaned forward to turn the steaks over, and when he sat back down again his arm brushed against mine.

They were wrong, I thought. There *is* life in me. I can feel it in my arm. Next to his arm.

The sky above the cliffs to the east now darkened. The bright star, Vega, appeared, and not long after that, the Swan rose on its side, flying down the stream of the Milky Way.

"Yat'eh ah' bin," I said to the children coming on to the ward the next morning. What was that, a chirp? I asked myself. An evening cook-out shouldn't make you chirp, you silly woman! Dr. Bowman, a silly woman? And that tingling of your face when Jim came in, was that a flush? Or a blush?

"There's a squaw dance on the divide on the road to Ganado," Jim said. He'd learned more about where things were going on in two weeks than I learned in a year. "I'll pick you up a little after six on Saturday." There was that confidence again, I thought. He didn't even ask me if I wanted to go.

I threw off my glasses the minute I got back to my room that Saturday evening. I looked at myself in the mirror. You know with just a little bit of a smile and a little bit of color in your cheeks, you're not half bad, really, I said to myself. He'd notice if I started wearing lipstick, I thought. What the hell. One of these days I'll pick some with just a little bit of color. Nothing flaming red, of course. I'm sure I'll find something just right in Gallup. No perfume. That would be too obvious. Just a little cologne. Cologne is more subtle and it doesn't hang on as long.

We swept southward on the east side of the valley on the highway toward Window Rock. The sandstone cliffs rose on our left. Across the valley to the west, on the lower slope of the mountain, I tried to find the canyon at the outlet of which lay the Natural Bridge. The bridge between the sexes. The bridge between the races.

"No, it's too far away and too small to see from here," Jim said when I asked him. "But it was a perfect spot, a perfect evening, wasn't it?"

The road west of Window Rock took us across the valley, past the fair grounds, and then on the way up the mountain. The juniper bushes on the lower slopes gave way to the piñons and, still higher, the ponderosa forest began. I sat quietly next to Jim, our shoulders almost touching.

"This is so much different from Ohio, Jim," I said. "Out here you can tell how high you are just by looking at the trees."

"It's that way in California, too. Only there, when you climb to a certain elevation out of the Central Valley, you run into the redwoods. The giant sequoias. I'd love to show them to you some day."

I got a little dizzy. He's thinking about me. He's connecting with me.

We drove several miles at the top of the plateau with scattered ponderosa pines and open meadows stretching in all directions.

"So this is what the top of the mountain looks like," I said. "The folks back home would never believe this was Arizona. Even I thought Arizona was all desert, heat, and cactus."

"Wait till you see the Tuolumne valley in Yosemite," Jim said. "Even though you think you know what it will look like from pictures, when you actually see it, you will never believe how beautiful it is."

A crude wooden sign attached to a fence post pointed to the left. Jim slowed down and turned onto a dirt road leading south. It was nearly dark now. In the rearview mirror we could see the headlights of several pickup trucks that had turned off the highway after us. Those headlights were shining through the dust we had kicked up.

"It looks like I found the right road. Everybody seems to be following us in."

Soon, through the dust, we caught up with the taillights of a pickup turning off to the right onto a less-traveled track.

"Looks like that fellow's going where we want to go." Our headlights caught the glow of the cinnamon-colored bark of an old ponderosa pine when we turned. Further ahead we saw a cluster of taillights, the rear ends of trucks that were parked in a circle in a meadow among the trees. Crowds of Navajos wandered about in the semi-darkness, light coming from a huge fire of logs in the center of a large circle.

We found a place to park and Jim took me by the hand. He pulled me as he threaded his way between the trucks and through the groups of Navajos. The Navajos moved about gaily, chatting and greeting one another as they came and went.

We stood quietly inside the circle. Our faces felt the heat of the great fire which churned smoke and spewed sparks into the night sky. On the other side of the circle a cluster of men and boys and an occasional woman had already begun to sing, loudly and in unison, accompanied by the beat of a small drum held by one of the men. Jim folded his arms around me from behind and I could feel his happiness and my happiness.

"We're going north this time," Jim announced. "We're going to the canyon."

"Which canyon?"

"Canyon de Chelly, the red rock canyon, the one with the Anasazi ruins. Be prepared for a half day's drive. I haven't seen it myself yet but I hear it's marvelous."

On an early Saturday afternoon, after rounds and after giving a report to the weekend duty doctor, I rushed back to my room. I put on the same peasant blouse with the ruffles around the neck, the same ankle-length Navajo skirt, a different set of earrings, coral this time, a pale blush of lipstick, and a touch, just a touch of Chanel Number Five.

We climbed the same forested plateau going straight up out of Fort Defiance, the day brilliant and blue with fluffs of white clouds accompanying us. At the higher elevation the air was cool in spite of the August sun.

"There's never been any clear-cutting on the Defiance Plateau," Jim said when we passed the sawmill town. "Hosteen Begay, whose little boy we had on the ward last week, works for the Tribe. He told me that the Navajos were among the first to practice scientific harvesting of trees. The largest trees, the ones with the cinnamon-colored bark, had never been cut. Some of those were always left standing for seed. The slender, smaller trees with the dark-colored bark are the new growth."

Past the sawmill town the road ran northwest and then north. After a steady climb we dipped down into a broad and open meadow. Just ahead of us, a vertical gray cliff rose about three-hundred feet high. It extended about a quarter mile east and west and it was made up of compact vertical columns.

"It's just as Hosteen Begay described it. He said the Navajos call it 'Tsilth da sa ahn,' which means 'Fluted Rock.' It's a volcanic formation where the rock cooled and crystallized to give it that fluted appearance."

The road curved to the left around the rock formation, then ran straight through the forest along a somewhat improved logging road for about twenty miles. When we began to descend, suddenly a vast space opened up before us.

"Look," Jim exclaimed, and pointed to the northeast. "Those must be the Lukachukais!" In the late afternoon sun the light fell on a line of deep red, sandstone benches, each bench separated by a small canyon. And mounted on top of each bench was a towering, gray, ragged peak of volcanic rock, the whole complex extending twenty or thirty miles in a south to north direction.

"'Like stout Cortes/Silent on a peak in Darien.'" I said.

"It's much grander than I imagined," he said. "Let's get out of the car and stand here for a while. I need time to let this sink in."

We stood side by side and held hands. I leaned my head against his shoulder and he kissed the hair on the top of my head.

We drove down the mountain in the gathering dusk, down through the piñon, then the juniper, then across a brush-covered plain where the penetrating aroma of sage greeted us through the open windows. We reached the paved road of the South Rim Drive and soon found the sign that said "To Spider Rock Overlook."

"This is a must. They say it's the grandest view of the canyon. Are you ready for it?"

"I'm ready," I said.

It took us longer to reach the overlook than I expected. There were only one or two cars in the paved parking area and the light was fading. Jim took my hand as we got out of the car, and we walked to the stone wall that marked the edge of the overlook. The gulf, the depth, and the darkness nearly swallowed me. The parapet was too low. I went down on my knees and pressed the solid stone against my chest. Only then did I dare to look into the canyon again.

"It's at least a thousand feet deep at this point," Jim announced. He stood his full height and leaned over the parapet.

"Don't! Get Down!" I shouted, and I crouched myself down still lower.

"You've got to look. It's the most spectacular sight in the West."

"Not until you get down a little yourself. It just scares me too much."

"O.K.," he said kneeling beside me. "Now take a good look before the light fades altogether."

Spider Rock, the column, a shaft of deep red sandstone perhaps seventy feet wide at the base and thirty feet wide at the top, rose nearly a thousand feet from the darkness at the bottom of the canyon almost to the level of the overlook. Perched at the top of the column and catching the last of the light of the day was a thin layer of cap rock, much lighter in color than the rest of the shaft.

"The Navajo legend says the cap of light rock is what is left of the bleached bones of the victims of Spider Woman after she devoured them. How do you like that for a gruesome tale?"

I held on a little tighter to the stones at the top of the parapet and gazed once again into the depths. Canyon de Chelly was wider where Spider Rock rose up than at other places because, in fact, three canyons came together there. Once more I felt the enormous power of the dark depth below. It was as if the gulf was drawing me into it.

"Thanks, Jim. I've had enough.' I wasn't ashamed at all to crawl on my hands and knees, back away from the wall, far enough back to where I felt safe.

"But you haven't seen the companion shaft, Talking Woman, on the other side of the canyon. Talking Woman is the one who tells Spider Woman which victims to choose," and with that Jim stood up and started to walk away from the protecting parapet and further out onto the promontory, further toward the edge.

"No, I don't want to see Talking Woman. Jim, I'm frightened. Get back here!"

Jim didn't answer but disappeared into the near darkness. I got up and ran back to the car, and then beyond the paved parking area that was as far away from either edge of the promontory as I could get. I threw myself down under the protecting, low branches of a juniper and flattened myself onto the flat rock from which it took root.

Jim could trip and fall in the darkness! He has no fear, no sense. The worst of all possible thoughts came to me. I hugged the ground, pressing myself against the rock as earlier I had pressed myself against the parapet.

"I won't do that to you again, Marion. I'm sorry"

"Jim, you're back! Thank God!" I jumped up and threw my arms around his waist. I pulled him down beside me and I held on to him. I wanted him all over me. I wanted his hands on my breasts. I pulled his hands down over me and I cupped his hands over my nipples. I pressed my mouth against his mouth and his arms tightened around me. I felt his rising and I pressed myself against him. This was the moment that was right for me, for us. That surge of heat rose within me, that aching within me and I pressed against him. I saw that he was struggling to free one of his hands as he reached into his pocket. A condom. That's O.K. if he wants it. I don't care. I just want him. I watched him roll over on his side to pull down his pants and I did the same. I helped him. I tilted myself so he could get to me, to get into me. And he did. Not gently but he did and I struggled now to wrap myself around him and I held on to him as he came. Too soon, but I wanted him and I didn't care. He laughed and I was happy for him that he came and I held him in me because I loved him and I wanted him. Then I laughed too. And he kissed me and I kissed him and we held each other as the wind blew across the promontory and across his sweaty brow and mine.

"I'll cook you a Japanese dinner," he offered two days later. He'd brought all his paraphernalia, his little electric cooker, his Teriyaki sauce, his Saki cups and warmer and the clear rice wine. He tossed bits of skinned chicken breast, cauliflower, and cashew nuts into the electric pan and added a dash of sesame oil.

"Now for the chopsticks. You hold the lower one against the middle finger and the upper one lightly under your thumb. And you don't use them like pincers; you use them like a shovel. Don't try too hard or you'll get a cramp in your hand."

I sat back and watched him work. He wore a bandana around his head to catch the sweat and a sash around his waist to fasten his kimono. His short, stiff, black hair glistened, and his epicanthal folds, when he smiled and laughed, caused his eyes to narrow to a slit. It must have been the whole cultural thing, the dinner, his dress, that made me more aware now of his Oriental features.

"You don't mind me being a Jap?" he asked, as if he'd read my thoughts.

"I don't mind, Slant Eyes. I love you. You don't mind that I'm so tiny?"

"You know what they say, don't you?"

"No, what do they say?"

"Big girl, big cunt; little girl, all cunt!"

"You bastard!" I shouted and I jumped up and pulled him down I ripped open his kimono and my mouth found his nipples. We wrestled and laughed and shouted and stumbled into the bedroom where we loved again, forgetting until afterward the cauliflower, the cashews, and the Teriyaki chicken.

We felt each other's presence during the days, so full were our nights. I watched with joy as Jim worked with the children on the pediatric ward.

"Deetch'eh," (Open your mouth) and take a deep breath," Jim instructed as he listened with his stethoscope to the lungs of the fat boy. "We'll have you out of here in no time, Ashki de Jollie." The child smiled that he'd pleased his doctor.

"Ee'zinn," (Stand up). Let me look at that leg of yours, Hosteen T'la pahe," he said when he came to the boy with the spider bite on his leg. The shy, tan boy stood up and let himself be examined.

Jim moved with that sort of skill from child to child and from bed to bed making his rounds. But our days together came to an end when the time came for Jim to move on to the surgical service.

"Well, how is it over there, Mr. Blood-and-Guts?" I teased after he'd been on the surgical service a few days.

"I like, I love it, I'm sorry to say. I don't want to hurt your feelings, but in surgery you *do* things. You find a woman complaining of abdominal pain. You find she has right upper quadrant tenderness. Her white count is elevated. You make the correct diagnosis: acute cholecystitis. You take out an inflamed gallbladder, you sew her up. She gets better, she's cured, and you're done. I gives you a tremendous sense of accomplishment."

"It doesn't hurt my feelings when you tell me this, Jim. Surgery is part of medicine. Being a caring person as you treat patients is what counts, and I know you're that kind of person. I'm happy for you if you're happy."

Boy, that was some speech, I thought. The great professor oration. I confess to myself I was jealous that he'd found such joy doing something away from me, not connected with me. But I tried not to let him see that. He had to be free. We still had our nights. We still had our time off together on weekends.

We had our nights. We were finding new ways to do it. Wild. Fun. Shouting and laughing. We had our world together. Nobody could take that away from us.

We had our weekends. We strolled together under the gaudy lights of the midway at the Navajo Tribal Fair at Window Rock. We ate the spongy, freshly-made fried bread, dipping it into the thin, clear mutton stew that we bought at the Navajos' stands. From the grandstand at the rodeo grounds we admired the Navajo girls as they leaned into their horses careening around the barrels in the barrel race. We cheered the tough, wiry Navajo boys with their sweaty, determined faces as they clung to the rope and to the backs of wild broncos and massive, churning bulls. We shouted encouragement at the team-work of the lean cowboys at the calf-roping: the swift running down of the calves, the lassoing of the feet, the quick flipping over of the young animal, the tying of the legs, and then we cheered the cowboy when he flung his arms up for the timer in triumph.

At night, with the Navajo audience, we watched the Grand Entry of the costumed tribal dancers: the feathered headdresses of the Plains Indians, the buffalo skins and the eagle wings of the Pueblo dancers, the flat, black headdresses of the Apache devil dancers, and the twin-feathered, blue Yei B'chei masks of the Navajos. Then one-by-one, tribe-by-tribe, group-by-group, illuminated by small fires on the sandy floor of the great arena, we watched their pride as each group danced to their respective drumbeat, chanted their song, stamped their feet, and threw themselves into the magic of their ancient rituals.

In the darkness where we sat, I reached for Jim's hand to hold in mine, and his dark, smiling, almost Navajo face, with his narrow, Asian eyes, looked back at me.

Our weekends took us eastward, over the forested Chuskas into New Mexico, across the tan, barren plains to Crownpoint, and then north to the ancient city at Chaco Canyon. We stood side by side in amazement at the smooth, rounded outer wall and at the tight masonry of the great house. We entered the giant, roofless kiva and I could imagine the shuffling feet and the chanting and the masks of long-dead dancers.

The trumpets, the fat, base guitars and the squeaky violins of the mariachis at Santa Fe at Fiesta brought us other delights. We danced to their music in the bricked courtyard of the old De Vargas Hotel while the little boys and girls of the old Spanish families pranced around us. The children were dressed in their finest communion suits and white dresses while their parents and grandparents, seated at tables around the courtyard, smiled and plotted family contracts for the future.

"The Zozobra! It's time for the burning of the Zozobra!" someone shouted. Old and young rushed for the passageway to the street and the courtyard was emptied. We followed the crowds outside. The throngs in the plaza were in motion too, out to the park where the paper and wood monster loomed in the darkness. The torchbearers approached and applied their flames to the giant effigy of gloom. The flames licked slowly at the base of the figure, then exploded in a giant roar. Loudspeakers at the base of the Zozobra blared forth the simulated moans and groans of the creature and the crowd rose in shouts and cheers. With one great flash of light, and with a burst of flames and sparks rising in the night sky, the monster was consumed, while the people applauded and raised their voices in peals of laughter.

"C'mon, let's get out here. I'm hungry for you," Jim said. We rushed back to our room upstairs at the La Fonda, undressed in a moment and soon, like the effigy of gloom, we too were consumed.

I had known she was there since I arrived at the hospital at Fort Defiance. Perhaps it is just in retrospect that I perceived her as the coldest of all the cold, distant, and aloof members of the hospital staff. She had always ignored me, looked past me when I went by, failed to recognize that I existed. Angela Thibault was a member of the establishment, the nurse anaesthetist. She had been there for seven or eight years and, in that time, had seen as many as three or four changes of doctors at the hospital.

"It doesn't really matter who you are," she seemed to say the few times she cast her hard, gray eyes in my direction. "You'll be gone like the others soon enough."

I never heard anyone say a good word about her. She was an Indian in an Indian hospital so she had a right, I suppose, to claim her position there if she liked, but she was not a Navajo. She was a member of some Oklahoma tribe, a light-skinned, light-eyed, mixed-blood.

I had to admit she commanded a certain amount of respect for what she did. I used to see her through the small glass window of the operating room door. It was her eyes mainly that I saw since, in the operating room, her face was always covered with a surgical mask, her head covered with a surgical cap, and her muscular body always swathed in a surgical gown.

"You'll have to come and watch me later today," Jim said. "I'll be assisting Dr. Kaplan doing the appendectomy on your patient, Ellen Tsosie. Dr. Kaplan agreed with your diagnosis of appendicitis."

Typical James Kobiashi, I thought. That boyish confidence, that I would have some thrill watching a medical student assist at a routine appendectomy!

But Ellen Tsosie was not a routine patient. I had only seen this eleven year-old once, earlier that morning, when she'd been brought to the emergency room with nausea and vomiting. The doctor downstairs had admitted her with a diagnosis of gastro-enteritis, but when I examined her, though she did not complain, I found she had tenderness in her lower abdomen. That's when I called for a surgical consultation with Dr. Kaplan. What I loved about this child was her stoicism and her bravery. The ambulance driver had told me that during the ride over from the out-lying clinic at Chinle he heard her vomit, but saw nothing on the floor of the vehicle. When he carried her little cardboard suitcase into the hospital, he felt something dripping down the side of his leg. She had opened her valise and had vomited into it rather than mess up the ambulance.

"Of course I'll come to watch you assist at surgery today. Ellen is very special to me." So I scrubbed and gowned up and I entered the operating room.

I have to admit that Jim looked very much the professional, the surgeon, gloved, gowned, with cap and mask, standing opposite Dr. Kaplan, holding the retractors. I watched his dark eyes move quickly, from Dr. Kaplan, to the scrub nurse, to Angela. Angela, at the head of the sleeping child, worked the dials of the anaesthesia machine, checked the rate of the intravenous infusion, and squeezed the Ambu bag with a steady, deliberate rhythm. I was happy for Jim. If surgery was what he wanted, that was O.K. with me.

"I saw Jim and Angela Thibault in Gallup on Saturday," This casual remark by Annie Notah, chief nurse of my pediatric unit, sent an electric charge through my chest.

Why is she telling me this? Is it to deflate me somehow, to drag me down to some common level? For the moment my anger was with Annie but soon enough I directed it at Jim.

"I heard you spent a little time with Angela in Gallup, Jim."

I could tell by the swift rising of color in his face that he was angry, too. And that I'd caught him so suddenly the moment I saw him.

"Look, Marion, I just ran into her. I was shopping for some Navajo jewelry. She said she had some gifts to buy too and she was on her way to the best places. So I followed her to Tobe Turpen's and to Richardson's Pawn."

"Is that all?"

"Of course that's all. Come on, don't do that to me, give me the third degree."

"I'm not grilling you for the fun of it. I just don't want you to hurt me, that's all," and I turned away so he wouldn't see that I was beginning to cry.

"I'll never hurt you, Marion. I love you. Let me see you tonight. I've got to get back to surgery now." He reached for my hand but I wouldn't let him, and when he disappeared down the hall, I ran into the staff bathroom and let the water stream from my eyes.

I was in a calmer mood that night. It was my turn to cook, just a simple roast chicken, wine, candles. It was patch-up time after our first lovers' quarrel.

"So what is she like?" I wasn't going to shove the thing under the rug. I needed to know something about the enemy.

"I can't tell you much about her. She doesn't say much about herself. What I know about her I heard from others: that she'd had a hard life in Oklahoma, part Indian, part white, never comfortable in either world."

"Yeah, so you've got a lot of sympathy for her, right?"

"Come on, Marion, don't be so sarcastic. We both know what it's like to be 'off-center.'"

"So what are you now, a sociologist?"

I was sorry I said that. The conversation was turning sour. I didn't want to start another fight. I thought I would just engage in a little gentle mockery.

"You know she's old enough to be your mother."

"Yeah, and you're small enough to be my daughter!"

"Bastard, bastard!" I said and we were both laughing, jumping at each other, our mouths together, rolling on the bed, hands in each other's shirt, the sex exploding, the fire blazing again, wild again, sweet again.

The rains came every afternoon that early fall, and with the rains, the chill winds that came with them. Bah Salt, age three, was brought in by a horse-drawn wagon from Piñon, Arizona with pneumonia. Why this previously healthy child became so suddenly, gravely ill with the X-ray showing infiltrate in both lungs, struggling to breathe, was a puzzle, so frighteningly swift it was. Her parents, bronze of skin, silent, polite stood at my side watching as the girl coughed, strained, turned blue with coughing, with crowing respirations. With each drawn breath she made a crowing sound, and the notch at the top of her sternum and the spaces between her ribs were drawn inward. The full flow of oxygen and humidification in the croup tent, and the intravenous antibiotics didn't help. I was on the point of calling in Dr. Kaplan to do a tracheostomy. The tracheostomy might make it easier to suction the thick secretions from her windpipe, but the shock of surgery might push her over the brink. Her respirations became more rapid, her eyelids failed to close completely and only the whites of her eyes showed between her lids.

"The parents want to find a medicine man to sing over the child," Annie Notah said coming up to me.

"That would be fine but the child cannot be taken out from here."

"They understand that. The sing can be done over an article of the child's clothing. The parents have relatives in town here, the Tabahas. The prayer can be done in the Tabahas' hogan."

"I prayed too as I reached into the croup tent for one of the child's undershirts and I handed it to Annie.

The rain and thunder, the splashing of water on the windows, and the rushing of water in the arroyo behind the hospital continued through the night. Toward morning the wind pushed the rain-laden clouds to the east and then the wind stopped.

In the morning Bah's respirations became quieter, coughing less frequent. The crowing quality when she breathed in, ceased.

The child would live.

The Salts came up to me, pressed my hand gently and said over and over again, "Ah-*shay*-hay, Ah-shay-hay," (Thank you, Thank you!) When I was preparing to leave that evening, confident because the child had made steady progress during the day, the Salts followed me out of the building. Mrs. Salt tugged at my sleeve and pulled me toward their green-painted wagon. She reached under a tarp that covered the bed of the wagon and pulled out a package about the size of a pillow that had been freshly wrapped in brown paper. She handed the package to me and gestured to me that I should open it. I was reluctant to accept it, knowing how poor they were, but I had to oblige them. When I tore open the wrapping paper the tears came. The gift was a Pendleton shawl, brilliant in its stripes of purple, blue, and red, fringed with a border of deep purple tassels, and soft and warm to the touch. My voice thickened but I was able to say the word of thanks that I'd learned.

"Ah-*shay*-hay, Ah-*shay*-hay." I held the package under one arm and threw the other around Mrs. Salt's neck. She pressed her wind-thickened face against mine, hugged me in turn, and we held on to each other.

"Ah-*shay*-hay, Azay-ich-*inn*, A*shay*-hay, Ason Yazzie."

I ran toward Jim's apartment with the package under my arm. I was giddy from the fatigue of staying up the whole of the night before and all of the day with the sick child, giddy with the emotion and the embrace of the Navajo mother whose child would live. I stumbled once or twice running up the stairs, fumbled for the key and opened the door.

I wasn't sure at first if I heard the sound because of the pounding in my chest from running up the stairs. I stopped and I knew what I heard. It was coming from the bedroom, the grunting, the breathing, the rocking. Fucking! It was her! Angela was on top, pushing and straining to reach her orgasm, and underneath, from below her hanging breasts, that laugh, Jim's laugh, the laugh that I knew and that belonged to me.

I'll try to describe what happened in the next two hours, the images of frantic flight, swift, uncontrollable, inevitable. I spun around, out the door, down the stairs, out the outer door, onto the paved parking lot. I reached for the keys to my car and in doing so I dropped the paper-wrapped shawl, the Pendleton, the striped, the fringed, the soft, the warm. I didn't care that it fell into a puddle from the rains of the night before. The trunk key, the ignition key, which is which? The one that works. The car started up quickly, the engine raced, the tires squealed as I reversed onto the street, then lunged forward on the road that lead north, out of Fort Defiance, up the mountain toward the saw mill town. The headlights led me on. The arms on the steering wheel, the foot on the accelerator were not my own.

Beyond the town the road pulled me west, uphill between the ponderosas, car lights falling on cinnamon-colored bark, north to the palisade of 'Dsilth-dah sah ahn,' halfway there. Gravel clattered against the underside of the fenders as the car turned to the left, around Fluted Rock, then up the straight graded road north, getting closer. Lukachukais somewhere out there in the dark, who could care now? Now spinning through the twisted road on the sage-scented plain, to the paved South Rim Drive, and to the sign, 'To Spider Rock Overlook.' The car door opened at the now-deserted overlook parking lot. There the parapet, over the parapet toward the rocky ledge, the edge itself. I heard the soles of my shoes scraping the pebbles of the flat rock of the edge. I stopped. A faint, waning force of life held me, caused me to hesitate at the brink. The great, black gulf hung before me. The shaft of Spider Rock rose from the depths. In the star-light the faint whiteness of the cap rock glowed dimly, the bones of the victims of Spider Woman.

I stood at the very edge when the darkness and the great dark depths sucked me forward.

They say when a person falls from a great height they die before they hit the ground. That's not true. As I fell into the blackness of the canyon, as my speed increased, as I felt the pressure of the wind in my face, I found I was struggling to keep my body in an upright position. I reached out with my arms to grab onto any tree or bush that might help to break my fall, but I was now rushing past too fast for that. Suddenly fear exploded within me. When my head struck the rock nearly a thousand feet down, a one millisecond-, a ten kiloton-, a sunburst of pain — then the blackness and the silence.

I can't explain why I chose to come back after nearly forty years to enter into somebody's dream, or why I chose Jack Berkowitz who had always despised my plainness, or what he thought was the absence of life or passion within me. Maybe I chose him as an act of forgiveness, arriving myself at a more charitable view of him. Perhaps he'd had been too busy with his Navajo girlfriend to shed any of his warmth and kindness (which people said he had an abundance of) in my direction. Or perhaps I know, since he married the girl and that they've had children and grandchildren, that he would visit Fort Defiance and that he would think of me and remember me.

I had tried to enter Jim's dreams in the past, but I'd succeeded only in the first few years when the memory of my suicide was fresh. I understand he is now a distinguished transplant surgeon, professor and chairman of a department of cardiac surgery at a medical school in California, that he married a Caucasian girl, that they, too, have had children and grandchildren. I'm told that he is still handsome and that his short-cropped, bristly hair is now largely gray. It has taken me many years to forgive his betrayal of me, his theft of my life, but I still love him that he did open my short life to me.

Cecile Comes West

﹌

I live now on the Arizona-New Mexico border, land that lies at 7,000 to 7,500 feet in elevation, the coolest and greenest portion of the Navajo Reservation. On the shoulders of the Chuska mountains, whose peaks reach 9,000 feet, three streams flow westward. These are the Whiskey, Wheatfields, and Tsaile Creeks, which, over eons, have carved the underlying red sandstone of the Navajo Formation to form the main branches of the Canyon de Chelly.

It was into this spectacular country that I brought my eighty year-old mother on her first visit to the West. I pass the spot every day where, on that trip many years ago, we left the paved road to cross a cattle guard and entered onto the rutted wagon track to reach my wife's summer sheep camp on the next wooded ridge. I still wonder at the curious juxtaposition of person, time, and place that brought my mother to this wondrous land.

My mother was born in 1893 on New York's Lower East Side, the first American-born child of newly-arrived Jewish immigrants from Poland. On the occasion of that first visit of hers to the West, we drove from Denver, a drive with its own splendid Western scenery, down the eastern face of, and then across the Front Range of the Rockies. It was during that day-long drive that she told me new details of the story of her life that I had never heard before. Those stories still vibrate in my mind as I pass that cattle guard each day and I wonder that in one lifetime a single human being can have lived so long and have traveled so far.

i.

I knew that my mother was the first child to be born in America to a family into whom a number of children had been born in Poland. My mother had spoken many times of her pride that her father, Reb Yitzhak Eliahu Zeitlin, had been a Cohen, a member of the ancient, honored tribe of Priests in Israel and that therefore she herself was a "Bat Cohen," the daughter of a Cohen.

"When my mother died, and my father had to remarry..."

"I know what that means, Mom. A holy man such as a Cohen must not cast his seed upon the ground. That means he *must* find a wife." I was enough of a yeshiva boy to know that.

"And furthermore," my mother went on, "As a Cohen, he couldn't just marry anybody. Certainly not a widow or a divorcee. A Cohen could only marry a virgin."

"I see that could have been a problem," I said. "Where would a man with eight or nine children find a young girl willing to marry him?"

"Well, she didn't have to be a *young* woman. She just had to be a woman who'd not been married before and at the same time one who would be willing enough to be the step-mother to eight or nine brats, some of whom would have been grown or at least half-grown."

"Well, I'm beginning to see what sort of a woman that might be. The good-looking girls or even those who at least had a pleasant disposition would have been married off long before. So that would have left an older woman, either a saint, or somebody desperate to marry for some reason."

"That's right, son," my mother said. "The woman my father married was desperate, all right. She was an old, humpbacked witch of a woman, with a big mole on her nose, and a mean disposition to go with it."

I'd never heard my mother speak so unkindly of anyone before. But I couldn't restrain a howl of laughter. "So she was the Wicked Stepmother, right out of the fairy tale!"

"Exactly. Except that it wasn't funny. Although I was only four when my mother died, I missed her terribly. And the new step-mother was, as you imagined, really awful both to me and to my younger sister, Birdie. Things got worse when the stepmother began to have children of her own. (So you see, she couldn't have be so old as we'd imagined.)"

"But you still had your father then, didn't you? Didn't he protect you, take care of you?"

"If he was there, it didn't seem to make any difference. As a matter of fact the memory of my father seems to fade when I try to think of him. But I do remember that my older sister, Beila, was at my side when I was accused of taking too big a portion of food at the table, or when I was rebuked for asking for fruit or candy or something sweet."

"It sounds as if, Mom, misery was mainly a matter of poverty, a large (and growing) family living in a tenement on Rivington Street on New York's Lower East Side as you'd described to me in the past."

"Yes, it's true we were poor, but meanness to a child, unkindness, is what cuts so deeply and that's what is remembered."

"You told me once that you were raised in Canada.. How did that come about."

"It was my older sister, Beila, who had a lot to do with it. I told you my father was unable to comfort me and my younger sister, Birdie. He just wasn't there. Beila realized my sister and I couldn't live like that, so she arranged for Birdie and me to taken as foster children by other families, and the family I was sent to moved to Canada."

"How did that turn out, Mom, being taken in by a strange family and then having them move so far away?"

"You're right, son, it was doubly hard in so many ways. The Smiths (that was the name my Jewish foster parents called themselves — how they picked that one I was never told) were poor themselves. They had four children of their own so I was an extra mouth to feed. While I don't recall they were ever as outwardly mean to me as my stepmother, I always had the feeling that I couldn't ask for anything. You know, a child might want a doll or an extra sweet or something. But there was that unspoken and understood, 'You must not!'"

"Was there anyone in the family you managed to get close to?"

"Yes. The next to the youngest child was a girl, Miriam. She was my age or a year or so younger. I remember her serious little face, her jet black hair and eyes. Miriam was a comfort to me and I, I suppose, was a comfort to her in that strained household. There was also a much younger boy, Eddie. He was a sweet thing but he was so little we couldn't really be friends. The two older boys were a bit strange and distant, like their parents."

"And what was it like for you in Canada? Where was it in Canada?"

"It was in Toronto, a city with poor neighborhoods like any other city and we lived in one of the poorest. It was a city crowded with Jewish immigrants and the immigrants always lived in those poor neighborhoods. So Toronto was another Jewish city where the Smiths found they could be feel at home."

"Did you live in crowded tenements like the ones on the Lower East Side of New York?"

"No, son, and for that I was thankful. The Smiths managed to rent a big two-story house, not new or fancy but with plenty of room. There were even a few trees on the street and I liked that."

"It sounds like there were some pluses then in your new life. You were not mistreated, you had in Miriam a little sister and a little friend, and there were trees on the street."

"That's right, son. And there was one more good thing, really good thing that happened to me at that time. I was sent to school and I learned English. You may not have realized this, but the only language I knew as a child up until that time was Yiddish. But English opened up a whole new, sweet world to me."

"Why do you say a 'sweet' world to you?"

"I suppose it was because the teachers were so good to me. They spoke to me sweetly in that new language, so I came to imagine, compared to the unhappy things in my life up to that point that had been spoken to me in the old language, that English was part of a new, beautiful world."

"I'll bet you were a good student."

"Yes, I did learn fast. I think at age six or seven, new things come easier. And I suppose I became sort of a teacher's pet."

"I'm not surprised. I'll bet you were a pretty little girl then, too."

"Did you ever see pictures of how little children were dressed then? You must have seen the middy blouse, that sort of sailor's blouse with the broad square collar with the piping on it that falls back over the shoulder, and the contrasting bandana that's tied in the front. I remember being dressed that way for Dominion Day, Canada's national day of celebration, something like the Fourth of July in the United States. Except instead of celebrating independence, we were celebrating our allegiance to Great Britain and to the Queen. You see the year must have been 1900 and Queen Victoria was still on the throne."

"What a bit of history you lived through, Mom."

"What made that day so memorable for me was that my teacher, Miss McCauley, who I loved so much, put her arm over my shoulder and drew me to her. I knew she was proud of me. Then she turned to Miss Brown, one of the other teachers and said, 'This is my little Cecile Smith. Look how prettily she's dressed, the little Kike!'"

"Oh Mom, that must have been devastating for you!"

"Those sweet tongues in those days were so full of hidden hate for us. Yes, it nearly killed me. I've never forgotten it. Even so, it didn't change my love for the English they spoke."

"I know Mom, growing up in Canada instead of New York, your speech is so pleasant, and it doesn't have that awful New York accent. I was always proud to bring my friends to meet you, to hear you speak."

"Well enough of sweet accents. Now your father, he had an accent all right. He came to America when he was sixteen so he was never able to lose his Polish-Yiddish accent. It wasn't as bad as most because he was an intellectual and a medical student when I met him."

"How did you meet him?"

"It was Beenah Sunshine who introduced us. She worked as a sewing machine operator next to me and she'd come from the same little 'shtetl' in Poland as you father. It was at a Socialist gathering in one of those Landsmanshaft clubs called the 'Yvansker Farband' after Yvansk , the little town he'd come from. He was handsome, self-assured, with dark, curly hair. When the political speeches were over and when the music started he came right up to me and said, `You're an American girl, I can tell. Do you care to dance along with me?' I knew the syntax wasn't right but it didn't matter."

"So it was a romance between an 'American' working class shop girl and an immigrant medical student."

"Come now, don't oversimplify. Yes it's true. Our both being Jewish had a great deal to do with it, but it was our love of music that drew us together. On my own, in the Smith household, I earned enough to buy a piano, and to take lessons. I learned two pieces, Schubert's *Moment Musicale Number Three* and Padrewski's *Minuet.* I think hearing me play is what sold him on me. And we went together to hear Ignace Jan Padrewski play himself."

"Well, there is another bit of history."

"When World War I ended your father had to respond to appeals from his family in Poland for help. He felt the only way he could do this *and* to marry me (he was over thirty at the time and I was twenty-six) was give up medicine and to get to work earning a living in business. So he proposed asking, 'Will you walk along with me?'"

"Touching. Same error of syntax."

"Exactly. But it worked. When we were to be married we came to New York and I became reacquainted with my sister Beila and with the rest of my family. 'He's a Socialist and obviously not 'Frum' (Religiously Orthodox). He probably doesn't even go to 'Shul' (synagogue) on Yom Kippur.' But he surprised them all when he sent you and your brothers to the Hebrew Institute of Boro Park, the first yeshiva in Brooklyn where the language of instruction in the Hebrew classes was all in Hebrew."

II.

My mother fell silent now. We had been talking, I asking questions, she revealing her personal history, which to me revealed bits of world history as well, for many hours. The Front Range of the Rockies, which, in the morning sun had been illuminated from the east, now gave way to interior valleys and then over Wolf Creek Pass. In the afternoon we descended into the valley of the San Juan and finally south into the arid valley of the Navajo Reservation east of the Chuska mountains. Now, in the gathering darkness, we climbed into the green of that mountain range and down into the valleys of Crystal, New Mexico.

I drove my new, 1976 Dodge pick-up slowly as the cattle-guard entry to the summer sheep camp road came into view in the headlights. There I turned off the paved road.

"You did very well, son, driving all the way on the highways, but are you sure you know where you are going now? I didn't see any road sign."

"It's all right, Mom. Once you get off the paved roads there aren't any signs on the Reservation. People just know where they're going. I know this road very well and you'll see I'll get you there." I began to pick my way down the narrow, rutted, sandy track, down off the ridge where we had left the paved highway. Though the headlights revealed mainly the dirt trail ahead, I pointed out to my mother that we were crossing a little valley.

"You can see a little of the sagebrush and dry buffalo grass on the side of the road."

"It looks like the road is washed out just ahead," my mother observed, a little apprehension in her voice. We had come to the edge of an arroyo.

"You don't have to worry, Mom," I said, and I shoved the manual transmission into the lowest gear. "The pick-up is the perfect vehicle to negotiate this kind of terrain. Driving across arroyos is standard operating procedure on the Reservation. "Hold on, Mom!"

With this I sent the nose of the pick-up down about forty-five degrees and allowed the truck to roll down to the bottom of the stream bed which lay only four or five feet below the level of the valley floor. At the proper moment I gunned the engine and the pick-up climbed easily to the top on the other side.

"This is one of the easier ones. People don't have much trouble with this one unless the rains have been very heavy. But, you don't have to worry. There won't be any more arroyo crossings the rest of the way."

I could sense that my mother was bracing herself against the armrest as I pressed on the accelerator. We started to climb up out of the valley. The first trees we encountered on gaining the next ridge were the short piñons and through the open windows we could smell the piney perfume they exuded into the night air.

"Ah, now that smells lovely," she said, relaxing a little bit.

"It's the piñon, Mom. It's always a treat."

Suddenly, the headlights caught the flutter of a flying creature crossing the road ahead.

"What was that?"

"It was an owl, Mom. The Navajos believe that seeing an owl at night is a bad omen. But I know you're not superstitious. You've got nothing to worry about."

The road now entered up a steeper climb and I kept the truck in low gear. Now, on a rough, stone-strewn, deeply-rutted road, we were climbing into tall ponderosa pine country. We could only see a narrow strip of night sky, filled with stars, through the windshield. Straight, dark trees on either side formed a narrow canyon through which the road now ran. At last, the road having attained the elevation of the plateau, the truck ran more quietly on a soft, sandy surface.

A line of fence posts appeared on the left in the beam of the headlights. When the fence line suddenly ceased, I slowed the truck and drove off to the left on a still less-traveled track.

"Are you sure you know where you're going, son?" my mother asked.

"Of course I know, Mom. We're very close. In a few minutes you'll see the camp."

"I never dreamed that you, a boy from Brooklyn, would be able to guide me through a forest at night like this," she said.

"Oh Mom, things change. I'm a long way from Brooklyn now and you're a long way from Rivington Street."

A short drive up the new track, and I guided the truck across a meadow of tall, rich grass. Then, with a turn to the left, down across a very shallow, dry-stream bed, up again to gain a rise, we entered among the tall trees again. Then, off to the left we saw the welcoming orange glow of a friendly fire illuminating the rosy trunks of the ponderosas. We had reached the summer sheep camp at last.

"There they are, Mom," I said as my Navajo wife and dark-eyed children came running to greet us.

"We were worried about you," my wife, Ida, said. "You did well to find a place like this in the dark."

"Yes, we were nearly lost," I teased. "But a friendly owl showed us the way."

Ida looked at me darkly, but a smile soon came over her face.

"Come, I'll help you get down off that truck," she said helping my mother down. "I'll bet it was a rough ride."

"It was, especially the last few miles. Your fire and your camp look so beautiful. I'm so glad to be here," she said as her grandchildren came running to embrace her, drawing her toward the warmth of the fire.

PRONUNCIATION GUIDE
FOR NAVAJO GLOSSARY

This guide is modified from "The Sound System of Navajo" in the introduction of the *Navajo-English Dictionary* by Wall and Morgan, Hippocrene Books, Inc., New York, 2nd Ed., 1995, for which permission has been requested.

VOWELS:

The vowels have continental values:
> **a** as in f**a**ther
> **e** as in m**e**t
> **i** as in s**i**t
> **o** as in n**o**te

Vowels may be either long or short in duration, the long duration vowel indicated by a doubling of the letter. This never affects the quality of the vowel, except that the long duration vowel **i** is always pronounced as in the English **see**.

Vowels with a hook (**a̧**) beneath the letters are nasalized. This means that some of the breath passes through the nose as the sound is produced.

Example: **Ta̧zhi** (turkey)

All vowels following **n** are nasalized though not marked. An accent mark above the letter (**é**) indicates emphasis, and the voice rises on that letter.

Example: **Tsé** (rock)

(') either after or before a vowel indicates a glottal stop. This means that the breath is held momentarily in the glottis (the throat) before going on to pronounce that letter or the next letter.

Example: **Yá'át'ééh** (expression, "hello," or "it is good")

CONSONANTS

Consonants are largely that same as in English with several exceptions:

h represents the sound of **ch** as in German **ich**.
Example: **ahéhee'** (expression, "thank you")

ł with a slash bar represents the sound tl.
Example: **łikan** ("delicious", "good to eat")

GLOSSARY

A-glani, **adláanii**, *You drunk!*

A-glanis, **adláanii**, *drunks, intoxicated persons*

Ah-shay-hay D'li kon at eh, **ahéhee' łikan**, *Thank you. It is delicious.*

Ah-shay-hay, Ason Yazzie, **ahéhee', Asdzą́ą́ Yázhí**, *Thank you, Little Woman.*

Ah-shay-hay, ah zah-ich-inn, **ahéhee' azee'ííł'íní**, *Thank you, Doctor.*

Ah-shay-hay, **ahéhee'**, *Thank You.*

Ah-zay-ich-inn, **azee' ííł'íní**, *doctor, physician, medicine-maker.*

Anasazi, **anaasází**, *The Old People, the ancient ones.*

Ashki de Jollie, **Ashkii Díjool**, *nick-name, "Round (fat) Boy"*

Ason Yazzie, **Asdzą́ą́ Yázhí**, *Little Woman.*

At'ed Pahe, **At'ééd Łibáhá**, *tan (light-skinned girl).*

B'nah t'lapahe, **Bináá' Łibáhí**, *His eyes are grey, "Grey Eyes"*

Bah Yazzie, a woman's name, *"Little Girl"*

Beh g'el chee, **Be'ek'id Halchíí'**, *Red Lake.*

Biligonnas, **Bilagáana**, *white men*, (corruption of the Spanish term "Americanos")

Cha d'eh shahn na a rhanh, **háadi shą' nighan?**, *Where is your home? Where do you live?*

Chad ish ahn b'ana nah? **Ha'át'íísh baa naniná?**, *What are you doing?*

Ch'indi, **Ch'į́įdii**, expression, *"What the devil..."* or a thing or object that is witched or cursed.

Chinle, name of a town at the mouth of Canyon de Chelly.

D'li kahn lah, **díí łikan lá**, *It was delicious (sweet)*

Deetch'eh, **diich'ééh**, Command, *"Open your mouth"*

Dilye'eh, **dilyéhé**, *the Pleiades*, ("The Seven Sisters") part of the constellation of
Taurus

Dsilth dah sah ahn, **Dził Dah Si'á**, *Fluted Rock*

Ee'zinn, **yiisįįh**, Command, *"Sit Up"*

Ee-yah!**Yíiyá**, expression of fear, dread, danger.

Gah-gee, **gáagii**, *crow, common raven*

H'leenh, **łį́į́'**, *horse*

Ha koh shi-mah, **hágo shimá**, *Come (over) here, Mother*

Ha ko sheenh, **hágo shį́į́**, Expression, *"that 's fine (OK) with me, I agree"*

Hosteen T'lpahe, **Hastiin Łbáhá**, nick-name, *"Tan Man"*

Inh ley Chinle, **nłéí ch'íníłį́**, *Over at (in the direction of) Chinle* (town near the
mouth of the Canyon de Chelly)

Lukachukai, name of a town at the base of the Chuska Mountains.

Mah-ee yahzha, **mą'ii yázhí**, *coyote*, literally *"little wolf"*

Na n'es kah'dah, **náneeskaadí**, *tortillas*

Na'acho'chai, **naa'ahóóhai**, *chicken*

Neh'massi, **nímasii**, *potatoes*

Ni'hi'cha'danih, **nihaadaaní**, *our in-law*

Ni'rhad'et'od'glod, **aghá'deeldlaad**, *X-ray*, *"light that shines through"*

Oh, shi-yahzh, **aoo' shíyaazh**, *Yes, my son*

Shash at eh!, **shash át'é**, *It's a bear!*

Shi mah, **shimá**, *Mother, or My mother*

Shi yahzh, **shíyáázh**, *Son, or My son*

Silah-o, **siláo**, *policeman, (sometimes used for soldiers)*

T'a chini, **Táchii'nii**, name of a clan (*"Red into Water"*)

T'lapahe, **łibá**, *grey* or *tan in color.*

T'senjikinnie, **Tsé Níjíkiní**, name of a clan (*"Rock House Clan"*)

Tra Trahzi B'kin, **Ta̧zhii Bikin**, *Three-Turkey House* (ruin)

Tsi-yeh, **tsiiyééł**, *a traditional Navajo way of tying long hair in a knot behind the head using a skein of white wool.*

Ya n'elgloshi, **yee naaldlooshii**, *witches, skin-walkers*

Yat'eh, sik'ess, **yá'át'ééh shík'is**, Greeting, *"Hello, my friend"*

Yat'eh, **yá'át'ééh**, Greeting, *"hello,"* or *(something) is good, fine, O.K.*

Yat'eh si zaydeh, **yá'át'ééh shízeedí**, Greeting, *"Hello, (my) cousin."*

Yat'eh shi yahzh, **yá'át'ééh shíyáázh**, Greeting, *"Hello, (my) son."*

Yat'eh shi mah, **yá'át'ééh shimá**, Greeting, *"Hello, (my) mother."*

Yat'eh-oh!, **yá'át'ééh aoo'**, Greeting, *enthusiastic, with emphasis.*

Yat'eh ah'bin, **yá'át'ééh abíní**, Greeting, *"Good morning!"*

Yat'eh ah-zay-ich-ihn, **yá'át'ééh azee' íłł'íní**, Greeting, *"Good morning, Doctor."*

Yei B'chei, **yé'ii bicheii**, *Holy Ones*, literally, *grandfathers of the holy ones.*

The logo for the Red Lake Press is Lewis's Woodpecker, a bird seen frequently in the valley below Red Lake and among the trees on the surrounding hills. It was first described by the explorer and naturalist Meriwether Lewis on his expedition of 1804-1806 with William Clark. This pink-bellied woodpecker, then, is an appropriate symbol for the Red Lake locale and for the West in general.